Intellectuals and the Public Good

Creativity and civil courage are major dimensions of an intellectual's authority and contribute towards the enrichment of democracy. This book develops a sociological account of civil courage and creative behaviour in order to enhance our understanding of the nature of intellectuals' involvement in society. Barbara A. Misztal employs both theoretical-analytic and empirical components to develop a typology of intellectuals who have shown civil courage and examines the biographies of twelve Nobel Peace Prize laureates, including Elie Wiesel, Andrei Sakharov and Linus C. Pauling, to illustrate acts of courage that have embodied the values of civil society. She advances our understanding of the nature of intellectuals' public involvement and their contribution to social well-being. In the current climate of fear and insecurity, as goverments are forced to deal with issues of increasing complexity, this is a pioneering sociological book with a highly original approach.

BARBARA A. MISZTAL is Professor and Chair of Sociology at the University of Leicester. She is the author of *Theories of Social Remembering* (2003), *Informality: Social Theory and Contemporary Practice* (2000) and *Trust in Modern Societies* (1996).

Intellectuals and the Public Good

Creativity and Civil Courage

Barbara A. Misztal

CAMBRIDGE
UNIVERSITY PRESS

CAMBRIDGE UNIVERSITY PRESS
Cambridge, New York, Melbourne, Madrid, Cape Town, Singapore, São Paulo

Cambridge University Press
The Edinburgh Building, Cambridge CB2 8RU, UK

Published in the United States of America by Cambridge University Press,
New York

www.cambridge.org
Information on this title: www.cambridge.org/9780521847186

First published 2007

Printed in the United Kingdom at the University Press, Cambridge

A catalogue record for this publication is available from the British Library

ISBN 978-0-521-84718-6 hardback

To Berenika, most lovable of daughters

Contents

Tables

Acknowledgements

I am grateful to the Department of Sociology, Leicester University, which generously assisted my research project and enabled me to take a six-month period of leave in which I was able to make substantial progress in writing. I am also thankful to my friends and colleagues who read different chapters in draft. I owe an immense debt to my husband for his help and unfailingly constructive support. Finally, my warmest thanks to my daughter, to whom this book is dedicated, for her forbearance and love.

Introduction

The aim of the book

This book aims to develop a sociological account of civil courage and creative behaviour. It looks at the careers, lives and works of creative and courageous public intellectuals in order to advance our understanding of the conditions that facilitate the production of public goods by intellectuals. By providing insight into the nature of the public involvement of intellectuals, the book also demonstrates the continuing importance of public intellectuals for the health of democracy. I understand the term 'public intellectuals' to include those scientists, academics in the humanities and the social and political sciences, writers, artists and journalists who articulate issues of importance in their societies to the general public. I argue that, in order to take on the role of 'democracy's helpers' (Kenny 2004: 89), public intellectuals need both creativity and courage, which are the essential building blocks of their authority to speak out on broad issues of public concern. While acknowledging that the public authority of an intellectual develops in the course of what he or she does and depends upon a variety of conditions and resources, I stress the significance of creativity and courage 'which embody the values of civil society' (Swedberg 1999: 522) as the twin major dimensions of the intellectual's reputation and standing with the public.

The tradition of the public intellectual as the guardian of universally grounded values and truths, enriched by tales of philosophers from ancient Athens, Enlightenment ideals, the Dreyfus Affair and the values of the mid-nineteenth-century Russian intelligentsia, has laid down the terms of discussion of the responsibility of intellectuals: belief in the value of science, readiness to confront repressive authority, defence of justice, reason and truth in the name of moral universalism. These narratives have also established the expectation that 'in the scientist the Greek prophecy of society governed by philosopher-kings would at last be fulfilled' (Rieff 1969: 340). It was anticipated that, in the developing scientific age, 'scientists would have duties like those of priests in the old society – duties superior to those of warriors ... But in the twentieth century ... something went astray ... ' (Rieff 1969: 340). In the last five decades the relationship between modern science and politics – or, more generally, the relationship between the public and public intellectuals – has evolved. The institutionalisation and the specialisation of intellectual life, together with the dominance of mass culture, are seen as responsible for the disappearance of the charismatic public intellectual and the decline in the quality of the public. As displaying academic credentials steadily becomes both less important and more dubious in the eyes of the lay public, and as increasingly egalitarian attitudes, wider access to higher education and the prominence of celebrity culture lower the deference accorded to academics, many talk about the decline of public trust in the infallibility and the authority of intellectuals.

Nonetheless, there are still voices defending the importance of intellectuals' social function as the arbiters of truth. Such claims reflect the dominance of the French model of public intellectuals, which established intellectuals' 'higher calling as moral watchmen over the modern state' (Lilla 2001: 203). As one of the results of this model's dominance, the study of intellectuals has frequently taken a normative form, offering visions of how intellectuals ought to behave and pleading for intellectuals to act in particular ways. This tradition, which began with Emile Zola and has continued with Julien Benda, Jean-Paul Sartre, Karl Mannheim, Russell Jacoby and Edward Said, remains alive and attractive and often affects the ways in which contemporary intellectuals think about their role and position in society. It maintains that being an intellectual entails not only engaging in creative mental activity but also taking social responsibilities and political positions. According to this moralising stance, best summarised in Vaclar Havel's (1991: 167) well-known phrase, intellectuals should 'speak the truth to power'.

These words suggest an inherent opposition between intellectuals and political rulers, yet throughout the last century there were many examples of intellectuals involved on both sides of the barricades. On the one hand, intellectuals have been deeply engaged in social and political movements that have brought about widely approved political and social change: anti-colonialism, revolution, student movements and the defeat of communism. But, on the other hand, intellectuals have also been prominent in the service of nationalism, fascism and authoritarian regimes. In the face of such diversity, it is necessary to approach the issues I discuss outside the shackles of the normative tradition. I do not assume, as that tradition has it, that being a public intellectual has to mean, by definition, speaking 'the truth to power' and generally acting as the moral consciousness of the nation. Rather, I claim that justification of the importance of the public intellectual for democracy arises from an appreciation of the pertinence of intellectuals to free public space. This Habermasian argument needs to be supplemented, however, by 'an appreciation of the relation between such figures and the multiplicity of "publics" that have emerged within democratic states' (Kenny 2004: 102), as well as by an understanding that the relationship between democracy and the intellectual is an uneasy one, characterised as 'love in adversity' (Bauman 1992a) or as a 'love–hate' relationship (Goldfarb 1998). Ideally, the leading thinkers of the time should be able to 'educate and to inspire democracy' (Leonard Trelaway Hobhouse, quoted in Collini 2006: 102). While recognising that reality does not often reflect this ideal model, that there are many instabilities inherent in the role of intellectual and that the intellectual cannot be seen as 'some sort of timeless entity' (Judt 1992: 296), the special role of intellectuals is worth retaining because of their potential contribution to matters of human significance: societal well-being and democratic standards. In other words, without the intellectuals' participation in the public sphere the quality of democracy can be threatened, because a democratic polity that does not draw upon all the sources of available information and good judgement is weakened.

Although intellectuals will always be caught in the tensions between specialism and generalism, engagement and withdrawal, a society can still benefit from their capacity to offer a broader perspective, as it is both necessary and desired by the public. Since, as Pierre Bourdieu (2004: 274) notes, there is no effective democracy 'without real critical counter-power', and since this power is 'the intellectual', it can be argued that intellectuals, because of their 'culture of critical discourse' (Gouldner 1979), or/and because of their 'monopoly of critical reflexivity', to use Bourdieu's (1988: 109) vocabulary, can be of crucial importance for the quality of democracy. Assuming that public intellectuals 'are particularly well equipped to bring to public view the complexities and multidimensionality of social problems and cultural differences' (Kenny 2004: 96), it can be said that the importance of public intellectuals for democracy is associated with their role in the establishment and cultivation of democratic discourse and culture. More specifically, intellectuals can help democracy to attain its potential by enhancing people's understanding, thinking and debates about political issues and actions and thus contributing to the creation of a broad public culture and the enrichment of the democratic imagination – that is, the repertoire of ideas, evaluations, skills and logics that citizens develop to inform their citizenship activities (Perrin 2006). Intellectuals also can enrich the political elite's ability to define and articulate innovative programmes and creative alternatives. In other words, if democracy is to serve people by protecting them and developing a sustained commitment to transparency and justice, it requires the active public participation of public intellectuals in expanding the democratic imagination and civic sensitivity of citizens and their leaders alike.

Intellectuals in a democracy not only cannot be, but also must not want to be, philosopher-kings. Yet, in order to serve democracy, they need an audience, and to summon it they must lay claim to some authority, which cannot be a claim to political authority (which belongs to elected politicians) and cannot simply be a claim to the authority of expertise (which the public views as narrow and merely academic). Since the proper conduct of democratic debate needs a model of independent rationality and since public intellectuals, as people privileged in this respect, are best placed to perform this service, studying the evidence of this special role of public intellectuals should focus on sources of intellectuals' public authority. The vital question of what does in fact provide intellectuals with the authority to earn the attention of a general audience is one of the main issues addressed in this book. My proposal is that creativity and courage are the two essential conditions for the public prominence of intellectuals, and therefore for their contribution to the public sphere. Creativity, by definition the principal characteristic of the intellectual, raises scholars to the status of public intellectuals as they gain the recognition and right to intervene in the public sphere on matters for which they have competence. This elevating role of creativity, 'perceived as a primary obligation of intellectuals' (Shils 1972: 6), places intellectuals in their public role by giving them licence to address a wider public on matters of common concern.

Intellectuals' standing is also built upon public intellectuals' capacity to voice a view 'which in some way goes beyond that available to those with a merely instrumental or expert relation to the matter in question' (Collini 2006: 56). Since it requires the courage of conviction to speak up on matters of human significance, civil courage, defined very broadly as disinterested and risky – but not necessarily rebellious – action for the purposes of institutionalising social or cultural change, must be seen as the other source of authority for public intellectuals. The ability to think independently, involving a willingness to challenge prevailing opinions and not merely follow conventional wisdom, is essential for the quality of public debates. In short, when the courageous stand of an intellectual forces people to rethink the very bases of their political allegiance, to re-evaluate the political order, and provides the basis for civic initiatives that affirm human rights and dignity, it performs a vital social function.

Recognising the significance of civil courage as one of the principal elements in intellectual authority – itself the primary requirement of the intellectual's contribution to just and pluralistic dimensions of contemporary politics – means insisting that neither consensus nor rebelliousness is an exclusive characteristic of the intellectual's involvement in public affairs.

Naturally, the scope of the courage required differs according to the nature of the particular socio-political context. A study of recurrent patterns in the courageous activities and types of public engagement of intellectuals therefore demands an investigation of the making of careers within specific historical contexts. Consequently, I move still further away from a merely normative approach by describing and analysing concrete empirical cases, which have not been selected on the basis of a specific ideological commitment or the personal qualities of the intellectuals concerned but, rather, on their distinctive achievements within national and international structures. Placing examples of civil courage and creative imagination within their social and historical contexts is the first step towards an adequate social analysis in the shape of the construction of a taxonomy of public intellectuals' courageous actions. I argue that the nature of contexts shapes the level of autonomy and the kinds of audience and media available to public intellectuals and therefore expands or constrains the ways in which public intellectuals can take a courageous stance. My analysis is built around the identification of courageous conduct by just four types of public intellectuals; to these types I have given the names of pioneer, dissident, hero and champion.

To provide these categories with life I illustrate them by reference to the careers of public intellectuals who have enjoyed international recognition. Since it is not easy to find good empirical material for studies of public intellectuals who have been widely recognised as having significantly contributed to the strengthening of the democratic values of their societies, I have decided to use the laureates of the Nobel Peace Prize as the catchment area from which my sample of public intellectuals is drawn. This prize, the best-known and most highly respected international peace prize, provides probably the most significant impartial validation of accomplishment (with a few notorious exceptions). The prize provides recognition of individuals who have made outstanding efforts to transform their respective societies to accept the idea of international peace and justice; and the laureates have received an extraordinary degree of attention as a result of the iconic status of the award. Since awakening and educating public opinion is necessarily a slow and complex process, some awards have been retrospective and honorific. Indeed, in the case of intellectuals in particular, it is often difficult to point to immediate tangible results of their actions or to particular events in public life with which their names may be associated, and recognition is thus more likely to come retrospectively. Awards have also been made to figures still heavily involved in the activities that have earned them recognition. My sample contains members from both categories.

In the more than 100-year history of the Nobel Peace Prize, alongside the activists, politicians, diplomats and leaders of international humanitarian organisations who constitute the majority of the winners, there appear several recipients who can be classified as public intellectuals. By scrutinising the biographical characteristics of these prize-winners, I have constructed a sample of the Nobel Peace laureates who worked in or around academia, journalism or related cultural fields, while also devoting themselves with great courage to changing the social and intellectual conditions of their own societies and, on occasion, of the entire international community. My sample therefore consists of twelve Nobel Peace Prize laureates who were (or are) writers, journalists, academics or scientists and who have spoken on important social, political or cultural issues to the general non-specialist public. The common characteristics of these public intellectuals therefore are, by definition, both creativity (which earns them recognition in their respective professional fields and helps them to legitimise their creative social initiatives and programmes) and courage (as, according to the formal criteria for the award, the Nobel Peace Prize is granted for brave and disinterested public involvement and for courageous action to defend and spread civic values, human rights, peace and democracy).

In summary, I shall examine intellectuals' real public involvement and recurrent patterns in the activities of my sample in order both to demonstrate that intellectuals can make a difference to societal well-being and to suggest that we can learn from what they have done. I am interested in the recognised cases of creativity and civil courage in which public intellectuals, those producers of ideas who take their ideas outside their professional fields to the general public, have managed to earn recognition for their contributions to social improvement. In other words, the focus of this book is on the successful achievement by intellectuals of their goals of spreading a specific message and winning people over to their point of view. It is not a book about the pre-eminence of intellectuals nor a nostalgic call for the return of the intellectual as the moral consciousness of the nation. Rather, it is, in the first place, a contribution to the understanding of intellectuals who have been the subject of many puzzling claims and contradictory evaluations. Second, despite the compelling reasons for attaching primary importance to creativity and courage, there is no major study of either from a sociological perspective. I therefore aim to fill this gap and to increase our awareness of the importance of both features for the enrichment of democracy. If, as Zygmunt Bauman (2002) suggests, one of the main tasks of contemporary sociology is to inform people about the social forces that threaten to reduce freedom and political democracy, it is essential to study the role of creative imagination in the elaboration of political goals and in the resistance to symbolic domination. It is similarly vital to explore the difference that civil courage makes to the functioning of institutions and to the scope and quality of civil society.

The outline of the book

As the book has both theoretical-analytic and empirical components, it is divided into two parts. The first part, Theoretical framework, is devoted to elaborating the conceptualisation of the main ideas, in particular the authority of intellectuals, creativity and courage. This part also contains the elaboration of a typology of intellectual engagements based on the categories of pioneer, dissident, hero and champion. In the first chapter I examine the debates on the definition of and change in the role and the authority of intellectuals. After a brief presentation of various ways of understanding the role of public intellectual, I address the question of what gives intellectuals the authority to speak to non-specialised audiences on matters of general concern. Chapter 1 develops the argument that, in order to establish a reputation for being likely to have important contributions to make to their societies and for having the capacity and courage to do so, intellectuals need to evince creativity and civil courage. Such a conceptualisation of public intellectual authority focuses our attention on the contemporary convergence of knowledge and public voice as the basis of intellectuals' public authority.

In chapter 2 I move on to analyse the notion of creativity, a topic long debated within a number of different research paradigms and traditions. I note its evolution from the aura of elusiveness, enigma and myth through being a mirror of modernity to its status today as both 'the weapon of the weak' (Lofgren 2001: 73) and a fashionable commercial strategy. I argue that, as both social and natural sciences shift towards stressing the conceptual centrality of contingency and context dependency, any account of different forms of creativity should incorporate the permanent reality of risk and of multiple relationships between the formal and the informal. I conclude by identifying forms of creativity and arguing that public intellectuals' engagement in shared projects of imagining a better democratic future concentrates our attention on one specific type of creativity, namely 'civic creativity', conceived of as a creativity that provides us with ideas on how to democratise and humanise the workings of modern societies.

Chapter 3 discusses what the social sciences, in general, can tell us about the complex phenomenon of courage and looks for answers to such questions as what is courage? And what are the relations between courage and risk, courage and loyalty to the group and courage and nonconformity? Starting with a classical view of courage as the greatest of all virtues, I construct a sociological account of civil courage as disinterested, nonconformist and dealing with difficulties and risky actions that are motivated by the ideals of civil society.

In the final chapter of part I, I develop a sociological approach to creativity and courage by proposing a general typology of intellectuals' public involvement. As the study of intellectual authority needs to be 'the study of the making of careers' (Collini 2006: 56), the first step towards the construction of a taxonomy of public intellectuals' courageous actions requires the analysis of recurrent patterns of intellectuals' activities in the public sphere. In the next step towards a typology of the involvement of intellectuals in the public sphere, the links between the configurations of social relationships and civil courage displayed by intellectuals are discussed. This discussion starts with debates as to the nature of the socio-political contexts that shape intellectual autonomy, and therefore the audiences and media available to public intellectuals.

Part II, Public intellectuals: the case of the Nobel Peace Prize laureates, consists of five chapters, each of which comes with notes that enrich our knowledge of the studied cases. In this part, I offer extensive material on a sample of those Nobel Peace Prize laureates who can be classified as public intellectuals. Detailed examination of their lives, creative achievements, courageous behaviour and disinterested contributions to public life illustrates the concepts and typology developed in part I. I present a compact history of the Nobel Peace Prize and its objectives, followed by a summary introduction to the public intellectuals to whom it has been awarded. The successive chapters provide both an illustration and a validation of my typology of the involvement of intellectuals in the public sphere. Chapter 6 presents three portraits of heroes. It describes the careers, works and lives of Jane Addams, Fridtjof Nansen and Elie Wiesel, who won the Nobel Peace Prize in 1933, 1922 and 1968 respectively. Chapter 7 offers the characterisation of the dissident, by examining the cases of three intellectuals who were politicised: Carl von Ossietzky (awarded the prize in 1935), Andrei Sakharov (1975) and

Adolfo Pérez Esquivel (1980). Chapter 8 depicts instances of the third category, champions. It portrays Norman Angell (1933), Emily Greene Balch (1946) and Alva Myrdal (1982) in their roles as campaigners for various kinds of social and political reform. Chapter 9, which is devoted to the presentation of the pioneer, examines the careers, works and lives of three scientists, John Boyd Orr (1949), Linus Pauling (1962) and Norman Borlaug (1970), who addressed some of the perennial problems affecting humanity at large, in particular hunger and war.

In the conclusion I revisit some earlier themes in the light of my analysis of the twelve individual cases and restate the case for the vital role of creativity and courage in the sustainable development of any democracy. If this case is accepted, it will be clear that the enhancement of civic sensitivity requires the deliberate cultivation of opportunities for civil courage and use of the creative imagination.

Part I

Theoretical framework

1   The authority of public intellectuals

The definition of the intellectual

In this chapter I look at debates concerning the definition, role and authority of intellectuals. After a short presentation of various ways of defining intellectuals and conceptualising their role, I try to answer the question: what gives intellectuals the authority to speak to non-specialised audiences on matters of general concern?

As we have already observed in the introduction, the rise of the social type of intellectual, the 'universal intellectual', is connected with the Dreyfus Affair of the late nineteenth century in France. The modern intellectual, whose rise and fall have become distinctive and indicative phenomena of modernity (Bauman 1995; Bourdieu 1989), is defined by his or her duty to intervene on 'behalf of rights and progress that has been delayed' (Habermas 1989: 73) whenever societal well-being requires. This responsibility is a more worldly and secular expression of the doctrine of 'defenders of the faith' and it authorises intellectuals in their universalistic ambitions to represent the realm of ideas beyond narrow specialisation. 'The Dreyfusard intellectuals believed that it was by virtue of their immersion in the world of ideas that they had the right, nay moral duty, to uphold universal ideals against even the state' (Coser 1965: 223). Their faith in universal ideas, together with their critical reflexivity, over which they have a monopoly, obliges them 'to associate the pursuit of the universal with the constant struggle for the universalization of the privileged conditions of existence which render the purist of the universal possible' (Bourdieu 1989: 110). The dominance of the French model has established intervention in politics as being 'constitutive of the definition of the category' and has provided the contrast for all national comparisons (Collini 2006: 49).

Nevertheless, this new image of the intellectual has, as Bauman (1992a) notes, functioned more as a project or mobilising call rather than an empirical definition, as it aimed to demonstrate the social value of the intellectual mission. It has been both forward-looking and nostalgic as it has tried to overcome the growing fragmentation of the knowledge class and to restore the unity of the public authority of women and men of knowledge (Bauman 1995: 224–5). Moreover, this popular but confusing definition of the intellectual has contributed to controversies over the reality of intellectuals' involvement, the responsibility they have, the forms of their public engagement, their definitions, their views, their class position and their level of integration into society. The description of intellectuals, as a result of this confusion, tends to oscillate in its emphasis of the extent to which they should be 'outsiders' or 'integrated', engaged or detached, conformists or rebels, dissidents or members of elites, prone to hold a critical view or not (see chapter 4 for further discussion). These frequently employed binary characterisations of the intellectual are responsible for long-standing and widely held contradictory convictions about the fate of and what constitutes the intellectual. Thus, since the end of the 1960s, the debate about intellectuals has consisted of several contradictory voices.

Firstly, there are those who believe that the role of the intellectual has been undermined by the processes of institutionalisation, professionalisation, and the commercialisation of intellectual life. These expressions of grief over the absence of intellectuals, about 'the salience of the intellectual' (Max Gallo, quoted in Fassin 1998), the invisibility of the intellectual (Bauman 1992a) and the vanishing of the non-academic intellectual (Jacoby 1987), often refer to Sartre as the ideal of intellectual responsibility and engagement. They lament that the death of the intellectual has left a void in public life (Ignatieff 1997) and complain that the voices of intellectuals are hardly 'audible in the noise of the mass culture and politics' (Goldfarb 1998: 216). In addition, postmodernists such as Jean Baudrillard (1990) and Jean-François Lyotard (1984) pronounce the death of the intellectual by pointing out that intellectuals could no longer retain their legitimation, which justified their credibility and which allowed them to speak on issues beyond their specific competence: they became mere citizens, devoid of any specific authority. Bauman (1995: 239) sees the end of the 'historical glory of intellectuals' as a result of the growing irrelevance of their ideas, especially those that were 'tied closely to other, now largely extinct, factors of the modern age – great utopias of perfect society'. The disappearance of the charismatic public intellectual is viewed by Jacoby (1987) as a consequence of the absorption of intellectuals into university faculties in an era of specialisation and professionalisation. In the same vein, Frank Furedi (2004: 25) blames the routinisation of intellectual life and the banalisation of cultural life for the transformation of the intellectual into 'a uniquely insignificant figure'.

Secondly, there are voices claiming that the death of the intellectual is greatly exaggerated (Fassin 1998) or even false (Collini 2006). According to this view, the notion of the decline of the intellectual, attributed to specialisation, institutionalisation, widespread access to knowledge and public platforms once restricted to elites, and the media culture, overlooks the existence of the conditions for intellectuals' independence. Writers who, like Alan Wolfe (2003) or Said (1994), defend the role of intellectuals insist that intellectuals, by providing broader perspectives that are both necessary and desired by the public, perform an important social function. Even those who want to retain the special role of the intellectual, however, also express a suspicion of the intellectual. This third position reflects on a present-day type of intellectuals' ambiguity by pointing not to the intellectual's lower status but, rather, to the fact that institutions of higher education and research seem to be more withdrawn from life, and to the decline in quality of the public (Bourdieu 1993).

Still others are more critical and view intellectuals not only as being the most indoctrinated part of the population (Chomsky 1989), but also as being guilty of irresponsibility by virtue of having been 'intellectual associates of Hitler and Stalin' (Fuller 2003: 20; see also Judt 1992). Some writers, following George Orwell's saying that 'No ordinary man could be such a fool' (quoted in Szacki 1990: 230), criticise the intellectual for 'getting things badly wrong' (Norman Stone, quoted in Jennings and Kemp-Welch 1997: 1). Others, such as Paul Johnson (1988), accuse intellectuals of being full of hypocrisy, selfishness and despotism as well as habitually forgetting that people matter more than concepts and ideas, or, such as John Carey (1992), expose the pretensions and elitism of intellectuals. Steve Fuller (2005) points to intellectuals' paranoia, impotence and inability to cope with the challenges facing them in the modern world. In similar vein, Richard A. Posner (2001) criticises the declining quality of intellectuals' work, which he attributes to the growing prominence of celebrity culture. Furedi (2004: 2) suggests that the marginalisation of intellectual passion and the compliance of the intellectual with a 'philistine social engineering agenda' are consequences of 'a new ethos of managerialism that dominates intellectual and cultural life'. Nonetheless, it is worth remembering that such a negative evaluation of intellectual work is nothing new. At least since Edmund Burke's time 'intellectuals have been blamed for virtually every ill that afflicts society' (Furedi 2004: 27). While Joseph Schumpeter (1947: 145–55) worried about intellectuals' hostility to capitalism, Sartre (1974: 230) saw the intellectual as someone who 'meddles in what is not his business and claims to question both received truths and the accepted behaviour inspired by them, in the name of a global conception of man and of society'.

These contradictory and confusing opinions about the fate of the public intellectual as well as the instability of the usage of the term make defining the intellectual a very difficult task. Moreover, this difficulty is increased by the fact that the intellectual is a historically constructed category, whose characteristics depend upon the cultural tradition of a particular society (Eyerman 1994). In addition, efforts to define the intellectual are made even more difficult by the fact that many of the writers who are making the attempts are themselves intellectuals and are therefore confronted by the problems of self-definition. Thus, the reality of the intellectual as a social category is always 'doubly in doubt: in the absence of a clear definition, and for a lack of a firm legitimation' (Fassin 1998: 23). It is not surprising, therefore, that definitions range from ones that focus on the intellectual's sacred role of priest, whose words sustain 'the cult of the final and the obvious as acknowledged by and contained in tradition' (Kolakowski 1971: 57), to ones that use the term 'intellectual' in its everyday sense – that is, as writers, philosophers, some journalists and some academics, or generally as people with advanced educations, producers or transmitters of culture or ideas, or members of either category who engage in public issues.

The majority of traditional definitions assume that intellectuals can be found in all modern societies and tend to stress intellectuals' function as producers of ideas. Talcott Parsons (1969: 4–6), for example, defines intellectuals by pointing to their primary concern with the articulation of cultural symbols, while Seymour Martin Lipset (1963: 311) views them as those 'who create, distribute, and apply culture, that is, the symbolic world of man, including art, science, and religion'. These definitions tend to see intellectuals as 'special custodians of abstract idea like reason and justice and truth, jealous guardians of moral standards that are too often ignored in the market place and the houses of power' (Coser 1965: vii). Furthermore, many of these definitions view the intellectual as an objective social category with distinctive relations to other social groups. Looking at the most celebrated definitions of the intellectual, we need to mention Benda's, Mannheim's, Antonio Gramsci's and Michel Foucault's usages of that term.

The most distinctive definition is Benda's ([1927]1980: 43) conceptualisation of intellectuals as individuals 'not of this world', whose reason for living is creation and knowledge, as those 'whose activity is essentially not the pursuit of practical aims, all those who seek their joy in the practice of an art or science or metaphysical speculation, in short in the possession of non-material advantages'. In his seminal work *The*

Treason of the Intellectuals (originally published in France in 1927, and in the United Kingdom in 1928), Benda portrays true intellectuals as serving the interests of mankind best by being committed to universal ideas, while at the same time staying detached from the political passions of the masses and not taking sides in politics. This book has initiated a long tradition of lamenting over the eagerness of intellectuals to attach themselves to mass movements, being followed, among others, by Raymond Aron (1957), Tony Judt (1992) and Posner (2001).

For Benda ([1927]1980: 43), real intellectuals – those 'whose activity is essentially not the pursuit of practical aims' – are the central figures in the account of the modern social order. In his words, the treason of intellectuals – that is, their betrayal of a disinterested mission, oriented towards the betterment of the whole of humanity for 'the service of their political passions' – results in the domination of national particularism or social partisanship (45). This criticism (52) was directed towards his contemporary intellectuals, whom he condemned for abandoning their role as the guardians of truth, for descending to the level of particularistic passions, for conceding their moral authority to the 'organization of collective passions' and for being interested solely in the pursuit of concrete advantage. Benda is guilty, notes Stefan Collini (2006: 297), of a double fantasy: firstly, that there is 'a form of intellectual activity which is entirely divorced form the world', and, secondly, that 'pure thought can be operative in the world without thereby being at all corrupted or compromised'. Furthermore, it seems that Benda, himself Dreyfusard, overlooks the fact that the heroic defenders of Dreyfus were also – in the light of his own definition – guilty of treason, as they deployed the intellectual's autonomy and authority in the name of France, a country that they 'unashamedly identified with reason, liberty and justice' (Jennings 2000b: 834).

Mannheim (1949: 160–1) also sees the intellectual as the main force in the shaping of the modern social order, the possessor of independent judgement and as the '*watchman* in what otherwise would be a pitch-black night' (emphasis in original). He, like Benda, sees rootlessness as a condition of criticism itself. In *Ideology and Utopia* intellectuals are presented as lacking a firm anchorage in the social order, and therefore as able to transcend their group of origin to pursue their own ideas. Mannheim (154) provides an explanation as to how the 'experimental outlook, unceasingly sensitive to the dynamic nature of society', can be developed 'only by a relatively classless stratum which is not too firmly situated in the social order'. The idea of free-floating, unattached intellectuals consists of two seperate arguments. Firstly, Mannheim suggests that intellectuals are capable of ideological diversity, since, as they do not form a class, they 'are differentiated' or heterogeneous in their political views. Secondly, being relatively unaffected by their class of origin, intellectuals can act as the 'carriers of the synthesis' – or, in other words, as 'the predestined advocate of the intellectual interests of the whole' (154, 158). Thus, the idea of a 'free-floating' position within a society is presented as both an explanation of intellectuals' actions and a justification for their privileged position in a new scientific politics. As Robert J. Brym (1980: 56–8) notes, Mannheim's view of the political attitudes of intellectuals, as simultaneously heterogeneous and homogeneous, is full of unresolved tensions.

Gramsci, like Mannheim, recognised the power of knowledge to influence politics, but, in contrast to Mannheim, the Italian Marxist treated intellectuals as primarily class-bound and argued that each social class 'creates together within itself, organically, one or more strata of intellectuals' (Gramsci 1971: 5). Organic intellectuals, unlike Benda's independent intellectuals, have surrendered their autonomy, as they are involved in supporting the interests of a particular group. They are distinguished not necessarily by their profession but, rather, by their function in 'directing the ideas and aspirations of the class to which they organically belong' (Gramsci 1971: 3). Organic intellectuals, who can be found amongst all social groups and who work within these particular locations and articulate these groups' interests, are contrasted with detached, traditional intellectuals operating in the realm of truth, who 'put themselves forward as autonomous and independent of the dominant social group' (7). Traditional intellectuals, unlike organic intellectuals, do not represent or serve any group interest; they are, like Benda's intellectuals, spiritual leaders who defend universal values. Gramsci's categories of organic and traditional intellectuals are not stable and are 'fantastically unclear and difficult to make clear' (Said 1996: 79). Yet his thoughts – especially his social analysis of the intellectual as a person who fulfils a particular set of functions in society, and his idea that intellectuals, not social classes, are essential to the working of modern societies – have been responsible for today's perspective, which argues that intellectuals should be organically linked to social groups and movements (Eyerman 1994; Karabel 1996; Brym 1980), and also for Foucault's formulation of the notion of the intellectual as the specialist.

Foucault (1977) replaces the traditional intellectual (who defends universal values and aspires to be a spiritual leader of mankind) by the expert specialist, who engages in and articulates the interest within his or her field of specialisation. He rejects Benda's vision of the universal intellectual as inhabiting a realm of pure value and points out that there is no value that is untouched by power. Foucault's model of the 'specific intellectual', with her or his limited, specialised involvement in selected public issues, also differs from the traditional French image of the 'total intellectual', who speaks on all issues of the day. Writing after the Parisian student demonstrations in May 1968, Foucault (1977: 207) contends that the masses no longer require the intellectual to provide them with representation. Instead, the task of the intellectual becomes reflexive: '[T]o struggle against the forms of power that would transform him into its objects and instrument by appropriating the "tools" of the intellectual, that is, knowledge, "truth", or discourse' (208). The increased intellectual specialisation and the displacement of the humanities by science has undercut the traditional cultural bases for universal intellectuals. The 'specific' intellectual, Foucault argues, is a 'professional' and an 'expert' in his or her particular field of enquiry, someone who works inside a discipline.

The traditional sociological definitions of the intellectual tend to refer to intellectuals as a group defined either by their primary occupational activity – such definitions stress that intellectuals' function is to develop and disseminate ideas – or by their class positions; such definitions view the intellectual as an objective social category with distinctive relations to other social groups. Looking at the latter type of definition of intellectuals, Charles Kurzman and Lynn Owens (2002) have divided them into three distinct approaches: the first treats intellectuals as potentially a class in themselves; the second assumes that intellectuals are primarily class-bound; and the third regards intellectuals as relatively classless – that is, able to transcend their group of origin to pursue their own ideas. For example, Alvin Gouldner's (1979: 21) description of intellectuals, or a 'flawed universal class', as 'a new cultural bourgeoisie whose capital is not its money but its control over valuable cultures' illustrates the first approach, Gramsci's idea of an engaged intellectual supports the second approach, while Edward Shils' (1972: 3) definition of intellectuals as those 'unusually sensitive to the sacred, [with] an uncommon reflexiveness about the nature of their universe and the rules which govern their society', represents the third perspective.

Nevertheless, by the second part of the twentieth century intellectuals had become distinguished not by their status as a class or collectivity but by their individual quality, vision of knowledge and strategies. 'What had begun as a collective identity, emerging in the uninstitutionalized interactions of a situated group, as a form of identity generated through a distinct cultural-political position, was now seen as rooted within the individual, a personal quality and a social role' (Eyerman 1994: 30). The continuous changes in the nature of the intellectual's role and the composition of the intellectual group mean that now, in the context of increasingly egalitarian attitudes, wider access to higher education, a decline in the deference accorded to academics and the prominence of 'celebrity culture', intellectuals cannot be conceptualised as a class or caste. New sociological conceptualisations tend to define intellectuals through their membership of an intellectual field (Camic and Gross 2004: 241–2). For example, Bourdieu (1989: 99) defines intellectuals as cultural producers who belong to an autonomous intellectual field, one independent of religious, political and economic or other powers. Bourdieu (2004: 59) uses his field approach to argue that every scientific choice is 'a social strategy of investment'. Incumbents of the field, seen as constituted of scientific habitus and endowed with different amounts of intellectual capital, employed individual and collective strategies in struggles to preserve, transform and reproduce this social space.

The notion of the intellectual field, understood as a contested terrain upon which the struggle for recognition as an intellectual occurs, therefore focuses our attention on a configuration of relationships, interdependencies among intellectuals and their struggles with one another and with various audiences to establish their legitimacy and credibility as intellectuals. To speak about the intellectual field as a social space made up of agents taking up various positions is to break with the idea that intellectuals form a uniform, homogeneous group, and to observe a universe of competition for the 'monopoly of the legitimate handling' of intellectual goods (Bourdieu 2004: 44–6).

Collini (2006: 57), who criticises Bourdieu's concept of cultural capital as importing 'too narrowly economistic nations of "competition" and "positional strategy" into areas of activity better understood in their own terms', proposes that the intellectual should be defined by reference to his or her performance in a role – or, more exactly, to 'a structure of relations'. In other words, 'the intellectual must, by definition, build out from a relatively secure basis in one specialised activity and simultaneously cultivate the necessarily more contestable perspective of a non-specialist' (57). In contrast to the sociological definitions' focus on intellectuals as an occupational group or on their class position, Collini's cultural definition of the intellectual refers to function rather than occupation or belief. It also directs our attention to 'the ways in which the role of intellectual is a role constituted by and performed *within* a set of historically specific cultural and social relations' (62; emphasis in original).

Defining the intellectual through performance in a role emphasises that the role of the intellectual involves the intersection of several dimensions, thus 'being intellectual will always be a matter of degree' (52). Such an approach brings into focus the fact that, since the most important elements are achievement and engagement with some of the general concerns of various publics, intellectual capital needs to be reinvested constantly, and the relationship between speaker and publics needs to be seen as a two-way street. It also provides an explanation of the structural tensions, such as the polarity between criticism and conformity, the dilemma of detachment and engagement and the subsequent confusing evolutions of the role of intellectuals, as stemming from the instabilities inherent in the role of public intellectual.

Collini (2006: 7) focuses on the mechanisms by which a culture enables academics, writers, journalists or artists to combine being recognised as having attained a certain level of intellectual or cultural distinction with addressing non-specialised audiences on matters of general concern. He rejects the notion that the political activity as such is constitutive of the intellectual, and instead argues that what is 'a constitutive part of the meaning of the term intellectual in the cultural sense' is his or her public role (51). Thus, although being politically active is one form in which that public role may frequently, but not necessarily, be performed, the intellectual is seen as not necessarily politically active. Moreover, there is 'no one set of topics, which it is the peculiar business of the intellectual to address' (56).

It seems that it is Collini's perspective, due to its concentration on the way in which successfully fulfilling the role of intellectual involves doing more than merely applying expertise, that grasps the nature and uniqueness of the notion of the intellectual, and thus best suits my research purpose. Because such a conceptualisation of the intellectual makes it possible to focus on the movement between the two notional spheres – the establishment of professional standing and the usage of it for the setting of the relationship with a non-academic audience – it allows us to address directly the core characteristic of being public intellectuals. In what follows, we look at the conceptualisation of and the tensions built into the role of the public intellectual.

The role of public intellectuals

Collini's (2006: 190) idea that the activity of the intellectual 'happens when specialisms "converge" and scholars go beyond their particularities' stresses that public intellectuals have always started out with some recognised expertise, on which they capitalise when speaking to a broader, non-specialist public. Thus, it can be argued that the importance of public intellectuals is associated with their role of restoring the link between professional producers of ideas (such as academics, journalists, artists and scholars) and a non-specialist public.

The term 'public intellectual' is well established now and refers to 'those few academics who enjoy a significant media presence and who use the opportunity to address current political and social issues' (Collini 2006: 231). Yet in the English-speaking world, despite the fact that in France the term 'the intellectual' has really meant 'the public intellectual' from the beginning, the concept of the public intellectual became popular only in the 1960s. It first entered academic writings on the wave of nostalgia for an independent intellectual that was initiated by Jacoby's book *The Last Intellectuals* (1987). The book's message that 'the universities virtually monopolized intellectual work' (8) dominated late twentieth-century discussion of the role of intellectuals and their autonomy – two factors seen as central to the intellectual's vocation.

Jacoby, unlike Allan Bloom, who in *The Closing of the American Mind* (1988) claims that leftist intellectuals 'are wrecking the university', thinks 'that the university is wrecking intellectuals' (Lemert 1991: 179). Jacoby insists that intellectual life has been distorted by the dominance of academisation, professionalisation and the specialisation of intellectual work, which has left little room for those willing and able to reach large audiences with their views. The absorption of intellectuals by the university meant that they lost their traditional rebelliousness (Jacoby 1987: 82). Following C. Wright Mills (1963), who already at the beginning of the 1960s was lamenting that intellectuals were surrendering to conformism, Jacoby (117) writes that 'in class, status, and self-image' the intellectual has become more solidly middle class, a man at a desk, married, with children, living in a respectable suburb. Despite Jacoby's normative and nostalgic stance, which romanticises the past role of public intellectuals, ignores the fact that intellectuals never were really independent and overlooks the role of non-academic intellectuals associated with new social movements (such as feminism or anti-racism), his appeal to intellectuals to uphold the 'politics of truth' has opened up the long-standing debate concerning the social and political significance of intellectuals and the discussion of the role of academisation in the undermining of intellectuals' autonomy.

While many support Jacoby's idea and claim that universities present a threat to serious intellectual work as their ethos fosters mediocrity and trivialisation (Luke et al. 1987), others, such as Said (1994), criticise his assertion that academisation poses a risk to the independent intellectual. According to Said (1994: 61), universities, despite many pressures, can still offer 'the intellectual a quasi-utopian space in which reflection and research can go on'. The main danger to the public intellectual today is not so much the academisation as the professionalism – that is, 'thinking of your work as intellectual as something you do for a living, between the hours of nine and five with one eye on the clock, and another cocked at what is considered to be proper, professional behaviour … ' (55). For Said, three negative consequences of professionalism – namely the pressures of professionalism, the cult of the certified expert and the drift towards power and authority – all kill the sense of excitement and discovery, and the critical and independent spirit of analysis and judgement. Therefore, a way of maintaining relative intellectual independence is to have 'the attitude of an amateur instead of a professional' (64). Said claims (61) that today the public intellectual ought to be an amateur, namely a lonely dissenter who 'raises moral issues at the heart of even the most technical and professional activity' and whose critical and independent analyses neither succumb to power or to thinking entirely from within the speciality or in favour of conformity. However, this rather romantic image of the isolated individual's heroic struggle with power in the name of solidarity with the oppressed exposes the instability of Said's usage of the term 'public intellectual'. 'Said's book does not really confront, let alone resolve, these tensions between lonely individuality and axiomatic solidarity, in part because it never rises to a sufficiently analytical level' (Collini 2006: 428).

Said's (1994) assertions, that being an intellectual is not at all inconsistent with being an academic and that an attitude of professionalism can be a threat to intellectualism, are not totally new, as the negative association between scholarly reputation and engagement fuelled by passion and affection rather than narrow specialisation has been pointed out by others. For instance, Friedrich Nietzsche, in *Beyond Good and Evil* ([1911] 1990), held up the philosopher who lives recklessly and rates himself constantly as superior to scholars and ordinary men, while José Ortega y Gasset ([1929] 1961) condemned the barbarism of specialisation. In the same spirit, Florian Znaniecki (1940: 134–5) wrote that scholarly discipline hampers originality, as scholars in 'their striving for absolute certainty put formal perfection above originality and prefer a thorough piece of work which brings little that is new but satisfies established standards to an important theoretic innovation which falls short of those standards'. Furthermore, some, such as Posner (2001), Michael Walzer (2002) and Fuller (2005), disagree with Said's claim that responsibility for truth can be experienced only if the intellectual stands apart from the field. For Walzer, true knowledge is the source of critical power, and social critics work as adversarial insiders relying on the work of specialists, while, for Posner, the amateurism of public intellectuals undermines the standards and norms of the scientific community. Said's (1994: 64) example of an amateur – that is, the intellectual who chooses 'the risk and uncertain results of the public sphere over the insider space' – is Noam Chomsky. Yet, as Fuller (2005: 123) points out, closer inspection reveals that Chomsky and other twentieth-century exemplars of the public intellectual amateur (such as Said himself, Bertrand Russell and Albert Einstein) have been 'trading' on their academic authority in 'that the character of their general claims and arguments bears the marks of their original expertise'. Posner (2001: 50–2) goes even further and argues that, in today's age of specialisation, the time when amateurs such as Chomsky could make a high-quality contribution of benefit to a general audience outside their particular fields has already passed, and, moreover, that amateurs' opinions carry little weight with professionals.

In the debate about the impact of academisation and specialisation, Posner, in his book *Public Intellectuals: A Study of Decline*, takes a totally different position from Said and Jacoby's admiration of the Sartrean, critical and oppositional 'total intellectual'. He is concerned not so much with the absence of the public intellectual but, rather, with the quality of the public intellectual's work. Posner praises the university as the proper place for intellectual activity and holds that the main public intellectuals' comments on larger public issues outside their narrow expertise come without any risk or cost and are not of impressive quality. Whereas Said (1994: 11) defines the public intellectual as 'someone whose place it is publicly to raise embarrassing questions, to confront orthodoxy and dogma (rather than to produce them), to be someone who cannot easily be co-opted by governments or corporations', for Posner (2001: 30) this is too narrow a definition, as 'it implies that the only opposition worth putting up is to governments and corporations'. Nevertheless, his own definition of the public intellectual, which states that 'a public intellectual is a person who, drawing on his intellectual resources, addresses a broad, though educated, public on issues with a political or ideological dimension', is also a narrow one, as it concentrates on those figures who are result-oriented and who use the mainstream of public media to comment on contemporary political issues (Posner 2001: 170). Although Posner (23) agrees with Said that the role of public intellectual involves 'disputing norms', his intellectual is someone who merely writes for the general public on public affairs for fame and money, rather than being someone who tries to engage with political matters in order to induce change in the direction of the recognition of rights and democratic freedoms for everyone.

Posner (2001) claims that it is the media market that presides over the formation of the intellectual, who more often than not then fails to deliver the promised quality. Noticing the ever-increasing power of the media to make intellectual reputations, he argues that the media's appetite for public intellectuals has grown not only in inverse proportion to the quality of public intellectuals' performance but also in inverse proportion to the risk faced by public intellectuals. Posner shows that the market for public intellectuals is becoming dominated by academics at the same time as the growth of academic specialisation has made it increasingly difficult for academics to fill the public intellectual role. To obtain academic credentials, seen as the chief and the best warrant of intellectual credibility, is not easy. Moreover, such credentials do not always impress that audience. Therefore, intellectuals rely on market-based devices for increasing buyers' trust, such as celebrity status and a reputation for commitment. Public intellectual goods are goods that must be taken largely on faith because consumers cannot check and evaluate their quality. Consequently, public intellectuals can exit the public intellectual market at low cost (Posner 2001).

Nevertheless, contrary to Posner's claim that market-based incentives do not ensure the quality of public intellectual products, some argue that market devices work, although for the majority of public intellectuals it is not the money that acts as an incentive. 'It is rather the notion that readers are not fools' (Wolfe 2003: 370). Even if it is appetite for money rather than a striving for wider recognition that is responsible for changes in the relationship of intellectuals to publicity, it does not need to mean that new market-created intellectuals – who came into being with the expansion of, and qualitative changes in, the cultural market, the audience, the press and publishing – are necessarily inferior to academia- or state-created intellectuals (Kauppi 1996: 1). For other scholars, for example Bourdieu (1993) and Regis Debray (1981), an examination of changes in the sources of intellectuals' credibility suggests that there are many more processes at play than Posner's denunciation of the media orientation of intellectuals admits.

These analyses of the evolution of the role of intellectuals show that, in this newly developed intellectual market on scholarly works, it is easy to become surpassed by other contenders more able to attract public attention (Debray 1981; Kauppi 1996). Public intellectuals' 'mistaken prophecy and superficial policy advice', according to Posner (2001: 99), are results of 'the absence of the usual gatekeepers who filter and police academic publication'. It seems, however, that evaluation of the intellectual input should be seen in a wider context of changes in political culture and in a broader framework of battles over the evaluation of the quality of public intellectual work – battles that are indicative of struggles for intellectual autonomy (Bourdieu 1989). In short, the assumed deterioration of public intellectual work can also be seen as a result of the fact that public debates are giving way to 'celebrity chat shows', and the fact that institutions external to the domain of cultural production determine the value of their work. Furthermore, it can be argued, contrary to Posner, that it is not just public intellectuals but academics as well who can be found guilty of failing in their commentaries and their predictions. As Eva Etzioni-Halevy (1985: 2) shows, Western academics are 'prophets who have failed', as their knowledge and advice 'have not contributed as much as some of them have claimed to either the moral rectitude or the socio-economic well-being of Western societies'. So, generally, Posner's book is more about celebrity than accomplishment, as he focuses on academics who enjoy media recognition rather than on intellectuals 'whose views have seriously influenced the public' (Wolfe 2003: 364). It overlooks the risks and uncertainties connected with entering the public sphere, and the issues of cost and risk involved in the pursuit of less 'celebrated' goals by less 'celebrated' intellectuals.

Among many other scholars who define public intellectuals by stressing what they do over and above their professional duties, the most interesting contributions come from Bourdieu and Bauman. Challenging the classical opposition of pure contemplation and engagement, Bourdieu (1992: 4) conceptualises the intellectual as having a civic mission to promote the 'corporatism of the universal'. Yet his assertion that intellectuals must deploy their specific expertise and authority in activity outside their particular domain of specialisation differs from Said's admiration for the lonely and oppositional figure of the amateur. According to Bourdieu (1993), intellectuals, in order to constitute themselves as an autonomous collective force, need to draw on their intellectual capital. This specific capital enables them to claim autonomy vis-à-vis the political authorities. Such a request by intellectuals for a privileged status within a society is justified, writes Bourdieu (1989: 103), because by 'defending themselves as a whole they defend the universal'. As intellectuals' entry into politics is rooted in the authority of their autonomous disciplines, this means that public intellectuals are, paradoxically, 'bi-dimensional beings' who – despite the antipathy between autonomy and engagement – are capable of extending both simultaneously. Yet this 'paradoxical synthesis of the opposites of retreat and engagement, typical of intellectuals, was neither invented in one shot nor instituted once for all' (Bourdieu 1989: 101). Being unstable and uncertain, the synthesis 'enables the holders of cultural capital to "regress" to one position or another as warranted by the historical pendulum, i.e. to "regress" to the role of pure writers, artists or scholars, journalists, etc.' (101). Despite the fact that intellectuals are exposed to all sorts of subtle constraints and censorship, they are the ones best situated to overcome the illusion of freedom and 'to extract from the present the laws that make it possible to dominate it, to break free of it' (1993: 44). Although initially Bourdieu saw intellectuals' gestures of political commitment as moves in a self-contained game, later he himself was 'eager to take place in the greatest tradition of public intellectuals like Zola and Sartre' (Robbins 2006: 19).

Bauman, while noticing the historical origin of the conceptualisation of intellectuals by what they do over and above their professional duties, says that being 'an intellectual means *performing a peculiar role* in the society as a *whole*' (1995: 225; emphasis in original). In such formulations the accent is on intellectuals' function outside their professional role, seen as providing intellectuals with authority of a particular academic discipline or area of expertise, and also on their unique ability to gain a universal outlook on the problems faced by a society. Nevertheless, while in modernity a mutual dependence and constitutive affinity between the political rulers and intellectuals allowed intellectuals to claim authority and, therefore, to serve the state as 'legislators' (Bauman 1987: 3), in postmodern conditions, in which politics becomes 'mostly about the reallocation of attention', intellectuals become 'interpreters' or translators, working from 'inside' various different systems of knowledge (1992b: 201). Thus, intellectuals, despite the fact that they are individuals who possess both the ability and duty to act as the 'collective consciousness' of the nation, or people who know how to put the law and the idea of justice above their personal interests, natural instincts and group egoism (1992a: 85–6), are limited to interpreting 'meanings for the benefit of those who are not of the community which stands behind the meanings' and to mediating 'the communication between "finite power" or "communities of meanings"' (1987: 17).

To sum up, the term 'public intellectual' denotes authors, academics, scientists and artists who communicate to the general public outside their professional role on the basis of their knowledge and authority gained in their specific disciplines. Viewing the public intellectual as combining 'the role of specialist in one or other field of intellectual work (writer, scientist, professor) and the role of one who for some reason feels the call to active participation, or even leadership , in some supra-professional community', Jerzy Szacki (1990: 232) points to the complexity of the relationship and tensions between the public intellectual's various functions. These tensions, inbuilt into the role of the public intellectual, have been dramatically enhanced by the growing

institutionalisation and professionalism of intellectual life, the commercialisation of journalism and the rise of electronic media cultural
production values. Consequently, both the intellectual capital allowing
for intellectuals' engagement with a broad public over some important
issues, and the engagement itself, need to be constantly re-earned,
rethought and reapplied. In other words, there is a continuous need for
the sources of intellectual authority to be subject to reinvestment.

Sources of authority

The source of intellectuals' authority has evolved as a result of the
growing importance of expertise/knowledge, academic specialisation,
and institutionalisation and the increasing power of the media. In the
classical model of the intellectual, the source of authority is connected
with the intellectual's belief in his or her mission to proclaim a 'truth'
and defend universal values and humanitarian causes. This first tradition's historical roots, the Enlightenment, the Dreyfus Affair and the
model of the Russian intelligentsia, constituted the intellectual as a
separate group 'only in the activity of *critique*' (Bauman 1995: 228;
emphasis in original). The second source of intellectuals' credibility is
their specialist knowledge, their academic/professional credentials.
More recently, the basis of intellectuals' authority has become their
celebrity status, their high media profile, which allows them to reach the
general public. These major transformations in the role of and in the
beliefs about intellectuals suggest that there is declining relevance for the
dualistic view of the intellectual as critic versus expert (Debray 1981).
The departure from the classical model of the intellectual, whose 'closet
and more troublesome kin is the philosopher' (Fuller 2005: 3), focuses
our attention on today's convergence of public voice and expertise/
knowledge as the basis of intellectuals' authority.

In the classical model, the intellectual is seen as a social critic whose
mission is to uphold universal ideals against the state and to represent
the realm of ideas beyond narrow specialisation. This tradition, while
presenting 'true' intellectuals as detached and critical, and therefore able
to provide society as a whole with ideas and solutions to its main problems, views experts as being compromised by their relations with
power and as unable to move beyond the pragmatic task of the moment.
Experts, as professionals who are 'absorbed in the pursuit of concrete
answers to concrete problems', are contrasted with intellectuals, as ones
who 'go beyond the immediate concrete task', who tend 'to penetrate a
more general realm of meanings or values' and 'who live off ideas'
(Coser 1965: viii). The job of the expert is to explore, discover and

communicate, however, without providing any judgements on ethical matters. In contrast to experts, who are condemned for the narrowing of the field of intellectual possibility, intellectual-critics are praised for having a broader outlook and for being committed, sensitive and reflective (Said 1994). All the same, despite this classic model's dualistic view of the intellectual as critic versus expert, it is worth noticing that even the Dreyfusards were basing their critical stance on their exceptional professional knowledge. The famous '*J'accuse*' open letter of Zola in defence of Dreyfus was signed not only by artists and writers but also by scientists who believed that their response as scientists was necessary, since 'the miscarriage of justice denoted a challenge to the status of science' (Jennings 2000b: 830).

In the second half of the twentieth century the classical model's division between the role of critic and expert was reinforced by theories of the so-called 'knowledge society', which view expertise/knowledge as the basis of intellectuals' authority and autonomy and their emancipatory projects. The initial debates on the nature of the knowledge-based society, by stressing the positive value and social utility of science itself, assumed that the intellectual had ceased to be a critic and had become an academic-expert. Theorists who emphasise the centrality of knowledge production in modern societies, in contrast to the traditional approach, locate a new type of intellectual-expert, identified as a collective actor, at the heart of the new type of society. The image of the expert as a collective force, as formulated in Gouldner's (1979) controversial idea of the 'new social class' or in Gyorgy Konrad and Ivan Szelenyi's (1979) vision of intellectuals as a ruling class *in status nascendi*, emphasises that in modern credential society the professional, as a 'technocrat', can establish her- or himself as a 'self-interested' collective actor. For Konrad and Szelenyi, intellectuals constitute a group that seeks to obtain power and reward for itself by exploiting its relative monopoly of complex knowledge as a means of achieving these goals. Gouldner (1979) associates the changing role of intellectuals with the idea of power by virtue of specialised knowledge, and assumes that their scientific culture of critical discourse would provide the basis for a collective identity that would create the foundations for their leading role in society. Contrary to the expectations of these two perspectives, the following decades have been dominated not by the rise of intellectuals as a new ruling class but, rather, by mourning the decline of the intellectual. In this context, the theories that identify the intellectual as the established collective actor capable of serving his or her own interests have been replaced with the image of the individual expert-intellectual.

Theories of this type, while emphasising the salience of the intellectual-social critic, promote the rise of this new kind of intellectual who occupies a specific position in the domain of knowledge production, testifying to the role of professionalism as the foundation for the credible performance of intellectuals in the public world (Pels 1995). It is also the case that, in liberal theory, the value of independent experts, as technically proficient specialists with no political agenda, is associated with their ability to inform and help people in making wise decisions. Such intellectual-experts should empower laypersons as partners in deliberation on all matters of science policy and help create a science fully rooted in the civic traditions of democracy. Experts, it is assumed, should play a role in defining the issues before they reach the stage at which decisions need to be reached. From the position of the non-involved, non-interested party, experts' main task is to empower laypersons as partners in deliberation (Ferree et al. 2002).

Yet, as we learned from Foucault, such practice, by making use of seemingly neutral categories of knowledge and expertise, could be a part of the mechanism of control and legitimisation. The specialist acts in the name of his or her field of expertise and advances a particular scientific competence, but, at the same time, the specific intellectual 'can take on a general significance by providing instruments of analysis ... – that is the intellectual's role' (Foucault 1977: 216). Her or his local struggle 'can have effects and implications which are not simply professional or sectoral', and it is even the case that the intellectual 'can operate and struggle at the general level of that regime of truth which is so essential to the structure and functioning of our society' (Foucault 1977: 217). The notion of the intellectual-expert is also viewed with suspicion by Ron Eyerman (1994: 190–5), who criticises experts for serving either as advisers to power or manipulators of public opinion. Arguing that the expansion of the role of experts leads to their developing a more individualised, instrumental and strategic orientation as their knowledge becomes a resource for those holding political power, Eyerman propagates the role of the intellectual as an activist in social movements. Nevertheless, with social movements today becoming increasingly institutionalised and incorporated into the state, intellectuals of this type seem to be less visible.

Another major transformation in the role of the intellectual, as we have already mentioned, is connected with the growing importance of intellectuals' celebrity status. This new development implies that the talent for publicity rather than the quality of their work can constitute a media intellectual and that the logic of media communication dominates the logic of intellectual criticism. The relationship of intellectuals to publicity has changed as cultural celebrity has become easily accessible and very profitable, symbolically as well as economically (Kauppi 1996). Since media intellectuals 'work in and against the mass media, in and against the convention of academia' (Goldfarb 1998: 204), their authority is only 'temporarily stable' and still constitutes a 'relatively uncodified social resource' (Kauppi 1996: 133). So, the public engagement of intellectuals in the role of celebrity stars – the most recent manifestation – is based on a very unstable status, which, when institutionalised, loses its 'exceptional character' (Kauppi 1996: 133).

Looking at the various definitions of the intellectual, it can be observed that their conceptualisations of intellectual authority tend to refer to at least two dimensions of the role: creativity and courage. The emphasis on creativity is the essential part of all main definitions of intellectuals. For Shils (1972: 7), for example, creativity is the most important characteristic of the intellectual, as the 'true' intellectual possesses qualities that can scarcely be ascribed to 'the ordinary run' of professors. Intellectuals, who 'elicit, guide and form the expressive dispositions within society', are by definition culturally creative and possess 'an uncommon reflexiveness about the nature of their universe and the rules that govern their society' (5). Although they differ in 'their creative powers and their knowledge of and attachment to the stocks of traditions and works' (154), intellectuals, who 'penetrate beyond the screen of immediate concrete experience' (5), are above all concerned with the elaboration and development of alternative potentials. Creativity, where acknowledged and prized, 'is perceived as a primary obligation to intellectuals' (6), and it is the key element in the definition of public intellectuals as it raises scholars to the status of intellectuals as they gain recognition in their exercise of the right to intervene in the public sphere on matters in which they have competency.

This uplifting role of creativity is also stressed by Znaniecki (1940: 165), who proposes to metaphorically term intellectuals 'explorers' as they 'are seeking in the domain of knowledge new ways into the unknown'. In other words, they 'specialise, so to speak, in doing the unexpected' (165). Znaniecki (198) notes that the scientist-explorer is 'a creator whose work, a unique and irreducible link between the past and future, enters as a dynamic component into the total, ever-increasing knowledge of mankind'. Such a concept of creativity, understood as an activity of scholars who aim at the creation of a world of 'relative truth, infinite in potential wealth, admirable in its trends perfection' (199), overcomes the bias inherent in the romantic model of creativity, which associates creativity solely with cultural innovators and artistic spirits.

Creativity's importance is associated with its ability to elevate the intellectual above the professional into the 'supra-professional community' (Said 1994; Shils 1972; Szacki 1990; Bauman 1995; Bourdieu 1989). Assuming creativity to be the main characteristic of the intellectual also permits us to argue that knowledge is the source of the critical power of public intellectuals and that intellectuals are of crucial importance for the quality of life in democratic societies. Thus, such a perspective offers us the ability to overcome the partiality of the tradition of humanistic knowledge, which, as Parsons (1969: 18) notes, 'perceives intellectuals as mainly members of a broad humanistic discipline rather than those in the natural sciences and which tends to confine the term "creative" to the humanistic side of culture'. Bourdieu (2004: 113) also recognises the role of 'creative imagination' as one of the foundations of intellectual competence and as one of the factors making intellectual life 'something closer to the artist's life than to the routine of the academy' (Bourdieu, quoted in Hobsbawm 2002: 297). In contrast to structural functionalism's vision of the scientific world as a legitimate regulatory institution in which the rewards system orients the most productive towards the most productive channels, Bourdieu (2004: 38) recalls Polanyi's (1951: 57) statement that 'scientific research – in short – is an art' and conceptualises creativity and the complexity of both 'crafts' as the foundation for drawing an analogy between artistic and scientific practice.

According to Collini (2006: 52), one of the most important sources of intellectual authority is intellectual achievement – that is, 'the attainment of a level of achievement in an activity which is esteemed for the non-instrumental, creative, analytical or scholarly capacities involved'. Intellectual creativity is one of the main sources of intellectual authority because it provides an individual with the reputation to speak out on broader issues, and therefore it is one of the essential preconditions for an intellectual's contribution to the public sphere. In other words, the significance of intellectual creativity relates to the fact that it is the essential feature of public intellectuals' authority and their input into public life. Such a conceptualisation allows us to move away from a rather narrow perception of the function of public intellectuals as people who simply inform the public and, instead, to view their task as one of enhancing political thinking – a process that can be liberating. Hence the importance of creative thinking and reflexivity, the privilege of intellectuals, which make possible both the growth of knowledge and the capacity for more responsible political judgement and action (Bourdieu 1992: 22).

Intellectual creativity is also important because the public rely on intellectuals' creative ideas to deepen their understanding of reality and to improve societal well-being. Put another way, for intellectuals for whom the crucial terrain of action is the public sphere, creativity in this area is also of importance. The significance of creativity, not only in science and the arts but also in the public sphere, according to Hannah Arendt (1958), lies in its role in struggle. Since the *polis* is a space where citizens can be involved in 'the free creative process' (Arendt 1961: 155), creativity in this realm is crucial for the expansion of its democratic potential. The importance of creativity in politics has been emphasised recently by Bernard Bailyn (2003), in his attempt to discover the sources of creative imagination for the fathers of the American constitution. In *To Begin the World Anew*, Bailyn defines creative political imagination as an ability to recast the world of power, to conceptualise reality in newer and fresher ways and to re-formulate the structure of public authority and the accepted form of governance. Thus, creative imagination is an indispensable ingredient for a successful re-engagement in the public arena.

Because intellectuals' fruitful engagements with public life are preceded by value judgements, it can be argued that there are two aspects to what makes intellectuals' contribution to the democratic project successful: their creativity in their specific field, and their democratic sensitivity and imagination, which is itself stimulated by their knowledge of a given area and their democratic values. When intellectuals display political judgement, they do not merely speak as experts in their specific field but reach beyond their 'professional' type of creativity. Expertise excludes any engagements for moral/ideological reasons, as it is valued for its neutrality: 'Experts should not be stakeholders in the conflicts, but disinterested and without any political agenda' (Ferree et al. 2002: 292). In contrast, public intellectuals' successful engagement with public issues depends, by definition, upon their civic concern with justice and other matters of human significance and upon their democratic imagination, which filters new and changing information about politics and the social world around them and which enhances their repertoire of strategies and the responsibility of their political judgement and action (Perrin 2006). If the necessary precondition for political judgement is a gift for synthesis, an exceptional sensitivity to certain kinds of facts or 'a capacity for integrating a vast amalgam of constantly changing facts, debating what makes the statesmen' (Berlin 1996: 27–8), such judgement is not built solely upon the foundation of knowledge, but on 'an acute sense of what fits with what, what springs from what, what leads to what, what the result is likely to be in a concrete situation of the interplay of human beings and impersonal forces' (Berlin 1996: 28). Therefore, when we talk about the engagement of intellectuals in the public sphere, we refer to their involvement as concerned citizens whose decision to get involved, and on what side of an issue, is the outcome of their civic sensitivity, helped by their creative imagination and stimulated by their specialised knowledge. Because such an involvement requires choosing the risk and uncertainty of the public sphere over the security and safety of their professional fields and because passing value judgements means being answerable for the ideas behind these judgements, the role of public intellectual also demands courage.

It is commonly assumed that the tradition of the courageous public intellectual began with Socrates. Relatively few political theorists have considered courage as being central to contemporary democratic processes, yet civil courage, defined very broadly, not only as resistance or rebellion but also as including disinterested and risky action for the purposes of institutionalising social or cultural change, performs a vital social function. Conceptualised in this way, the importance of courage as the source of public intellectuals' authority becomes evident. The courage of conviction performs an essential social role in creating and sustaining cohesive, just and pluralistic dimensions of contemporary politics, as it creates incentives for the upholding of core civic values and a commitment to persistence and resolution in the face of risk. It is also essential for the quality of public debates and provides the basis for civic initiatives that affirm human rights and dignities. The importance of courage as the source of public intellectuals' authority has been noted by many writers, who view intellectuals as taking risks in the name of universality, acting courageously in order to 'go beyond the easy certainties provided us by our background, language, nationality' (Said 1994: xii). Public intellectuals need courage because they, being never 'satisfied with things as they are' (Coser 1965: viii), 'rock the boat' (Said 1994: 55). In other words, courage, like creativity, is a vital factor in advancing the intellectual above the professional, as it is the crucial condition for reconciling the intellectual's role as specialist with his or her role as critic.

The role of courage in the combining of these two roles is well captured in Max Weber's argument that an intellectual's engagement in the world calls for the ethics of a hero, as it requires moral courage to face up to the consequences of action taken in the public domain. The intellectual's courage, the refusal to let fear govern the life of the mind, the refusal to submit to anything but the truth, is inherent in Weber's conception of intellectual integrity, seen as a duty to be followed at whatever personal cost. Weber ([1915] 1946a: 155), who endorses 'the plain duty of intellectual integrity', which demands 'the courage to clarify one's own ultimate judgements', argues that intellectuals' commitment to public problems consists essentially of a moral choice, and as such it requires courage. The role of courage in Weber's approach is connected with his preference for an ethic of responsibility, based on what is feasible, though not without influence from the ethic of ultimate ends, based on what is most desirable. Thus, although 'in the lecture-room of the university no other virtue holds but plain integrity', the intellectual duty to 'remain faithful to yourself' can lead to the rejection of institutional constraints (155–6).

Bourdieu, in contrast to Weber, who perceives intellectuals as champions of individuality and advises against their entry into politics as a group, thinks that scientific autonomy can be secured only by the joint mobilisation of scientists against the intrusion of external powers. According to Bourdieu (1989), intellectuals' specific authority, which itself is granted in their specific expertise (e.g. the scientific authority of a Robert Oppenheimer or the intellectual authority of a Sartre), expands in line with their independence from economic and political powers. Science is the best tool for achieving the intellectual's civic mission to promote the 'corporatism of the universal', yet scientificity itself 'comes at the cost of a kind of a little courage of every moment, a vigilance and commitment to critically scrutinize each word, each line, to track down polemical adjectives, slight connotations, unconscious innuendos, and so on' (Bourdieu 1992: 4). Courage is also required of intellectuals in order to ensure and increase the autonomy of the scientific field, seen as a site of contestation over boundaries and membership (Bourdieu 1988).

In short, courage is the essential characteristic of those who, while devoted to the *vita contemplativa*, are also intent on the *vita activa*. Following Collini (2006: 52), who sees the intellectual's engagement (or 'the expression of views, themes, or topics which successfully articulate or engage with some of the general concerns of the publics') as one of the main sources of intellectual authority, we can say that one of the essential preconditions for an intellectual's contribution to the public sphere is courage. The challenges faced by scientists, artists or writers venturing into the public sphere confirm and confer 'upon them the "supreme dignity" of the risk-taker' (Walzer 2002: 14). While – according to Arendt (1961: 156) – the very nature of the public realm demands courage, and while – according to Said (1994: 74) – it is reprehensible for an intellectual to avoid or turn away from political engagement out of fear, many liberal theorists take the view that the requirement for courage applies only in countries with undemocratic political systems (Robin 2000: 1087). Thus, in modern democratic societies, claims Posner (2001), being a public intellectual is 'no big deal', as there is no risk attached to any public stance. In addition, as the penalty for the public intellectual caught selling a defective product is reduced to 'trivial level' (Posner 2001: 388), public intellectuals are prone to 'think about themselves as being on holiday when they are writing for the general public' (105). Yet public intellectuals also face some risks and challenges even in democratic societies. Firstly, we need to remember that democracy, defined mainly by elections and the exercise of power in the name of the majority, is capable of being repressive of individual freedom and minority rights. Secondly, some major obstacles to intellectuals' engagement have emerged more recently, connected with the growing power of the media to limit the public agenda, with the increased influence of business schools and think tanks, the limited capacities of intellectuals and public suspicions of intellectuals (Goldfarb 1998; Furedi 2004; Fuller 2005).

Although modern intellectuals rarely face the challenge of the Dreyfus Affair kind, intellectuals even in their role of academic expert still need to reflect with courage on the problems and challenges confronting their societies. The risk faced by intellectuals cannot be ruled out, for the same reason that we need public intellectuals, which is not 'because rulers are never just but because they are never perfectly just' (Walzer 2002: 43). If we see the public intellectual's job as 'to be the bearer of bad tidings – not cynicism, but difficult truths that cut across lines of political affiliation and enthusiasm, that may put us at odds with those we would much rather be linked up in harmony with, that may, from time to time, give ammunition to those we would much prefer to see disarmed' (Jean Bethke Elshtain, quoted in Posner 2001: 386), we should expect intellectual engagement when it is the order of the day. In other words, the issue of courage is one of the preconditions for a public intellectual's civic involvement.

To sum up, public intellectual authority comes as a result of several dimensions of the role, with creativity and courage being the most important qualities. Generalising, it can be argued that it is creativity and courage that endow an intellectual with the authority to speak out on broader issues, as both determine the intellectual's position within the intellectual field and her/his relationship to the powers outside it. Such an approach permits us to identify public intellectuals as academics, writers, journalists and artists who, as high-quality specialists, are uniquely qualified to make contributions to societal well-being. Creativity is a means that enables intellectuals to participate in the realm of knowledge and to transcend their professional specialisations into critical sensitivity, and by this process to ensure their authority as critic-specialists. By emphasising creativity as one of the main characteristics of the intellectual role, we can hold that the creative achievements of intellectuals are the source of their authority while avoiding, at the same time, too narrow an image of the specialist. The creativity of public intellectuals, while taking place against a background of specialist knowledge, also refers to the movement from specialised domains of scholarship into domains of public debate and back. The courage of conviction, as the necessary precondition for speaking in defiance of the established powers and the public, also contributes to public intellectuals' special authority.

In order to enhance our understanding of public intellectuals' creative engagement in democratising and humanising the workings of modern societies and to construct a sociological account of civil courage, the following chapters discuss theories of creativity and courage.

2 Creativity: the problem of the new

What is creativity?

Any attempt to define creativity is faced with the question as to whether creativity is a property of people, products or cognitive processes. And, if we assume that creativity is not a personal but a social phenomenon, we need to ask: what do we mean by creative work? Is creative work common or rare? And how are the attributions of creativity made (Mayer 1999; Sternberg 1988b)? All these difficulties are reflected in the variety of definitions of creativity. Dictionary definitions present it as the ability to bring something new into existence, the ability to use the imagination to make new syntheses and the ability to produce something that is considered both novel and original, while also stressing that the notion is connected with unusual brightness or intelligence. Moreover, dictionary definitions also tend to suggest that this concept is used to describe such people as Albert Einstein or Leonardo da Vinci, who have changed our culture in some important respect (*Collins Dictionary of Social Science, Oxford English Dictionary, Encyclopaedia Britannica, Encyclopaedia Americana*). The existence of more than 200 definitions (Weisberg 1993), ranging from the oldest conceptualisations viewing creativity as a talent reserved for a particular type of gifted personality – a 'genius' (for example, Kris 1952) – or as emerging from the associations of ideas in the unconscious (Arieti 1976) to definitions stressing dynamics of collaborative creativity (Kohut 1985), prompt some to argue that creativity defies precise definition. Others collect and classify existing definitions. For example, Calvin W. Taylor (1988) has divided some sixty definitions of creativity, on the basis of their main theme, into five mutually exclusive classes.

Although almost none of the current sociological dictionaries, and none of the standard dictionaries of literary and cultural studies, have an entry on 'creativity', works in these areas addressing this issue offer a broad view of creativity as a movement through the 'known' into the 'unknown' (Williams 1977: 212) or 'the problem of the new'

(Arendt 1978). In a similar way, Rob Pope (2005: xvi) identifies creativity as 'the capacity to make, do or become something fresh and valuable with respect to others as well as ourselves'. Such a broad definition suits our preliminary purpose here. Since it is beyond our capacity to offer here a comprehensive history of the idea of creativity, what follows is a compact summary of the main meanings that creativity has taken on over the centuries.

Creativity and the issues relevant to it, such as creation myths, myths of individual genius and the concern with insight, inspiration and imagination, have been debated for centuries and studied within a number of different research paradigms and traditions. The idea of creativity has been evolving through history, from being seen as elusive, enigmatic and surrounded by myths, through being a mirror of modernity, to its status today as both 'the weapon of the weak' (Lofgren 2001: 73) and a fashionable commercial strategy. While questions regarding creativity originally puzzled mainly philosophers, since the last century the discourse on creativity has become more specialised, with psychologists, historians and philosophers of science leading the debate. Now, when all disciplines seem to agree that it is best regarded as a complex and multidimensional social phenomenon, creativity is no longer seen as being located exclusively in the elevated circles of science and the secluded atelier of the artist; it seems to be everywhere.

The earliest traditions of thinking about creativity, from the Bible through the ancient Greeks and the Middle Ages, associated it with spiritual and mystical beliefs, and put the emphasis on divine inspiration. In such accounts, creativity was seen as something purely mystical and divine, an act of God or as one of the divine qualities endowed by God on man (Joas 1996; Ericsson 2002). 'The creative person was seen as an empty vessel that a divine being would fill with inspiration. The individual would then pour out the inspired ideas, forming an other-worldly product' (Sternberg and Lubart 1999: 4). The classical Greeks stressed the metaphysical source of creative achievements and placed their emphasis on an individual daemon (guardian spirit). Plato, who argued that a poet is inspired directly by the gods with wisdom concerning the human and divine conditions, thought that it was impossible to explain or understand creativity (Asmis 1992). 'A poet is holy, and never able to compose until he has become inspired, and is beside himself and reason is longer in him ... for not by art does he utter these, but by power divine' (Plato, quoted in Boden 1994: 1). Since poets have divine access and duty towards a god, their creativity ought to be beneficial to the order of the state. Hence, artists who create deceptive images and who produce without knowledge of the truth pose a threat to the integrity of the mind and spirit, because creativity 'apart from moral concern loses its soul' (McLaren 1993: 137). In the *Republic*, Socrates warned against creativity's dark side and argued that poets who are deceived by their own images should be banished from the ideal republic.

During the Middle Ages discussions of creativity and creation, due to their potential threat to Christian monotheism, were limited, and it was not until the Renaissance that creation began to be seen as a human act (Williams 1983: 82). The Renaissance not only brought liberation from seeing creation as an exclusively divine act, it also led to the revival of the ancient idea of divine inspiration, which offered creative artists a new means of expression of their self-esteem (Joas 1996: 74). It was also this period in which references to the creative abilities of artists themselves entered into narratives about art for the first time (Williams 1983: 74). All the same, the modern sense of creation as a human and aesthetic act became firmly established only in the eighteenth century. During the Enlightenment, with the emergence of a clear difference between the mythical and the historical, with the growing recognition of reason, experience and intelligence and with natural science's belief in natural law becoming widely accepted, the idea of creativity gained in importance. At this period '[n]o word in English carries a more consistently positive reference than "creativity"' (Williams 1961: 3). Creativity took on the forms of rational scientific discovery and the material inventiveness of engineers. It was viewed as being located in the renowned spheres of science and as being the mark of engineers and scientists (Albert and Runco 1999; Liep 2001).

One of the most significant distinctions made in the middle of the eighteenth century was one connected with the difference between the idea of creativity and the ideas of genius, originality, talent and formal education (Albert and Runco 1999: 21). By the end of that century the prolonged debates about the nature of creativity and its relation to the notion of genius led to the conclusion that genius, while distinguished from talent and seen as exceptional, was unconnected with the supernatural (Albert and Runco 1999; Engell 1981). The rise of the model of rational science, which stresses science's power and the practical use of research, did not totally eliminate the attraction of the myth of the scientist as the hermit genius, who draws 'inventions out of his intellectual and psychic innards' (Burns and Stalker 1961: 21). While attributing scientific and technological advances, which were now seen as simply 'happening', to singular and isolated geniuses, the myth of accident and inspiration left out of the picture much significant information about inventors' social conditions and about the informal ties that connected many of them. The creative Scots of the eighteenth century (such as inventors James Watt, Joseph Black and John Roebuck) belonged to a society that was small in number and closely integrated, which served as a social medium for technological development (Burns and Stalker 1961: 25). By the beginning of the next century there was a clear awareness of the need to institutionalise these informal connections. The establishment of various learned societies, which were 'at the same time friendly and scientific' (Samuel Smiles, quoted in Burns and Stalker 1961: 25), meant that for some time the responsibilities for scientific advance and for technical innovation were passed to them.

As the Enlightenment's quest for liberation from the hierarchical and immobile order of the *ancien régime* was followed by the emphasis of Romanticism upon individual self-fulfilment, a new way of defining creativity emerged. In this second model of creativity, produced by the historical process which has transformed the traditional world, creativity is seen as being located in the atelier of the artist and as being an expression of the artist's inner feelings, associated with the power of imagination. The Enlightenment had transformed itself from an age of reason to an age of imagination since the end of the eighteenth century, and therefore 'imagination' was accepted as the governing impulse in artistic creativity (Engell 1981: viii). This second model of creativity found its expression in the Romantic movement, at the heart of which was the concept of creativity as a 'counterweight to scientific rationalism' (Albert and Runco 1999: 23). Nineteenth-century Romanticism declared that each historical period has its unique character and rediscovered the links between imagination and poetry. The idea of creativity, which emphasised the power of imagination, the role of inspiration and the wisdom inherent in feelings, and which is referred to either as 'the ideology of creativity' (Albert and Runco 1999: 23) or as the metaphor of expression (Joas 1996: 71), was grasped in Johann Gottfried von Herder's idea of self-expression. Herder, who understood art as the sphere in which the human being articulates herself or himself as a whole person, emphasised the idea of cultural diversity as intrinsic to human history and asserted that history does not move in straight lines and that 'there is not a single key to the future or the past' (Berlin 1999: 36). Herder, by the same token, helped Romanticism to destroy the Enlightenment's axiom that, if we applied proper scientific methods, valid and objective answers could be discovered to all questions. In other words, the Romantics, on the one hand, 'subjectively secularised' creativity, and on the other hand they re-mystified it, into 'something for the divinely inspired few' (Ericsson 2002: 11).

In short, the rise of modernity produced two models of creativity, representing 'the contrast between the material and the spiritual: secular, rational scientific discovery and the emotional, spiritual creativity of the artist' (Liep 2001: 3). In the nineteenth century these two models – one of rational science, which stresses science's power and the practical use of research, and the second of 'the ideology of creativity' – were accompanied by two additional images of creativity, namely the metaphors of production and revolution (Joas 1996: 71–9). The idea of production, which relates creativity to human beings' material lives, and which therefore eliminates any liberating possibilities or powers, was formulated in Karl Marx's action theory. In his deterministic perspective, creativity, seen as externalised and depersonalised, is attributed entirely to objective circumstances or contingencies, while the real activity of human beings is ignored. On the other hand, Marx's call for radical political and socio-economic change, in an attempt to get people 'not only to *think* differently and to *act* differently but to *be* different' (Fromm 1998: 145–6), introduced the revolution-based model of creativity.

At the end of the nineteenth century the creativity discourse was dominated by yet another image, namely the metaphor of evolutionary progress in nature. The power of this naturalising metaphor can be illustrated by the nineteenth-century assumptions about the hereditary nature of genius and the process underlying natural selection, which followed evolutionary theory's basic principles (Albert and Runco 1999: 24). Charles Darwin's emphasis on the role of biological adaptation in survival as well as his emphasis on conflict, competition and inheritance in the progress of evolution shaped Francis Galton's ways of thinking about creativity. In his *Hereditary Genius* (1869), the first attempt at an empirical study of human abilities, Galton, a cousin of Darwin, offered the operational definition of broad evolutionary diversity as manifested in specific individual differences that could be measured. Galton, a propagator of sociology as the science of good breeding, studied men of genius as representing the extreme end of the distribution of intelligence (Rogers 1973: 147). The biological-evolutionary reading of life histories also influenced Sigmund Freud, who read Darwin and met Galton. His psychodynamic theory, which took the view that creativity is the result of working through the repressive control of forbidden impulses, was 'the first major twentieth-century theoretical approach to the study of creativity' (Sternberg and Lubart 1999: 8). Freud saw creativity as arising from the tensions between conscious reality and unconscious drives and proposed that writers and artists produce creative work as a way to express their unconscious wishes in a publicly acceptable fashion (Albert and Runco 1999: 24). Nonetheless, even though it influenced the search for the personal characteristics of creative people, the psychodynamic theory did not provide a scientific foundation for the investigation of creativity within the emerging field of psychology in the early twentieth century. While Freud conceived of works of art as the product of sublimation, by which energy, originally instinctual, is displaced and discharged (or derived from the instinctive sexual impulse, for which they were, ultimately, substitutes), later developments in the field recorded a progressive shift from seeing creative motives as being 'psychopathological' to paying more attention to the 'normality' of creative traits.

None of these attempts to interpret creative action as scientific, expressive, productive, revolutionary or evolutionary offered a systematic theory of creativity. 'It was not until the latter half of the nineteenth century that attempts were made to define creativity in a more profound way than simply by reference to one single type of human action, which obviously could not encompass all actions' (Joas 1996: 71). Two new and different ways of trying to elucidate creativity – the concept of the 'will' in the philosophy of life, as developed by Arthur Schopenhauer, and the concept of intelligence in pragmatism – offered crucial insights into the phenomenon of creativity. The pragmatic theory of intelligence (the prototype of creativity) encompasses all types of creativity. Pragmatists emphasise that it is important to recognise the intelligent and creative aspects of all human activity, and that creative action, like all action, is infused with meaning. Their theory of situated creativity assumes that we should not extract or eliminate the individual action from its situational context (Joas 1996). The pragmatists' viewing of creativity as actions performed within situations that call for solutions owes much to George Herbert Mead's (1932: xiii, 29) belief that past experiences arose in such a way as to enable 'intelligent conduct to proceed' against situational problems, and to John Dewey's (1917: 63) view of creativity as the liberation of the capacity for new actions. While pragmatism locates creativity in everyday human activity and regards science as a more pronounced development of such potentials, the philosophy of life, which depicts the whole of life itself as creative, offers too totalising an understanding of creativity (Joas 1996).

During the second part of the nineteenth century, with the growing development of science and with its increasing specialisation, the nature of discourse on creativity was shaped – due to the new and elaborate organisation of professional scientists – by the establishment of new forms of relation between scientists and their audiences. Furthermore, institutional barriers between science and industry and between 'pure' and 'applied' science were constructed. 'In the twentieth century the new and elaborate organization of professional scientists has been eventually matched by one of technological innovators into groups overlapping teaching and research institutions, Government departments and agencies, and industry' (Burns and Stalker 1961: 36). At this stage of the development of capitalism, according to Schumpeter, the driving force in the process of innovation was the entrepreneur. Assigning the crucial role to innovative entrepreneurs in giving birth to new technical paradigms for future growth relies on the conceptualisation of innovation as 'a feat not of intellect, but of will. It is a special case of the social phenomenon of leadership' (Schumpeter 1991: 65).

The specialisation of the discourse on creativity in the twentieth century has, on the one hand, fragmented and, on the other hand, enriched our understanding of the creative process. Philosophers' questioning of creativity continued, with Nietzsche's emphasis on the free play of creativity and on the idea that valuing is creating, with Henri Bergson's understanding of creativity as the human impulse to improvise and with Charles Sanders Peirce's introduction of the concept of scientific methods as consisting of, alongside deduction and induction, abduction, defined as 'the production of new hypotheses in a creative act' (Joas 1996: 134). In the second half of the last century the issue of creativity became the subject of studies by psychologists, historians and philosophers of science, whose works have contributed to a growing recognition of the social nature of science. The debate was initiated by Karl Popper's (1959) distinction between 'discovery' and 'justification' and his rejection of the assumptions that we gain knowledge by induction and that the reliability of knowledge comes from the quantity of inductively collected observations. According to him, science progresses only when a theory is tested, falsified and replaced by a new one. Popper (1959) assumed that creative 'inspiration' is fundamentally irrational, and therefore scientific discovery (and artistic creativity) cannot be predicted and the psychology of creativity is not merely philosophically uninteresting but actually impossible. 'This Popperian view of creativity is as pessimistic as Plato's, to which indeed it is significantly similar' (Boden 1994: 3).

Popper's idealised image of the solutions provided by core scientists, his failure to recognise the 'puzzle-solving' activities of normal science and his account of the scientific revolution were all criticised by Thomas Kuhn. In *The Structure of Scientific Revolutions*, Kuhn (1962: 52) argues that the adoption of a new paradigm is the result of a scientific revolution, which inaugurates a new period of 'normal science' – that is, the kind of science in which an intellectual paradigm for research is taken for granted and which 'does not aim at novelties of fact or theory and, when successful, finds none'. He draws attention to the discontinuities in the development of science and makes it clear that the evaluation of new ideas by scientists is a less rational process than Popper assumed. In Kuhn's (1962) view, discoveries are events judged significant by the scientific community, but this consensus can be explained only by non-rational factors. In all domains of the natural sciences originality is attributed by social processes that are relative and fallible, and that are sometimes reversed by the next generation. Thus, creators are the individuals who have a great mastery of the accumulated collective resource and who are recognised by their 'scientific communities'. While scientific innovations do require the rejection of acceptable theories, the formulation of research questions is rooted in engagement with the scientific tradition. Yet Kuhn, for whom 'normal science' has no more force than that of custom and habit, overlooks the fact that even during periods of 'normal science' quite significant changes also take place, and that therefore 'true creativity cannot be bound or limited to periods of revolution alone' (Bohm and Peat 1987: 27).

Kuhn's contribution to the sociology of science has been of seminal importance. This field, following the impact of Karl Mannheim's (1949) idea of 'thought styles' and his claim that innovations are shifts in styles of thought, has become dominated by the structural-functionalist per-spective. The structural-functionalist perspective in the sociology of science owes much to Robert K. Merton, the founder of the scientific sociology of knowledge, who conceptualised scientific research as being determined by previous findings, the logic of science and scientific rationale and by societal – that is, extra-scientific – factors. In *Science, Technology and Society in Seventeenth-Century England* ([1938] 1970), the landmark text in this tradition in the sociology of science, Merton identifies the process of discovery as 'less individual and specific and more like a lengthy process of hard work and negotiations within a set of complex social networks' (Schaffer 1994: 16). In a later reformulation of his approach, Merton (1973) emphasises that successful developments in science arise not from the mere accumulation of evidence but from the combination of its rewards system with its institutionalised norma-tive system. The scientific world offers a system of rewards that operates to give recognition to significant researchers and also encourages ori-ginality, which, understood as the commitment to the pursuit of new knowledge, is also an essential safeguard to ensure continuing scientific development. The value of originality, however, counts only if it is 'disciplined originality' (Sztompka 1986: 52) – in other words, when it is not just novelty for novelty's sake but the search for the new reinforced and constrained by the value of objectivity: 'The institution of science actually calls for variants that will better meet the goal of new knowledge. Each variant must be shown to satisfy the norms of evidence' (Merton 1959: 181). Merton's (1973) vision of science, as being characterised by universalism, communalism, disinterestedness and organised scepticism, pays insufficient attention to the contingent aspect of scientific practice. As a result, it has not established a basis for the analysis of creative activities but, rather, has enhanced structural-functionalist studies of the internal mechanisms and processes operating within the scientific community.

At least until the mid-1980s, almost no empirical work had been carried out on the impact of specific social features on creativity. For a long time the understanding of creativity had been dominated by the gestalt approach, with its concern with the nature of insight and the question of where creative ideas come from (Taylor 1988). These issues were popularised in the 1960s by Arthur Koestler's famous book *The Act of Creation* (1964). His explanation of creativity as 'bisociation', or the combination of ideas from different, and incompatible or unrelated, frames of reference, emphasises that the most creative moments in science involve the recognition of novel analogies between previously unrelated fields. His concentration on unconscious rather than conscious combinations of dissimilar or unconnected ideas and his reliance on bibliographical material made his approach very attractive to psychologists, especially ones viewing creativity as a life story. Yet the focus on insight lost its popularity when cognitive psychology opted for the precision of measuring traits of creativity, with creativity researchers concentrating primarily on empirical testing and the assessing of individual indicators of creativity. During the last fifty years the dominance of psychological empirical research guided by a definition of creativity based on personality traits, which assumed that creativity is a continuous quantity, and therefore can be measured in normal and not just unusually talented people, has led to the democratisation of creativity and a growing focus on creativity enhancement and education.

At present there is a growing consensus in the social sciences that creativity is a complex social phenomenon. Despite many contentious issues concerning definitions and methodologies, there is, moreover, a clear new interest and a new desire among social scientists to overcome the existing fragmentation in the field. It remains the case, however, that various areas of study continue to carry out their own independent discourses. For example, today's anthropology, where the notion of creativity plays a prominent role, being a discipline interested in studying change, conceptualises cultural creativity as 'an ever-emergent feature in the world' and as a moral force (Hastrup 2001: 31). As anthropologists became aware that the 'healthy perpetuation of cultural traditions requires invention as well as rote repetition' (Rosaldo, Lavie and Narayan, 1993: 5), a number of approaches have been developed that highlight the social, performative and political dimensions of creativity. Anthropologists, in arguing that invention takes place within a field of culturally available possibilities and that it is as much a process of selection and recombination as one of thinking anew, bring to our attention the playfulness of everyday creativity. Seeing creativity as stepping out of seriousness follows Johan Huizinga's (1955) and Mikhail Bakhtin's (1968) argument that play and laughter can break the grip of taken-for-granted realities and thus free us for new potentialities. 'For this reason great changes, even in the field of science, are always preceded by a certain carnival consciousness that prepares the way' (Bakhtin 1968: 49). Bakhtin's (1981) dialogic imagination, placed at the heart of his dialogic literary theory, suggests that the potential of imagination can evoke holistic engagement by making the mundane creative.

The idea of creativity has also entered cultural studies where it is assumed that the social construction of reality implies an element of creativity. Creativity is thus perceived as part of a 'strategy of underdogs' (Lofgren 2001: 71–7). The best illustrations of the way in which discussions of everyday creativity have become counter-arguments against the presupposition that creativity is an elite resource as well as against the notion that consumption is a pacifying, homogenising force in people's lives are Paul Willis's studies *Learning to Labour: How Working Class Kids Get Working Class Jobs* (1977) and *Common Culture: Symbolic Work at Play in the Everyday Cultures of the Young* (1990). Willis views creativity as a positive strategy of resistance or 'tactics for beating the system', as a special type of cultural competence, developed to compensate for a difficult situation (Lofgren 2001: 77). He rejects 'a self-interested view of elite creativity' and insists that 'there is a vibrant symbolic life and symbolic creativity in everyday life, everyday activity and expression – even if it is sometimes invisible, looked down on or spurned . . .' (Willis 1990: 1). The importance of creativity as an egalitarian resource has been enhanced further by studies of creative consumption and various investigations of subcultures and analyses of consumption and shopping practices, as symbolic production made the concept of creativity into 'a very positive concept' (Lofgren 2001: 77). Additionally, the development of creative industry, such as media, fashion and public relations, has boosted the value of creativity further by making it into the highest achievable good.

While creativity is seen as a moral force in anthropology, and in cultural studies as an egalitarian resource, in management studies the significance of creativity is more connected with its commercial value, on the one hand, and its empowerment value, on the other. The obsession with 'innovation' in organisational discourses tends to be premised on claims that 'global competitive forces', new structures that are open and flexible, demand creativity. As mangers are increasingly being selected for their creative visions of how to turn a company around, they themselves, alongside psychologists, are becoming 'our contemporary ideologues of creativity' (Osborne 2003). They preach creativity, arguing that in a post-industrial, informalised, global economy the name of the game is innovation and everybody can be empowered by creativity. The necessity of creativity as a job requirement for managerial positions is followed by managers' attempts to impose, as part of a demand to give up forms of protection in routine and law, a requirement of creativity on all employees. Thus, as the economic attractiveness of anything connected with creativity increases, even relatively mundane jobs are labelled 'creative' in order to attract people. Organisations, empowered by technologies and aiming to become 'creative organisations', increasingly rely on 'creativity' as a buzzword to provide a remedy in the future. In short, creativity, often reduced to practices and techniques such as brainstorming or mind-maps, has become one of the hottest issues within the organisational discourses of the last two decades (Ericsson 2002: 7). Some worry that the unintended consequences of such a commercialisation of the interest in creativity could trap us in something resembling a Weberian iron cage. 'The renewal of working life through creativity and the managerial obsession with creativity' could lead to 'an iron cage of creativity', in which 'leaders have become trapped by their own notion of creativity' (Ericsson 2002: 1).

To conclude, in recent years the notion of creativity has received renewed attention in many disciplines. As the aspiration to be creative becomes a part of our life, at work and outside it, creativity is seen as a positive force and as a valued commercial strategy. The twentieth century enhanced the process of democratising creativity as increasingly specialised studies fashioned creativity into an objective, cognitive trait that is quantifiable, measurable and controllable. 'In other words, creativity functions as a mirror of modernity – it is a post-war attempt to treat everyone as equals, yet at the same time create an instrument that discriminates between equals' (Ericsson 2002: 11).

Although the interest in creativity has not yet manifested itself in an expansion of the multidisciplinary perspective to the study of creativity, we observe a growing recognition of the role of social aspects in creativity. Since at present it is psychological studies that dominate research and the discourse on creativity, in order to discus the different types of creativity we need to analyse psychology's more comprehensive approach to studying the subject.

Where is creativity?

Psychological approaches to creativity used to focus on any one of its four aspects: person, process, product and environment (Mooney 1963). Now, however, creativity is seen in a more holistic or systemic way. In contrast to the traditional perspective's conceptualisation of creativity as a process existing in a single person, the new alternative stand debates creativity as existing in the larger system of social networks, domains and fields of enterprise. Many psychologists have contributed to the development of this systems view of creativity. Apart from Howard Gruber, Howard Gardner and Mihaly Csikszentmihalyi's ideas, which are briefly discussed below, the systems approach has also benefited from Robert J. Sternberg and Todd I. Lubart's investment theory and Teresa M. Amabile's theory of creativity in context (1999).

Gruber (1981), who was one of the founders of the holistic approach, focuses on the unique experiences of each creative individual within the context of his or her social and emotional world and pays attention to multiple influences on creativity. He sees creativity as a slowly evolving process of reflection and discovery made possible by the existence of the closely intertwined and interacting system of social networks, rather than a 'Eureka' moment. Gruber's (1980: 311) studies of individuals whose creativity is beyond dispute (such as Darwin and Jean Piaget) show that 'creative people have a network of enterprises ..., which describes the individual organization of purposes' and which facilitates 'diverse simultaneous or parallel activities'. For Gruber (1983: 9), networks of enterprises are central to the creative process, as within an individual's unique network every idea 'seems to be implicated within innumerable other ideas in an intricate network'.

Gardner (1988; 1993), much influenced by Gruber's tradition, takes into account cognitive, developmental psychological approaches and the motivational aspects of creation. He favours the use of individual case studies, which he places in the context of a specific environment, and examines the ways in which creators and their surroundings interact. Gardner's biographical approach, which he employed to study Freud, Einstein, Pablo Picasso, Igor Stravinsky, T. S. Eliot, Martha Graham and Mohandas Gandhi, emphasises the cognitive domain associated with the creator as well as social and historical contexts. Gardner (1993: 23–5) sees creativity as a confluence of intrinsic motivation, knowledge of a field and particular cognitive skills. Thus, 'the creative individual is a person who regularly solves problems, fashions products or defines new questions in a domain in a way that is initially considered novel but that ultimately becomes accepted in a particular cultural setting' (Gardner 1993: 35).

The systems view of creativity has been further enhanced by Csikszentmihalyi, who is also known for his idea of creativity as *flow* – that is, the state of mind we get into when we forget about time and become absorbed in an activity. According to him, creativity is the process that can be observed only at the intersection where individuals, domains and fields interact. Thus, creativity is the product of these three shaping forces: '[a] set of social institutions, or *field*, that selects from the variations produced by individuals those that are worth preserving; a stable cultural *domain* that will preserve and transmit the selected new ideas or forms to the following generations; and finally the *individual*, who brings about some change in the domain, a change that the field will consider to be creative' (Csikszentmihalyi 1988: 325; emphasis in original). Creativity is not the product of single individuals, but of 'social systems making judgements about individuals' products' (1999: 313). The level of creativity depends just as much on individual creativity as on 'how well suited the respective domains and fields are to the recognition and diffusion of novel ideas' (1996: 31). Because creativity is constructed through an interaction between producers (who draw on different materials, skills and knowledge) and their different audiences (who judge according to their own values and standards), the criteria for what constitutes creativity vary from one domain to another. Csikszentmihalyi (1999: 316) postulates that we need to view each mode of creativity in relation to the communities, social organisations and institutions in which creativity is judged and endorsed. 'What is meant by creativity is not a real objective quality but refers only to the acceptance by a particular field of judges' (1999: 316). Csikszentmihalyi's approach can be criticised for being too consensual, as it overlooks the fact that creative acts can be ignored or suppressed by judges. 'In other words, he plays down the personal and political struggle that characterised the making and breaking of authorities and institutions themselves' (Pope 2005: 68).

Gruber, Gardner and Csikszentmihalyi, the three main representatives of this holistic or systemic position, share many common ideas. They all suggest that creativity – identified as contributions to original ideas, different points of view and new ways of looking at problems – takes time and involves an active search for gaps in existing knowledge. They demonstrate that creative work can be carried out only in the social and historical context of its making. Their definition of creativity as 'any act, idea, or product that changes an existing domain' (Csikszentmihalyi 1996: 28) focuses on the creative product rather than the creative process or person, and sees creativity as a phenomenon that results from the interaction between these three elements or systems. The systems-oriented approach combines two of the key elements of the conceptual definition of creativity – novelty and acceptability or appropriateness – as any contribution to an original idea rests on the consensus judgement of some social group at some point. This holistic perspective, in contrast to the more atomistic view of creativity, perceives creativity as a process that takes place within the context of a particular environment and that can be observed only at the intersection at which individuals, society and culture interact. The three writers are also in agreement that creativity should be defined as the production of both novel and appropriate work, where 'novel' refers to original work, work that could not be predicted, and where 'appropriate' refers to the usefulness of the product towards a certain need (Sternberg and Lubart 1999).

In general, this new systems approach, in contrast to the traditional psychological view of creativity as a process existing in a single person, conceptualises creativity as existing in the larger system of social networks, domains and fields of enterprise. As a consequence, the individual responsible for products that are judged to be creative is seen as only one of the many elements necessary for the process of creation. The systems view of creativity, while pointing out the role of social networks and contexts, does not preclude the notion of the creator as an individual. Although systems-oriented approaches range from views that are more socially oriented to views that are more individual-oriented, none of them totally loses sight of the creative person or the creative process. Sternberg (1988), for example, argues that all aspects have to interact to generate creative performance. Furthermore, all researchers within this paradigm suggest that to understand creativity it is necessary to know what characteristics are associated with creative individuals, how the attributions of creativity are made and what conditions are most favourable to creative performance.

In sum, in the last fifty years the psychological study of creativity has shifted from attempting to answer the question 'what is creativity?' to posing the question 'where is creativity?' (Csikszentmihalyi 1988: 325). As researchers have come to the conclusion that creativity is never the result of individual action alone, this question cannot be answered solely by reference to one person and that person's work. Without a culturally defined domain of action in which innovation is possible, the person cannot even get started. And, without a group of peers to evaluate and confirm the adaptiveness of the innovation, it is impossible to differentiate what is creative from what is simply statistically improbable or peculiar.

Although psychological studies are still in need of 'effort to synthesize the various approaches of the past into an integrated theory' (Csikszentmihalyi 1988: 338), their proposed holistic theory of creativity is very relevant for any sociological attempt to understand the phenomenon.

What is the nature of creative action?

Despite the importance of creativity, the phenomenon has occupied only a marginal position in the sociological tradition (Joas 1996). Even twentieth-century sociology, with the sole exception of pragmatism, which located creativity in everyday human activity and conceptualised creativity as a natural endowment of human beings that allows them to infuse reality with meaning and to create a social world (Dewey 1934), preferred to shy away from studying creative activity. There are several reasons why a systematic sociological theory of creativity has not so far been attempted. The first reason why creativity has not been consistently integrated into general sociological theory may be found in the fact that there is an important individual dimension to creativity that is hard to get at from a sociological perspective. Secondly, the idea of creativity has failed to capture sociologists' attention, as most social science relies implicitly on a teleological conception of action, and therefore neglects indeterminacy and ambiguity of action. Another reason why sociologists have not been interested in creativity is connected with the fact that they often pay more attention to the establishment of patterns, constraints and social reproduction rather than creative activity. For example, both structuralism and systems theory paid more attention to established patterns and forms than to change and innovation.

Nevertheless, although creativity has been, by virtue of its individualistic flavour and the nature of sociologists' interest, marginalised in a sociological approach, this discipline is well equipped to bring out the social and group dimensions of the phenomenon. A sociological argument that 'creativity does not belong to persons, but travels in groups; it is concentrated in space and time' (Fuchs 2001: 188) offers a conceptualisation of creativity that leads us in the direction of investigating unusually creative periods and schools. Recently, moreover, several sociologists have discussed creativity, whether directly or indirectly. Cornelius Castoriadis's *The Imaginary Institution of Society* (1987) was one of the first books to focus on the notion of creativity and the role of judgement in identifying it. Castoriadis discusses the operation of creativity at the level of the individual subject and at the level of society, as well as the creative and imaginary character of language. According to him, individual-radical imaginaries and social-collective imaginaries are mutually constitutive. Castoriadis proposes that the creative nature of praxis results in the self-creation of humanity; in other words, that each society brings into being its own mode of self-alternation in the process of institutionalisation. While we explain the new in terms of the old narratives or in terms and categories of situations already experienced, to recognise the new as such one must be in a position to judge it. In short, without disregarding categories brought in by language, we are unable to grasp the new. The difficulty related to the problem of the new escaping logical insights can be exposed, according to Castoriadis (1987: 108), by focusing on the tension between what is new (the instituting society or history in the making) and what is given (the instituted society or history already made). Thus, from Castoriadis's perspective, the question of the new is a question of judgement; at the same time, the practice of judgement does not necessarily include logical reasoning.

The crucial role of judgement in our understanding of the problem of the new can also be also found in Hans Joas's insightful book *The Creativity of Action* (1996), which revises action theory based primarily on the pragmatist understanding of human action as situated creativity. Criticising the predominant models of action, Joas accords a central role to the notion of creativity as something that is performed within situations that call for solutions. *The Creativity of Action*'s model of creative action, developed with the help of the pragmatist's viewing of creativity as the liberation of the capacity for new action, presupposes that the routine dimension of action and the creative dimension of action complement each other. This argument, together with Joas's (1996: 197) claim that 'even acts of the utmost creativity assume the persistence of a bedrock of underlying routine actions and external conditions which are simply taken as given', offer a conceptualisation of the relationship between habit and creativity that establishes a duality between the two. Yet such an approach ignores routinised creative action; therefore, Joas's perspective misrepresents the pragmatist view, which recognises that there are some 'tensions' between creativity and habituality in its action-conception, 'but not in the manner suggested by Joas' (Kilpinen 1998: 178). Furthermore, Joas's assumptions about the agent's capability to monitor the world and reflexively process the information received are not clearly stated (McGown 1999). In addition, Joas's theory does not acknowledge the highly problematic nature of our judgement of situations and the importance of pre-existing social categories for forming judgements (McGown 1999). Although Joas has failed to construct a fully satisfactory action theory and to ensure a shift from philosophical analysis to sociological theory, he has nonetheless convincingly shown that the concept of creativity should have a much more central place in sociological theorising.

Our discussion of the sociological approaches to creativity suggests a need to take into account the creative dimension of all action by incorporating into analyses of action the notion of reflexive rather than purposive intentionality. It also implies a need to accept the central role of judgement in identifying creativity and a need to acknowledge the highly tentative, problematic nature of our judgement of situations and the importance of past experiences in forming judgements in the present.

What are the forms of creativity?

In order to expand a sociological analysis of creativity, we need to search for an approach that can help us to address the unresolved problems and tensions of the main sociological approaches to creativity. This task can be accomplished by moving beyond the conceptualisation of the notion of creativity as a single, unproblematic unitary concept and beyond the viewing of creativity as something independent of social and cultural contexts. A good starting point is Joas's (1996) argument that, in order to see creativity as both an exceptional and a ubiquitous phenomenon, we should take account of the creative dimension of all human action and include the concept of 'situation' as a basic category in such an approach. The pragmatic theory of situated creativity means that the individual action should always be considered within its situational context. Under this approach, situations are defined in relation to our capacities for action and actors are seen as testing out and revising their courses of action. In William I. Thomas's (1923) elaboration of the definition of situation, which allows us to take account of both the subjective and objective aspects of the situation, the distinction between means and ends is only an analytical and temporal one. Joas finds Thomas's conceptualisation of situation a suitable replacement for the means–ends schemata as the primary basic category of a theory of action. According to him, in this conceptualisation of situation not only is full recognition given to the subjective components involved, but also the emergence of the problem is not seen as 'constructed as the result of subjective caprice because the actors are confronted by problematical qualities of the world which provoke them into performing definition work' (Joas 1996: 131).

Following the reviewers' argument that Joas makes too much of the dichotomy between habitual and creative action, Benjamin Dalton addresses this shortcoming by stressing the simultaneous presence in all action of habitual and creative elements, and by incorporating Bourdieu's idea that creativity can arise directly from the interaction between habit and specific concrete situation. The characteristics of Bourdieu's idea of habitus 'are extremely useful for deepening Joas's conceptualization' (Dalton 2004: 614). The core of his conceptualisation of habitus offers us 'the possibility of unifying habitual and creative elements in a theory of action that neither depends on ascribing a separate origin and operation to creative "tendency" nor on toggling between habitual and creative moments in the unfolding course of practical challenges' (614). As habitus organises the way in which individuals see the world and act in it, dispositions and frames of perceptions are at once historical, social and individual. Although people internalise 'the immanent law of the structure in the form of habitus' (Bourdieu and Wacquant 1992: 140), they are still capable of creativity within the limits of the structure. Bourdieu's concept of habitus, like the pragmatists' notion of situation, allows us to argue that prevailing situations are imposed on us (although our reactions to them are not), and to see creativity as the necessary adaptation of practices to specific contexts of action. Nonetheless, this notion, although it permits us to conceive of creativity as the interaction between habitual action and specific environmental conditions, fails – because of its rather reductive assumption about human nature being motivated solely by a self-interested competition for status – to 'incorporate a robust conception of creative agency' (Dalton 2004: 613). Therefore, the revised notion of creativity should combine the strength of Bourdieu's concept of habitus with Joas's conceptualisation of creativity as a response to the 'frustration of prereflective aspirations'.

Starting with Joas's (1996) description of creativity as a response to the interruption of habitual activity or an innovative adjustment so as to re-establish habitual intentions, it can be argued that the situation-relatedness is constitutive of all creative action. Such a recognition that every situation contains a set of possibilities for innovative adjustments, together with an understanding of creativity as the reinvention of meanings so that they can 'fit' into already existing patterns and into newly emerging patterns, suggest that innovative inputs originate at the point of the intersection of situation-rooted and socially valid relevance systems. 'We are always in the act of fitting an ever-changing reality so that there is no fixed or final goal to be attained. Rather, at each moment the ends and the means are both described as the action of making every aspect fit' (Bohm 1998: 58). In other words, creativity occurs in a wide range of situations, and in order to account for it we need to know something about both the subjective and objective dimensions of the situation. To start with the subjective component of situation, it can be argued that a person's individual definition of a situation prompts her or his search for solutions or necessitates innovative adjustment. Our judgement of a situation reflects the correspondence, or the lack of it, between the actors' expectations or aspirations and their perception of the situation. As such, it is associated with our past experiences and knowledge that we have as a result of living in our culture.

In other words, it is habitus, 'the system of durable dispositions to act that are produced by objective structures and conditions but are also capable of producing and reproducing those structures (Bourdieu 1977: 72), that organises the way in which individuals see the world and act in it. Since it does not determine our actions totally, as it still permits 'regulated improvisation' and the 'conductorless orchestration' of practice (Bourdieu 1977: 72), it allows us to see creativity as our response to the 'frustration of prereflective aspirations' caused by a given situation (Joas 1996: 144–5). When the fit is imperfect, when the expectations, based on past experiences, provide an unsatisfactory comparison and when therefore routine conduct based on habitual confidence is simply not enough, such a situation inspires and mobilises creative responses. In addition to the perceived level of imperfection in the correspondence between aspirations and a given situation, another factor that galvanises people to search for creative solutions is a threat or risk to their aspirations and routines. However, it is not only situations perceived as representing high levels of frustration or risk that may assist creativity. The perception of a situation as fitting expectations can also be conducive to creativity, because feelings of comfort and ease release the actor's attention and, by the same token, facilitate flow – the state of mind we enter when we become absorbed in a creative activity (Csikszentmihalyi 1988: 325).

As creativity originates at the point of intersection of the objective dimension and the subjective definition of a situation, we also need to consider the objective aspect of the situation. Although this is discussed in more detail in chapter 4, we can note here the fairly obvious point that the nature of the social order, seen as embedded in the informality and formality of interactional practices, determines the objective characteristic of the situation. Consequently, the relationship between formality and informality decides the amount of pressure put

Table 2.1. *Forms of creativity*

The perception of the situation	The nature of the system		
	Formalised	Balanced	Informalised
Ease/comfort	Invisible elbow	Improvisation	Insight
Uncertainty	Charismatic inspiration	Collaborative exploration	Rationalisation
Frustration/risk	Taming anxiety	Taming chance	Taming ambiguity

on people to conform and influences the nature of people's creative responses (Misztal 2000). In other words, the relationship between formality and informality determines not just the scope of peoples' freedom to innovate and be creative but also the directions and kinds of possible creative actions. In short, creative responses are contingent on the nature of the relationship between formality and informality, with both a high level of informality and a high level of formality seen as responsible for actors' search for creative solutions to a situation.

To sum up, as formal and informal rules both go into making the social order, the relationship between formality and informality, together with the perception of a given situation as putting people at ease, satisfying or not satisfying, or presenting risk to their pre-existing aspirations and routines, provide us with a good description of situations facilitating creativity, offering therefore an opportunity to investigate various forms of creativity. If, instead of focusing only on extreme situations, we add a third type, an 'in-between situation', the two axes, the type of situation and the nature of the relationships between formality and informality, generate a matrix with nine possible forms of creativity (see table 2.1).

While the first axis refers to different types of situation as measured by the perceived level of required adjustment, the second axis, referring to how formal or informal the nature of the system is, also allows the identification of three positions on this scale. The process of formalisation, located at one extreme of the scale, describes a trend introducing formal ways of regulating interaction and therefore contributing to an increase in the predictability of social life. Formalisation, by removing the responsibilities for negotiation from the participants, may reduce their mutual trust and understanding and can lead to 'a reduced concern for particulars of situations and to an increasing rigidity of action' (Wagner 1996: 99). At the other extreme there is the process of informalisation, which ensures emancipation from external constraints and contributes to the demise of predictability as it brings a higher level of structural insecurity. It also provides for a large space for interactive indeterminacy or uncertainty and a higher level of reliance on informal negotiations. Here the emphasis is on the indeterminacy of interaction and the fluid nature of social reality, and on the role of spontaneity and creativity in shaping social encounters. In the middle of the scale we can place the balanced relationships, those somewhere in between the processes of formalisation and informalisation.

We start our discussion of the nine cells of the matrix with the three forms of creativity that are located in the first column of the matrix and that are characterised by the same relatively high level of formality but by different levels of the perceived danger in a given situation, respectively a high level of ease/comfort, some uncertainty (the middle line of the matrix) and a high level of frustration/risk. The first form of creativity in this formalised institutional framework plotted along the comfort/frustration axis is the kind of innovative action that emerges from conditions of routine, which can be called the 'invisible elbow' principle (Tilly 1997). The idea of the invisible elbow draws, of course, on Adam Smith's concept of the 'invisible hand', which suggests the optimisation of collective consequences from narrow self-interest. Charles Tilly's (1997: 39) substitution of 'the invisible elbow principle' for the invisible hand aims to show that, while social life contains errors that result in unaccepted consequences, it also 'teems with error correction and responses, sometimes instantaneous, to unexpected outcomes'. The invisible elbow form of creativity points to the varied and constant adjustments we make to the existing constraints and conditions and to correct and improve the unintended consequences of prior actions. This type of episodic innovation is illustrated by the situation in which, not having a hand free to close a door, we use an elbow to slam it – sometimes successfully, sometimes missing it completely. To some degree this type of action is similar to *adhocism*, particularly in the sense that both of these two actions serve an immediate need. While both forms of creativity are answers to a particular purpose, the invisible elbow type of creativity takes place under conditions of limited choice, where the existence of rules, barriers and restrictions puts limits on our choice and demands creative adjustments or innovative arrangements that can immediately fulfil specific requirements. As examples of the invisible elbow form of creativity we could quote various strategies of coping with the limitations of authoritarian systems.

At the mid-point between the two extremes there is a space occupied by 'charismatic inspiration', where dynamic changes responsible for increasing the system's capability to react flexibly to internal and external challenges are produced. According to Weber ([1914] 1968), who places great emphasis on the role of charismatic leaders and their movements in the shaping of social dynamics, social change is brought about by a set of values and institutions, and charismatic heroes and prophets are truly revolutionary forces in history. For Weber, charisma, as a revolutionary force in history, involves the attributes of authority by disciples and followers. The charismatic breaking of tradition may be regarded as creative insofar 'as a personality and mind of originality of imagination perceives a profound gap in the adequacy of the prevailing tradition and seeks to fill that gap, while acknowledging his derivation from it' (Shils 1981: 229). Charisma is opposed to all institutional routines, and challenges formalised structures; a genuinely charismatic situation is 'direct and inter-personal', and the 'creative entrepreneur' is characterised by 'the inner freedom', an imaginative, spontaneous 'flight of genius' (Gerth and Mills 1946: 52–3). However, an emphasis upon the exceptionality and spontaneity of the charismatic man or woman does not minimise 'the mechanics of institutions' (54). On the contrary, Weber tries to grasp what is retained of the heroic and enthusiastic work in the institutional order. 'The achievement of the charismatic person is an accomplishment of an original imagination working within a tradition and modifying it in important respects but not leaving it completely behind him. His imagination is aroused by incompleteness in the tradition for what he perceived as a task which must be reckoned with' (Shils 1981: 229). We can point here to the role of Nelson Mandela in initiating political creativity in South Africa, in the recasting of the field of power and in the re-formulation of the structure of public authority and the form of governance.

At the end of the spectrum, under conditions of high risk and formalisation, creativity takes on the form of the taming of anxiety. This type of innovative action occurs when structural conditions undermine consensus or an old definition of the situation. It can occur in the case of science due to the persistence and accumulation of anomalies, which resist assimilation. According to Kuhn (1962), whose account of scientific revolutions relates decisions to change a given paradigm to the social psychology of the scientific group involved, such a loss of consensus can result in radical change. When a new definition of the situation becomes public and acted upon, the group rejects the old paradigm, or the previous conventional basis for evaluation. It can also happen when people acting contrary to the restrictions imposed by the political authority constitute a transformative political power. The creativity of political action, seen as a result of the construction of an interactive definition of the situation in an authoritarian political setting, has been described by Arendt (1963) as a lost treasure of the revolutionary tradition. Arendt's description of the experience of public freedom by the French Resistance suggests that such dissenting action grants a sense of freedom, not only because they 'acted against tyranny and things worse than tyranny ... but because they had become "challengers", had taken the initiative upon themselves and therefore, without knowing, or even noticing it, had begun to create that public space between themselves where freedom could appear' (1963: 4). Dissidents' radical work therefore expands the scope of freedom, calls into question the old paradigms and conventions and radicalises the public definition of the situation.

Our next three forms of creativity are located in the middle column of the matrix and are characterised by the same balance of formality and informality but by different levels of the perceived danger in a given situation. The first form, a successful creative interaction between people who are at ease, free from formalised rigid rules and regulations and in a relatively safe environment, can be described as improvisation. Improvisation occurs under conditions of informalisation and comfort and refers to a spontaneous, collaborative process of creating and sharing experiences in real time. This first form of creativity, rooted in the relationships that are established by the reciprocal sharing of others' experiences and not using scripted lines, is founded upon the common experience of living simultaneously in the same dimension of time, and can be illustrated by such activities as improvisation in jazz, where participants work within a framework of agreement on procedures and outcomes yet avoid too rigidly prescribed texts (Tilly 2000: 723). It describes something more than just the process of coordinating human action as it is a creative process in action, unplanned, without a basic script as one is performing some activity. In an improvisational performance the collaborative role of the audience is also of importance (Sawyer 2001: 102). Jazz-style improvisations generally rely on relatively fragmented and variable social structures and proceed 'through improvised interaction, surprise, incessant error and error correction, alternation between solo and ensemble action, and repeated responses to understandings shared by at least pairs of players' (Tilly 2000: 723). Improvisation, as a social phenomenon, is 'an organised, collaborative social practice occurring in the context of a specific artistic community' (Martin 2002: 134). Seeing improvisation as a social phenomenon 'in which the impulses and aspirations of individuals must somehow be reconciled with the configuration of normative conventions that confronts them' (Martin 2002: 141) makes the point that it is not so much the free play of individual creativity but a collaborative and collectively organised practice.

The second form, a successful creative interaction between people who are relatively free from immediate rules and regulations, yet embedded within wider formalised structures that provide them with codes of behaviour and a relatively satisfying environment, can be described as collaborative exploration (or 'exploring the world together'). Creative achievement is accomplished mainly through purposeful work, which indicates a certain degree of mastery of a domain, and is characteristic of science, in which discoveries become a formalised part of a shared knowledge. While jazz-style improvisations generally rely on free and real-time collaborative adaptation, a science-style creativity typically rests on complex and relatively balanced formal/informal structures. Whereas the first form of creativity can be seen as coming close to balancing proximity and individual autonomy, this second form faces a difficult task in trying to balance autonomy and control. This is a result of the fact that, with the growing size of the group, new channels of monitoring are needed, leading to the emergence of administrative structures, although it does necessarily mean the reduction of actors' autonomy (Schutz 1964: 77). This requires the introduction of a type of monitoring that will reduce people's suspicions about the inequality of burdens without, however, infringing on their autonomy. Consequently, collaborative exploration can be successful only when the distinctions between the formalities of the front of the stage (techniques, methods, procedures, administration) and the backstage informalities (collegiality) are drawn up in a flexible manner, to allow for any specific adjustments required in particular conditions. Kuhn's (1962) investigation into what research is typically like, most of the time, in any well-established and productive scientific field fits this picture. It is devoted largely to the elaboration and extension of some generally accepted concrete scientific achievement. The attraction of the achievement is that it can, when given the status of an authoritative model, serve as the basis for further research (as a scientific paradigm that is never judged or tested; it itself is the basis for judgement in normal science, which relies upon consensus).

The third form of creativity, marked by a relative balance between informality and formality and a high level of frustration, is a 'taming of chance', or normalisation, since it refers to the kind of breaching of the normal registered as 'chance'. The taming of chance can be seen as 'the most ideological tool of the twentieth century', as it allows for an evaluation of events in terms of normalcy and deviation from the norm (Hacking 1990: 169). The positive valorisation of the 'normal' has ensured the widespread appreciation of the notion and it has been built into many projects in social sciences, medical practices and public policies, as well as resulting in the growing significance attached to the collection of social statistics in terms of normality and pathology (Canguilhem 1989: 246). 'Throughout the Age of Reason, chance had been called the superstition of the vulgar. [...] The rational man, averting his eyes from such things, could cover chaos with a veil of inexorable laws. The world, it was said, might often look haphazard, but only because we do not know the inevitable workings of its inner springs' (Hacking 1992: 1). From the beginning of the nineteenth century the taming of chance was assumed to be a part of the notion of progress as it was seen to be capable of imposing order on variations and enhancing the processes of regulation and normalisation (Foucault 1975). Thus, it can be said that taming chance is a form of creativity that manifests itself through the development of something new to bring order out of chaos or eradicate the abnormal.

Moving now to the third column of our matrix, we can observe that there are three forms of creativity plotted along the comfort/frustration axis. First, at the top of the spectrum characterised by high levels of comfort and informality, creative actions can best be described as 'creative insight'. A low level of frustration, in combination with a lack of formalisation of the rules of conduct, can enhance the chance of an original insight or intuition and facilitate this type of creativity, which brings together intense intellectual and emotional involvement. Such creative intuition, which arises from a degree of vagueness (James 1890), can be illustrated by, for example, artistic groups or so-called 'hot groups'. Hot groups are spontaneously emerging groups that are characterised by openness and flexibility in their organisational structures and that generate excitement and intuitive solutions. Although they are rare, their fluid structures and small size, alongside their members' exceptional intellectual and emotional involvement, make them very successful (Leavitt and Lipman-Blumen 1995: 113). Puzzling over the sources of creative imagination in science, politics and arts, Bailyn (2003) notes that creative minds stimulate each other, interaction and computation have a generative effect, sparks fly as a result of disagreement and rivalry, and whole groups become creative. Similarly, Isaiah Berlin (1999) explains the unusual creativity of the decade of the 1840s in Russia in terms of the intensely personal nature of the contacts and the frequency of exchanges between intellectual friends.

Second, at the middle of the comfort/frustration scale, we can talk about the process of rationalisation. According to Weber (1968), the establishment of a new order can be achieved not only through charismatic personal forces but also through the process of rationalisation, which brings about an impersonal adaptation to values or material goals and which serves to demystify and disenchant the modern world. Rationalisation involves many features, among which the most important is the growth of procedural formality and goal-setting behaviour.

Rationalisation is a socially and historically differentiated and multi-dimensional process and has a variety of meanings; for example, Weber draws a distinction between practical, theoretical, formal and substantive rationality. Without going into great detail, Weber's view is that it is possible to say that all types of rationality are changing the world; for example, theoretical rationality involves an attempt to transcend the world by according it some sort of logical meaning, while substantive rationality involves a choice of means to ends guided by some broader set of human values (such as Calvinism, for instance). The process of formal rationality – 'the best means to an end is chosen on the basis of universally agreed-upon rules, regulations and laws' – can be illustrated by 'bureaucratic rationalization ... revolutionizes with technical means, in principles "from without"' (Ritzer 2001: 181). It first changes the material and social orders, and through them the people, by 'changing the conditions of adaptation and perhaps the opportunities for adaptation, through a rational determination of means and end' (Weber [1914] 1968: 1116). In short, the process of ratio-nalisation results in the creation of more complex, more calculated, coherent and abstract systems.

Third, at the end of the spectrum, there is the 'taming of ambiguity', which is an innovative process occurring under a relatively high level of frustration/risk. The taming of ambiguity, by bringing irregular events under control and by developing imaginative solutions to emergent problems, reduces the complexity of and the hardship experienced in the system. Such a lowering of the level of difficulties, when successful, is followed by a process of routinisation, which is 'one of the principal continually operating forces in everyday life (Weber [1914] 1964: 372). In other words, this form of creativity is 'purposeful action aimed at routinizing and ordering life to make shared existence predictable from one day to the next' (Davis 1994: 99). The taming of ambiguity, being a result of 'striving for security', is a form of creativity that manifests itself through the development of something new and through explorations of uncharted areas in order to meet 'the objective necessity of adaptation' (Weber [1914] 1964: 370). Since such pioneering achievements tend to be routinised, it can be said that routinisation is a final stage of creative actions, helping to tame ambiguity in a situation underwritten by a high level of informality.

To sum up, viewing creativity as being socially and culturally con-structed offers some interesting possibilities for our study of the role of public intellectuals. However, since creativity is seen as occurring in a wide range of situations, we need to ask if creativity in science or business is one thing and creativity in politics another. Among the main theorists of creativity there is no agreement whether creativity is domain-specific or not, with some asserting that creation is local to a particular domain of expertise, while others assume a lack of difference between the various kinds of creativity and stress the universals in creativity (Tardif and Sternberg 1988: 431). Although there are universals in creativity (Tardif and Sternberg 1988: 431), it can be argued that creativity is context-specific. The main reasons for this claim are that creativity, as interaction between producer and audience, is directly connected with social systems making judgements about individuals' products (Csikszentmihalyi 1999: 313), and that this evaluation varies from one context or domain to another and can be fully appraised only according to the criteria of a particular field of activity. Since 'creation can be democracy and the Parthenon and Macbeth, but it is also Auschwitz, the Gulag ... ' (Castoriadis 1996: 8), the role of judgement is especially important in the public sphere.

Since our main focus here is on public intellectuals' engagement in shared projects of imagining a better democratic future, we are interested in one specific type of creativity, namely 'civic creativity', conceived of as creativity that provides us with ideas on how to democratise and humanise the workings of modern societies. Creativity of this type, although expressed in various forms, is characteristic of all the public intellectuals in our sample. The twelve public intellectuals who won the Nobel Prize, apart from creative activity within their different domains, responded creatively to challenges posed to the health of democracy and the well-being of their nations. The particular forms their civic creativity took depended on their specific social and political contexts.

Drawing on Arendt's (1958; 1978) observation that politics is an inherently risky and uncertain enterprise, as well as on her conceptualisation of creativity as 'the problem of the new', it can be said that public involvement requires both creativity and courage. Because of the very nature of their activity, which consists of nothing less than changing the world, public figures' creative imagination – that is, the ability to recast the world anew and to think freshly, originally and innovatively – is rooted in a disposition to take risks. Its cultivation depends upon enhancing our ability both to break through conventional wisdoms, old habits and affiliations and to re-formulate the old structures in fresh ways (Arendt 1958). Since such creative contributions to societal well-being frequently demand courage, in the following chapter we scrutinise the nature of this essential aspect of public intellectuals' engagement.

3   Courage: acting on conviction

The changing nature and status of courage

In this chapter I discuss what the social sciences, in general, can tell us about the complex phenomenon of courage, and look for answers to these questions: what is courage? Does courage require a particular knowledge or belief component? What are the relationships between courage, risk and difficulty, courage and loyalty to the group and courage and nonconformity?

The notion of courage, which – alongside love – is the most popular topic in world literature (Miller 2000: 8), is still commonly discussed in terms derived from the Greeks, for whom courage was one of the most important virtues. Our contemporary understanding of this notion comes from Plato's and Aristotle's analyses of courage as virtue, while Socrates, a historical exemplar of someone risking death for his beliefs, is seen as the epitome of intellectual and personal courage. The argument that the flourishing of democratic values is associated with the cultivation of courage also goes back to classical Greek democracy, where the courage to speak up (*parrhesia*, or an act of truth-telling that involves risk) was an essential element of the functioning of democracy (Rossbach 1999: 3–4). As Arendt (1958: 186) notes, courage was the main political virtue, and only 'that man who possessed it could be admitted to a fellowship that was political in content and purpose and thereby transcend the mere togetherness imposed on all – slaves, barbarians and Greeks alike'. The centrality of courage to political life meant that courage was an indispensable characteristic of the hero and the core condition of democratic freedom. 'Classical Athenians believed not only that democracy was founded on courage, but also that democracy had special resources to aid in producing courage' (Balton 2004: 83). Pericles, in the famous funeral oration in honour of the dead during the first year of the Peloponnesian War (421 BC), praised the Athenian democracy for making the good life available to its citizens by guaranteeing the joy of a free society and stressed that this guarantee is based on courage (Balton 2004: 84–5).

For the Greeks, courage was one of the most important virtues to be tested on the battlefield. This view of courage, as embodied in the accounts of Plato and Aristotle, assumes that the courageous person had to have noble ends and had to be credited with possessing courage in battle. Aristotle retains physical courage as the primary case, although he extends its exercise to a political and moral context. For him, courage, the first moral virtue, must be performed for the sake of nobility, and the honour of courage is found in deeds that are not subject to necessity or utility (Kateb 2004: 48; Comte-Sponville 2003: 57). Aristotle's definition of courage as the disposition to act appropriately in situations that involve fear and confidence moves towards transforming it into 'a generalized enabling virtue' (Rorty Oksenberg 1988: 305). Courage is a matter of ethical consideration, and therefore people's responses to fear depend on their degree of virtue; for example, a virtuous man would not fear poverty but would fear dishonour in battle (Aristotle [350 BC] 1962: 68–70). The link between courage and honour means that courage is inseparable from the choice required for moral responsibility, and from the human capacity for deliberation and its demands (Miller 2000: 149). Since courage is the virtue 'both worthy of practice by morally serious individuals and as emphatically honourable from the perspective of the community's political leaders' (Ward 2001: 84–6), Aristotle insists on the cultivation of a courageous disposition for the sake of the city's political needs. He also argues that courage, as a kind of 'balanced deliberation in a tight situation' (Walton 1986: 6), requires moderation, which means that the risks we take must be in proportions to the ends we seek; it is admirable to risk your life for a noble cause but unreasonable to do so out of sheer fascination with danger (Comte-Sponville 2003: 58). As Lee Ward (2001: 85) notes, the ultimate effect of Aristotle's discussion of courage is to challenge the simple distinction between the moral and intellectual virtues.

Plato, through the literary device of Socrates debating with two generals in *Laches*, also reworks the notion of courage into a more broadly defined concept. In the Platonic dialogues, Socrates proposes that courage consists in 'knowledge of what is and is not to be feared' (quoted in Schwartz 2004: 351). Plato's image of a courageous philosopher who never confronts any fear identifies courage with knowledge and assumes mastery of the fear. This concept of courage, as a form of moral virtue that involves knowledge both of the self and of the ends for which a danger was faced, exposes the importance of the intellectual elements of the courageous action. Although Plato does not offer a positive theory of what courage is, his reworking of it proposes a shift of emphasis from military courage to political and moral courage – an attitude identical with practical wisdom. The definition that Plato proposes in the *Republic*, when Socrates defines courage as the 'reservation of the belief inculcated by the law through education about what things are to be feared' (quoted in Kateb 2004: 42), has moved far away from characterising the particular dispositions exercised in courage and stresses the cultivation of the virtue. This more intellectualist definition of courage that is being put forward claims that courage is synonymous with knowledge and wisdom, that 'the extremely wise are the extremely bold, and being extremely bold are extremely courageous' and that the practice of philosophy requires courage (Socrates in *Protagoras*, quoted in Hobbs 2000: 116). This concept of courage is illustrated by the life of Socrates himself: a life of perpetual philosophical questioning, and a life without fear either on the battlefield or in the civic arena. Despite the fact that such a conceptualisation is too idealistic, its account of the relationship between knowledge and courage has maintained its appeal for centuries.

The Greek debates about courage placed it among the most important virtues, and presented it as standing out from the other virtues not only on account of the 'mysteriousness of its psychology and its capacities to generate good stories' (Miller 2000: 77) but also because of its links to knowledge and honour. Nevertheless, the ancient Greek philosophers have left us with many unanswered questions, and with the realisation that courage 'is an impossible subject' (Kateb 2004: 39). Consequently, despite the richness of the debates and despite a long history of fascination with and glorification of the idea of courage, this value is still the subject of many controversies, and it continues to demand scholarly rethinking.

The existence of contradictory views on the nature of courage and on its role in the public realm can be explained, to some degree, by the concept's links with historically bound values and ideas – or, in other words, the fact that each civilisation 'has its fears and its corresponding forms of courage' (Comte-Sponville 2003: 44). The fact that we in the West have given up on the aristocratic search for military glory these days and do not appreciate the masculine culture of courageous warriors illustrates the changing nature and status of courage, and supports the assertion that there are connections between each civilisation's views of what is good and its chosen heroes – and, by the same token, its idea of courage.

This line of arguing has been proposed by Niccolò Machiavelli ([1513] 1988), who holds that the role of courage, and therefore also its main traits, reflect the dominant activities of the city. When the main preoccupation of the city state was statecraft, risky and courageous actions by the wise prince were in demand. In the changed conditions, when the primary activities of the city are mercantile, courage calls for radically different dispositions from those required on the battlefield: 'An energetic, inventive, bold imagination, a capacity to envision a distant benefit and unexpected means – a whole set of entrepreneurial capacities are required to carry out the exercise of courage' (Rorty Oksenberg 1988: 307). This new bourgeois ethic's valuation of commercial life means the recession of the aristocratic honour ethic, which stressed glory, won in military pursuit (Taylor 1989). A next step in the historical evaluation of the value of courage is illustrated by Alexis de Tocqueville ([1835] 1968: 248), who shows how democracy modifies courage in a new and democratic direction.

The classical definition of courage also calls for reconsideration because of its masculine overtones, its accent on the physical and military aspects of courage and its assumptions about the role of courage in political and moral life. Firstly, today we object to the fact that women used to be excluded from the category of great heroes, and we reject the definition of courage in gendered terms as solely a characteristic of men. Such a conceptualisation of courage is a result of the fact that courage began as *andreia* – that is, as military manliness (Rorty Oksenberg 1988: 304) – and therefore it tends to be commonly associated with the physical, usually violent, actions of soldiers. The Latin word for courage, *fortitudo* (strength), also indicates the military connotations of the term (Tillich 1961: 5), and therefore it too prompts the question as to whether courage has a role to play in peacetime.

The military connotation of the classical definition is the second reason why this earlier approach to courage strikes an antiquated note to people today. The idea that true courage has to be tested on the battlefield, in conjunction with the original association of the notion of courage with war and with physical, masculine, militaristic bravery, have been criticised by feminist writers in particular (Sparks 1997; Bethke Elshtain and Tobias 1990). They all argue that the close ties between courage and soldiering had institutionalised masculinity and located women symbolically and politically as lesser civic beings, and that such praising of courage in war projects a view of women that not only reinforces women's secondary status but also lays the basis for all other forms of social oppression (Bethke Elshtain and Tobias 1990: xi).

Another area of divergence between the classical Greeks' and our perception of the role of courage is connected with the fact that we attach less importance to the role of courage in public life. Granted, we frequently use the classical perspective in political rhetoric, of course. For example, Winston Churchill described courage as 'the first of human qualities, because it is the quality which guarantees all others' (quoted in Arendt 1961: 156), while John F. Kennedy ([1956] 1965: 21) praised courage as 'the most admirable of human virtues'. But the claim that courage by itself is not necessarily an attractive quality for public life has also been voiced frequently since the beginning of modernity. For Voltaire, for example – in contrast to Aristotle ([350 BC] 1962: 68–70), for whom courage was the premier value and a good person was one who feared 'the right things, for the right motive, in the right manner, and the right time' – courage was not a virtue 'but a quality shared by blackguards and great men alike' (quoted in Comte-Sponville 2003: 44). Moreover, the main representatives of utilitarianism did not appreciate the importance of courage as a public virtue.

In addition, we have a problem with the Greeks' claim that a courageous soldier is one who discounts his fear in his deliberations and therefore feels no fear, and for whom the goal of victory is superior to all other values. To surrender to fear is, according to Aristotle, an evidence of a failure of moral education, whereas acting courageously in the face of particular dangers suggests that one had properly internalised the rules of moral life (Robin 2000: 1085). In Euripides' ([410 BC] 1978: 77) play *Iphigeneia at Aulis*, Agamemnon's declaration that 'it is Greece that compels me to sacrifice . . . Greece must be free' represents Aristotle's notion of courage, seen as a virtue the main characteristics of which are derived from the political and moral shape of the political community. Today, in contrast to the Athenians' ethical guidelines, which praised physical courage in the service of the political community, we are less sure that the personal sacrifices should at all be necessary or that they should outweigh legitimate self-interest. Not only we have moved away from the unquestionable celebration of the warrior's courage but our attitudes are more complex as we tend to aspire, as Foucault suggests, to a more modest heroism, and to heroism rooted in reflections on the right of an individual. As well as admiring war heroes we also honour such people as Giuseppe Garibaldi, who spared the life of an enemy soldier out of respect for his courage, and such people as Joseph Schutz, a German soldier in World War II who – when he had been ordered to execute captured partisans – crossed over to them and got shot together with them (Swedberg 1999: 521–2). Furthermore, as the sense of belonging to national communities and its corresponding moral obligations are now often questioned, some go even further and argue: 'If I had to choose between betraying my country and betraying my friend, I hope I would have the guts to betray my country' (from E. M. Forster's 'What I believe', quoted in Singer and Singer 2005: 249).

Finally, the classical Greeks' view of courage as the most honoured virtue, of the greatest importance to the 'good life', differs from our modern, less definite, less solid and less affirmative ideas about the relationship between courage and morality. In contrast to the classical view of courage as 'the greatest of all virtues: because unless a man has that virtue, he has no security for preserving any other' (Samuel Johnson, quoted in Boswell [1791] 1998: 298), sceptics, such as Machiavelli and Thomas Hobbes, argue that humans are incapable of acting out of any other motives than self-interest and do not view courage from within a moral framework (Kateb 2004: 39–42). Machiavelli ([1513] 1988), who professed the primacy and the necessity of interest over reason and morality, rejected the classical understanding of courage as being too idealistic and not practical enough for ensuring political power. Not being concerned with courage's indiscriminatory capability to serve good or evil, Machiavelli ([1513] 1988: 59) stressed the political significance of a risky and courageous action by a wise prince, for whom, in order to enable a city to rise to prosperity and fame, it was much safer 'to be feared than loved'. In short, Machiavelli appreciated courage as a crucial instrument in the building of state power. In his view, courage is by no means a morally positive quality in itself (Rorty Oksenberg 1988: 306). The recent debate initiated by Susan Sontag's remark that the hijackers responsible for the 11 September 2001 attacks were not cowards since they were willing to die for a cause they believed in has again raised the question of whether courage is morally neutral or not (Pears 2004). We are faced here with the existence of contrasting views as to whether courage is moral or immoral in itself, and this lack of consensus is one of the main obstacles in today's theorising about courage.

Our understanding of the notion of courage is also not helped by the lack of consensus among political theorists on the role of courage in public life and liberal political theorists' relative silence on the subject. The main voice stressing the importance of political courage in the public domain belongs to Arendt (1961: 156), who asserts, while following the classical tradition, that courage is 'one of the most cardinal political virtues' as it is the necessary condition for political action. Courage is 'demanded of us by the very nature of the public realm' because 'in politics not life but the world is at stake' (156). In contrast to the argument that the essential quality for politics is courage, many liberal theorists 'have strived to tame the concept of politics, emphasizing the importance of gentler qualities such as toleration, civility, compassion, and reasonableness over the more bellicose quality of courage' (Scorza 2001: 637). For numerous liberals, the traditional political concept of courage is seen as being outdated, too anachronistic and vital solely to aristocratic character (Shklar 1989). They reject Hobbes' idea that rational fear must be taught on the grounds that not only does it sustain selfhood but it also helps to transform civil society into an instrument of the state. Hobbes ([1651] 1991: 483) saw courage as a form of hope that is particularly destructive because it could lead to irrational resistance, acts of private revenge and disruption of the public peace. Since one of the main assumptions of contemporary liberalism is that fear arises in the absence of laws, education, moral principles and institutions (Robin 2000: 1087), liberal theorists, in contrast to Hobbes ([1651] 1991) but like Baron de Montesquieu ([1748] 1989), identify fear with undemocratic political systems. They claim that citizens in democratic societies do not need to respond to fear or demonstrate courage (Shklar 1989). In similar ways to Montesquieu ([1748] 1989), who asserted that learning fear is a dehumanising goal of despotic education, today's liberals assume that fear is predicated upon the destruction of civil society. Additionally, following Montesquieu, who was among the first to praise the allegedly gentler manners and habits of commercial society, liberals argue that modern states have no special need for courage as this virtue impedes rather than promotes commerce (Scorza 2001: 645).

The fact that in Western culture the notion of courage has been closely connected with the idea of the 'hero' – that is, an individual who commits an approved act of unusual courage – has also contributed to this concept's complexity and unwieldiness. Courage, in the ancient literary conception of the hero, 'is virtually taken for granted in a man who is favoured by the gods, as the hero is presumed to be, and who is even endowed with certain inherited traits of divinity' (Trilling 1972: 85). Throughout history the ideas of courage and the hero have been more important in some literary strands than in others. For example, the Romantic period is connected with the notion of Byronic courage, seen as deriving from the militancy and passions of spirit, whereas the Victorian era is perceived as being characterised by calm submission to the law of things without any emotional personal engagement. Whereas in twentieth-century American culture, at least as exemplified in its movies, there was a predilection for powerful moral dramas in which courage is 'grace under pressure' (Ernest Hemingway, quoted in Kennedy [1956] 1965: 21) and a hero 'is one who looks like a hero' (Robert Warshow, quoted in Trilling 1972: 85). Furthermore, each culture has a different notion of how courage encounters fear and what constitutes the public sphere of life, the arena in which courage can appear (Schwartz 2004). Moreover, not all cultures develop the idea of courage. For example, the Jewish tradition is characterised by an indifference to the virtue of courage. The Hebrew Bible and rabbinic commentators provided a different conception of courage and its relation to fear, and seem to suggest that the life of virtue and religious devotion does not require the heroic quality (Schwartz 2004: 349–358). 'In the Rabbinical literature there is no touch of the heroic idea. The

Rabbis, in speaking of virtue, never mention the virtue of courage, which Aristotle regarded as basic to the heroic character. The indifference of the Rabbis to the idea of courage is the more remarkable in that they knew that many of their number would die for their faith' (Trilling 1972: 85). In this alternative tradition from Jerusalem, the greatest examples were the courageous Hebrew prophets who were intellectually perfect and morally good, although not free from fear (Schwartz 2004: 355).

And, finally, another impediment in theorising about courage is connected with the fact that there are many different kinds of courage. For example, we can differentiate between intellectual, military, physical and moral courage. This diversity also suggests the multiplicity of mutual links, which further enhances the difficulties in understanding this phenomenon. Although the term 'moral courage' did not appear in English until the nineteenth century, the notion of *fortitudo moralis*, as 'the capacity and resolved purpose to resist a strong but unjust opponent' (Immanuel Kant, quoted in Rorty Oksenberg 1988: 300), was employed in philosophical texts. Today this notion seems to mean 'the capacity to overcome the fear of shame and humiliation in order to admit one's mistakes, to confess a wrong, to reject evil conformity, to denounce injustice, and also to defy immoral and imprudent orders' (Miller 2000: 254). Though acts of moral courage – that is, acts 'in the service of others and more or less free of immediate self-interest' (Comte-Sponville 2003: 47) – are not the same as civil courage – that is, acts of courage 'which embody the values of civil society' (Swedberg 1999: 522) – we cannot easily separate moral and civic motives. This difficulty is a result of the fact that there are some moral, individual reasons for taking the duties of citizenship seriously. Moreover, acting on moral principle is often a political act, in the sense that 'you're not doing it for yourself. You don't do it just to be in the right, or to appease your own conscience; much less because you are confident your action will achieve its aim. You resist as an act of solidarity – with communities of the principled and the disobedient; here, elsewhere; in the present, in future' (Sontag 2003: 6).

Although Plato had already noted that philosophers are the most truly courageous of people and Cicero had already suggested that 'the courageous deeds of civilians are not inferior to those of soldiers' (quoted in Miller 2000: 10), the modern term for civil courage (*Zivilcourage*) was coined in 1864 by Otto von Bismarck, who contrasted it with courage in war situations where it is a form of obedience; thus, courageous soldiers are simply followers of orders (Schwan 2004; Swedberg 1999). Civil courage, as 'behaviour that relies on an individual decision motivated and legitimated by the fundamental value of human dignity for whose protection the courageous individual behaves in a nonconformist manner and takes a personal risk' (Schwan 2004: 113), describes courage differently from both military courage and civil disobedience. Civil courage does not necessarily include acts of physical courage. Yet, because we 'will always need physical courage', which means that we should aim not to 'confine it morally' (Kateb 2004: 68), democracy, in order to take full advantage of courage, needs to make sure that both types of courage – physical and non-physical – are inspired by civil values. Courage that has no civic value in itself, regardless of whether it involves a physical component, does not enrich democracy. Richard Swedberg (1999: 522), who recognises the increasing importance of civil courage for the health of democracy, gives an example of an act of physical courage that is not at the same time an act of civil courage. He suggests that racists who stand up to an audience of anti-racists may be showing physical courage but they do not show civil courage, because racists are hostile to the values of civil society and want to impose their own values. Therefore, when we describe courage as a civic virtue, we have to speak of 'civil' courage.

Courage: risk and difficulty

Following the ancient Greek view that courage is to be found in the mastery of fear, empirical psychology identifies this character trait primarily with a low sensitivity to fear (Rachman 1978; 2004). Experimental psychologists, who lack interest in the normative element of the notion, delineate courage as a functional relationship between sets of stimuli and responses (Walton 1986: 80). Such an approach, and a definition of 'courageous behaviour' mainly in terms of observable events such as bodily signs and chemical processes, orient psychological studies towards the measurement of less psychophysical reactions in people subjected to stress under controlled conditions. One of the main results of clinical studies that assume that courage is 'persistence in dealing with a dangerous situation despite subjective and physical signs of fear' (Rachman 2004: 173) is the discovery that 'individual characteristics might make some particular contribution to the execution of acts of bravery' (169).

Empirical psychologists, searching for proof that courage is synonymous with the absence of fear, study various groups of people who are capable of carrying out fearless acts. Investigations into courageous actions by astronauts, firefighters, bomb disposal specialists, parachutists and soldiers come up with evidence that people performing such fearless acts 'appear to be unusually resilient' and show 'a muted psychophysical reaction when subjected to stress under controlled conditions', and that their declines in fearfulness were accompanied by increased levels of self-confidence (Rachman 2004: 159–60). Drawing conclusions on the basis of studies into wartime experiences, such as air raids and combat operations, it is argued that people are capable of adjusting to living with and coping with fears, and that they became increasingly courageous as they became more experienced (Rachman 2004: 149).

Although the majority of scholars accept the definition of courage that suggests that risk is involved in courageous actions, studies of fear are often criticised for identifying courage with the absence of fear and overlooking the importance of the object of courage (Walton 1986: 82). One such study that identifies courage with the absence of fear is the landmark sociological research into American soldiers in wartime carried out by Samuel A. Stouffer et al. (1949). Rejecting this investigation's claim that airmen displayed significantly more courageous behaviour than other combat soldiers, Douglas Walton (1986: 81) points out that such an approach does not set soldiers' psychological belief that the situation is dangerous against a background of their expectations about normal fears and desires. According to him, although fear is often present in the initial stages of a courageous act, 'the emotion of fear is not, as such, an essential characteristic of the courageous act' (82). Judgements about courageous acts should be not tied to the emotion of fear, not only because there are people who are fearless but not courageous but also because the level of perceived risk and the level of competence could be different. A courageous act must be worthwhile or the risk acceptable, which means that an act of courage requires that the agent justifiably believes that her/his act is dangerous, but it will have good results or benefits (Wallace 1978: 81). Furthermore, to be truly courageous, an act must overcome real difficulty or danger.

So, courage contains an element of 'difficulty' as well as an element of 'danger'. Since it has to do with the overcoming of an obstacle to gain some end, it therefore refers to an outstanding determination – for example, a disabled person who overcomes his or her disability through persistence and ingenuity (Walton 1986: 94). We may call such a person courageous even if overcoming fear was not the main problem in her or his action. Defining courageous actions by their difficulty follows Thomas Aquinas's view of courage, which notes that 'it belongs to the virtue of fortitude to remove any obstacle that withdraws the will from following the reason' (quoted in Walton 1986: 94). In other words, we can say that a courageous individual is a person who opposes obstacles, overcomes difficulties, tends to set aside the normal fear and is capable of taking risk. 'Courage is identified against the background of beliefs about what is objectively difficult, risky or dangerous; its attribution rests on assumptions about what is normally feared or found difficult'

(Rorty Oksenberg 1988: 302). If moral courage – that is, the virtuous act that serves others – is a matter of readiness to take risks and to cope with oppositional confrontation, it can be argued that courage is the necessary element of altruistic behaviour in institutional settings in which a concern for the plight of others requires courageous conduct. This is confirmed by Samuel P. Oliner and Pearl M. Oliner's (1988) study of courageous people who rescued Jews under the Nazis, as well as by Nechama Tec's (1986: 163) investigation, in which the overwhelming majority (85 per cent) of the Jews rescued described their helpers as courageous.

For their study *The Altruistic Personality: Rescuers of Jews in Nazi Europe*, Oliner and Oliner interviewed 700 people: 406 rescuers, 150 survivors and 126 non-rescuers. They found that the courageous individuals cared more than the others about people outside their families. It can be said that what distinguished rescuers from non-rescuers was 'their strong sense of attachment to others and their feeling of responsibility for the welfare of others, including those outside of their immediate family' (Oliner and Oliner 1988: 249). The ethical values of care and inclusiveness that characterised rescuers, together with their ability to follow their own moral imperatives, even when these were in opposition to the values and norms pervasive in their environment (Tec 1986), make them exemplary cases of civil courage. Their brave conduct is explained by their 'sense of being a certain kind of person: of living by some standards rather than others' (Glover 1999: 383). Firstly, their strong sense of moral identity is connected with the fact that their parents had set high standards for them. Moreover, the parents of rescuers were significantly less likely to emphasise obedience, as only 1 per cent of rescuers (as against 9 per cent of non-rescuers and 12 per cent of bystanders) said that their parents taught them obedience (Oliner and Oliner 1988: 162). Secondly, their brave conduct is a result of high standards being imposed by their other networks and affiliations. There are many examples of courageous actions that had their origin in people's dedication to professional standards, religious beliefs, patriotic commitments or an academic or scientific truth. Finally, the studies suggest that people's courageous behaviour is also connected with their ability to sustain and cope with risk, or their 'readiness to act despite perceived risk' (127). The people who helped, while being fully aware of what punishment was attached to the rescuing of Jews, 'refused to focus on it', and consequently did not allow 'these negative forces to overpower them and saw life-threatening activities in less threatening ways' (Tec 1986: 190).

There are also some useful ideas for analysing civil courage in studies of whistle-blowing cases. Whistle-blowers are people who disclose the illegal, illegitimate or unethical practices of their companies to persons or organisations that may be able to effect action (Near and Miceli 1985: 4). The violation of professional standards is the most common cause of whistle-blowing. As professional ethics can often take on the status of a moral absolute, whistle-blowers are a good example of individuals with the courage of their convictions. Their willingness to pay the penalty for dissent suggests that whistle-blowing, as a process of speaking out in the public interest, shares many features with non-violent dissident action (Martin 1999). Seeing formal channels as tending to be ineffective, whistle-blowers, in order to achieve some success, must often base their tactics on mobilising the public. Whistle-blowers seem to be 'ethical dissenters', whose efforts can be influential in initiating protest movements (Jasper 1997: 137–46). For example, James Jasper (1997: 134) shows how a protest by a scientist whistle-blower, 'a man sustained by a clear moral vision, a belief in a set of rules: those of scientific methods', contributed to the anti-nuclear movement.

The ethical dilemma faced by whistle-blowers refers to conflicts between the ethics of their professions and their other obligations. The disclosure of information by whistle-blowers can involve risk because, especially in organisations in which there are no legal provisions or ethical codes that protect such actions, they frequently put their careers on the line and personal relationships at risk. Consequently, they 'usually finish up pariahs rather heroes' (Singer and Singer 2005: 213). While altruism, in situations when compassion demands courage, takes on the quality of civil courage, whistle-blowers' willingness to defend their ethical concerns demands courage in situations in which such a defence presupposes endangering the membership of, loyalty to and safety of the group. Although, typically, whistle-blowers are mainly concerned with the truth and the reality of their employment, while courageous citizens are concerned with a wide range of civic values and public issues, both groups, in order to be successful, need to challenge the existing rules (Donaldson and Werhane 1995). Moreover, whistle-blowers' actions, such as, for example, their concern with the quality of public services, can also benefit a wider public and, in turn, enrich civil society (Hunt 1995). Nonetheless, as the actions of whistle-blowers are indications mainly of employees' anxieties over work-related problems and dangers rather than indications of a public concern with the state of civil society, studies of whistle-blowing cases can illuminate only specific aspects of acts of courage.

In addition to situational demands, competence and confidence also contribute to the execution of courageous acts. Studies show that there is a positive relationship between self-confidence and people's capacity to sustain and cope with risk, which in itself is an important factor in explaining their courageous acts (Rachman 1978; 2004). 'The best preparation for courageous action is the preparation for action; competence and confidence in competence' (Rorty Oksenberg 1988: 303). Moreover, it seems not only that competence and confidence contribute to courageous performances but also that they are both strengthened by repeated and successful practice (Rachman 2004: 173). In other words, it can be argued that it is not fearlessness that account for courageous behaviour but competence, experience and self-control (Ruff and Korchin 1964). Such a conceptualisation of courage, which includes as a part of it the confidence connected with one's ability to cope with risk and difficulties as well as one's experience in coping with risks and difficulties, stresses self-control. It therefore contradicts Aristotle's approach, which assumes that a really courageous soldier is one who feels no fear rather than one who feels fear but controls it (Pears 2004). The Aristotelian view of fear, in contrast to our view of fear as an involuntary, affective emotional reaction, was morally informed and grew out of the particular political requirements of a society (Robin 2000). For Aristotle, 'discounting fear is a rational procedure and not an exercise of the will in self-control', and because such a discounted fear is no longer the problem there is no need for self-control, which is – according to Aristotle – 'an inferior substitute for virtue' (Pears 2004: 19).

All the same, the difference between these two concepts of fear is not unbridgeable. Although, on the one hand, today's psychology and neuroscience enrich our knowledge about fear as emotion, on the other hand the social sciences also enhance our understanding of the social roots and social effects of fear. Defining fear as not simply a matter of individual psychology, as developed in studies of fear that show that politicians and the media frequently contribute to public anxiety (Glassner 2004), in studies of the political use of fear (Heller 2004) and in studies of the impact of fear on an increased conformity to cultural norms (Pyszczynski 2004), helps us to recognise the validity of a more comprehensive, comparative and contextual approach to fear, and therefore also to courage. The dilemma caused by the existence of the two views of courage – as true virtue and as a special case of self-control, each rooted in different evaluations of self-control and two different concepts of fear (Robin 2000; Pears 2004) – can be solved by analysing the case of courage in a particular social context and by seeing courage not as primarily a matter of readiness for danger but, rather, as the very practical matter of being able to carry out the relevant actions to overcome difficulties in risky situations. In short, courage refers to an outstanding determination, despite danger, to remove obstacles or solve problems.

Allegiance to the group and nonconformity

In Aristotle's notion of courage, its main characteristics are derived from the moral duty to one's community. Yet many studies show that, although courage, as a virtue, presupposes some form of selflessness, it is not necessarily directly motivated by moral obligation to a wider community. For example, the study by Stouffer et al. (1949) shows the great importance of primary group loyalty. Stouffer's team (450–3) learned that soldiers returning from the war most often said that their actions on the battlefield were sustained by the strong group ties that developed during combat, and that they kept fighting to get the war over so that they could go home. This conclusion has been supported by many studies showing the role of close ties in sustaining soldiers' war effort. For example, Shils and Morris Janowitz (1948) confirm that it was the influence of primary group loyalties rather than Nazi ideology that sustained the fighting of Germany's Wehrmacht soldiers, even as Berlin fell. Many further studies have also confirmed that 'the execution of courageous acts will be enhanced by the support of a tightly integrated, familiar, small group of people' (Rachman 2004: 172).

Some input on the role of allegiance to the group in shaping people's conduct can be found in Emile Durkheim's theory of societal integration, which grants centrality to norms and values and sees solidarity as rooted in either commonalities or social differences. Durkheim argues that no society could exist unless its members acknowledge and make sacrifices on behalf of each other. His definition also centres on selflessness and relinquishing one's own interest in favour of obedience for the sake of society. According to Durkheim ([1915] 1973: 151), morality begins with 'disinterest, with attachment to something other than ourselves', and therefore there is no moral act that does not imply a sacrifice. Though absolutely disinterested behaviour 'is an ideal limit which can never be attained in reality', it is not merely 'a sort of agreeable ornament to social life' but its fundamental basis (152–3). Furthermore, Durkheim, like Weber, in an indirect way connects courage with religion. He argues in *Elementary Forms of Religious Life* ([1912] 1971) that the believer gets strength from his or her contact with God; and it clearly seems as if people with courage have more strength than others. 'The believer who has communicated with his god is not merely a man who sees new truths of which the unbeliever is ignorant; he is a man who is stronger. He feels within more force, either to endure the trials of existence, or to conquer them' (44). Despite the fact that they are the underlying cause of those 'great creative rituals' that give birth to new ideals, Durkheim is totally silent on the issue of variations in the structure of religious beliefs. Although Durkheim 'indicates that anomie is somehow associated with moral innovation' (Lockwood 1992: 131), he does not have much to say about morally challenging action and normative innovation, which can raise aspirations and create expectations that cannot be realised within the existing system of social hierarchy and therefore facilitate nonconformist action. It was Merton, not Durkheim, who developed the theory of anomie, which considers various forms of individual nonconformity as consequences of normative innovation.

Merton, while discussing nonconformity as a type of reference group behaviour in *Social Theory and Social Structure* (1968: 185–248), shows how dissenting behaviour can be analysed from a sociological perspective based on reference group theory. He proposes that criminal deviance might be studied as a specific variant within the larger social process of 'innovation'. After distinguishing two major forms of deviance, nonconforming behaviour and aberrant behaviour, Merton ([1949] 1968: 235–6) argues that some 'degree of deviation from current norms is probably functional for the basic goals of all groups. A certain degree of "innovation", for example, may result in the formation of new institutionalized patterns of behaviour which are more adaptive than the old in making for realization of primary goals' (236). He also assumes that nonconformity and deviant behaviour initiate two different paths of normative morphogenesis – that is, normative innovation and norm evasion (220). In the process of normative innovation, unlike in the case of norm evasion, the agent questions the validity of norms themselves, and this is therefore of relevance to our discussion of civil courage.

While rejecting the idea that civil courage can best be analysed as a form of deviant behaviour, Merton ([1949] 1968: 413–15) suggests that, although there are some similarities between the behaviour of the nonconformist and the criminal (neither lives up to the morally founded expectations of the others with whom they are engaged in the system of interlocking statuses and roles), the differences are even more important. Firstly, nonconformity, in contrast to criminality, is public, as the nonconformist does not try to hide her or his departures from the prevailing norms of the group. Secondly, while the criminal does not have an interest in changing the values of society, the nonconformist challenges the legitimacy of the norm from the beginning. Thirdly, the criminal is not driven by disinterested motives, while the nonconformist aims to change the norms of the group, and therefore he or she supplements the norms that he/she takes to be morally illegitimate with norms having an alternative moral basis. Merton, looking at 'courageous highwaymen', such as Oliver Cromwell or Jawaharlal Nehru, calls this type of nonconformist public behaviour 'rebellion': 'Rebellion involves a genuine transvaluation, where the direct or vicarious experience of frustration leads to full denunciation of previously prized values' ([1949] 1968: 209–10). This concept has a very wide denotation, while at the same time referring to exceptional episodes. It applies to a wider category of occurrences than only courageous defenders of civic values, as it can include innovators, pioneering scientists and religious prophets.

Merton ([1949] 1968) defines courage as being 'functional for the persistence and development of groups in accord with ultimate values – it elicits respect, even in those complex instances where it is apparently being used, not for the group but against it'. Courage, while fitting into a general category of nonconformist behaviour, is, according to Merton, a unique type of behaviour, because it is driven by disinterested motives and aims at changing the values of society. He views the 'courageous nonconformist' as somebody who departs from prevailing norms for wholly or largely disinterested purposes. Merton ([1949] 1968: 418–19) says that the nonconformist is 'prepared to accept, if not to welcome, the almost certain and painful consequences of dissent'. In short, Merton rejects the idea that civil courage can best be analysed as a form of deviant behaviour and argues that crime and delinquency, on the one hand, and nonconformist behaviour, on the other, represent two different sociological types of behaviour.

Merton's concern with the consequences of the power of allegiance to the group is indicative of a broader interest of American sociologists in the post-war period. While reflecting on Weber's anxiety connected with a pervasive institutionalisation of the 'iron cage', US researchers in the 1950s and 1960s focused their attention on the relation between organisational life and conformity. Investigations of conformity in bureaucratised contexts, seen as a prime threat to the American spirit, dealt indirectly with the issue of the conditions obstructing civil courage. Many American studies written in this tradition, such as David Riesman's *The Lonely Crowd* (1950), W. H. Whyte's *The Organization Man* (1956) and Herbert Marcuse's *One-Dimensional Man* (1966), have become sociological classics. This type of study was inspired by Tocqueville's warnings about the consequences of mass democracy, and by the writings of John Stuart Mill on the role of public opinion as the new barrier to freedom.

According to Tocqueville ([1835] 1968), citizens of democracies follow popular opinion not because they are forced to obey it but because such nations accord them with material sameness, which enhances isolation and conformity. It is a culture of fear, with its main characteristics – namely conformity and anxiety – reducing people's ability to form their own independent judgements. In contrast to weak conformists in democratic societies, aristocratic 'individuals have something of greatness and strength which is all their own' (643). They are courageous and have trust in their own superiority because they 'are tied by history to a long tradition of heroic exploits, and this gives them a sense of buoyancy, enabling them to rise above the tides of common opinion' (Robin 2000: 1096). Like Tocqueville, Mill was apprehensive of the tyranny of the majority, and saw the freedom of the individual as the first criterion of social good. He identified conformity and a lack of unorthodox thinking as one of the main societal dangers. Mill saw questioning and challenging the dominant views as one of the highest forms of virtue. He held that 'the mere example of nonconformity, the mere refusal to bend the knee to custom, is itself a service' to society (Mill, quoted in Riesman 1950: 301) because not giving in to the fear of what people might say is a way of promoting the long-term interest of society and thereby performing a social role of exceptional value.

For Riesman (1950: 301), as for Mill, the freedom of the minority stands in danger of being encroached on by the majority, as today people are governed 'by signals from outside'. Riesman follows Tocqueville's argument that, under equality, the intimacies of life become more important and the culture of equality produces conformity. Since, in the culture of material sameness, there are no common links between people to hold them firm and together, citizens abandon their concern for what is occurring outside the intimate sphere. Riesman (373) argues that 'men are created different; they lose their social freedom and their individual autonomy in seeking to become like each other'. Contemporary conditions produce 'conformity in the adjusted majority and force great numbers into anomie' (300). Only autonomous individuals, people who have freed themselves of the restrictions that their culture imposes, are courageous, because autonomy comes about 'always as the result of a continual struggle with the forces of the culture which opposes it' (300). Even more importantly, only autonomous individuals can be courageous, because only nonconformists can undertake unpopular actions or can stand up in defence of their values. Contemporary autonomous nonconformists' ways of rebelling and finding their own values are much less clear-cut than they were in the past. Because of contemporary societies' style and sensitivity, courageous actions are becoming more complex than they were in the more regulated societies of the past. Consequently, Riesman (305) asks: 'In what spheres does autonomy exist today, when the older barriers have crumbled and can serve neither as defence nor as observable for a life-long agenda of attack?'

At least a partial answer to this question is provided by Whyte's 1956 study, which echoes Tocqueville's and Weber's concerns that the process of rationalisation and democratisation would 'wipe out diversity and creativeness' (Tocqueville [1835] 1968: xi). According to Whyte, in the world of large corporations and complex bureaucracies, it is the organisation man who illustrates a conformist adjustment. The more democratic atmosphere has, moreover, made the individual's independence more difficult. The organisation man, intimidated by a belief in belonging as the ultimate goal for individuals, thus becomes 'more adept at concealing hostilities and ambitions, more skilfully "normal"' (Whyte 1956: 397). Nevertheless, despite his loyalty to the organisation and suburban community, he knows he is different: he feels isolated and 'a fraud who is not what he seems' (397). As the denial of any conflict between the individual and the group, and a belief in the group as the source of creativity, lead to considerable mutual deception, a lack of autonomy and courage to stand up for one's beliefs is the cost paid for the adjustment.

The same problem is noticed by Marcuse, who suggests that non-conformism and criticism are not valued in a society capable of satisfying the need of its citizens. 'Independence of thought, autonomy, and the right to political opposition are being deprived of their basic critical function' (Marcuse 1966: 1). American democracy, although on the whole providing for a better and safer society, appears to be the 'most efficient system of domination' (52). Seeing comfort and safety as instruments of social control leads Marcuse to question the value of cultural equality and to admire the dying of 'the oppositional, alien, and transcendent elements' of the higher culture (57). Since to 'liberate the imagination ... presupposes the repression of much that is now free' (250), he attempts to inspire an acknowledgement of the real meaning of one-dimensionality – that is, its role in preventing 'genuine self-determination' (42).

Riesman's, Whyte's and Marcuse's works demonstrate that large-scale social trends that shape allegiance to the group and the main institutions are responsible for changes in modes of conformity, and, by the same token, for changes in the nature and status of courage. In order to further our understanding of the significance of courage in public life, we need to enquire into what it is that inspires or motivates courageous actions.

Civil courage as value-rational social action

In Durkheim's perspective, in contrast to Merton's approach, which sees courage as the essential part of normative innovation, there is no explicit discussion of courage. Nonetheless, since social solidarity in modern societies does not mean uniformity and since social harmony is best served by not denying the differences, Durkheim ([1895] 1966: 71–2) is forced to acknowledge that it 'would never have been possible to establish the freedom of thought we now enjoy if the regulations prohibiting it had not been violated before'. Thus, in order to explain moral innovation, Durkheim introduces examples of courageous behaviour. For instance, while discussing the trial of Socrates in *The Rules of Sociological Method*, Durkheim points out that Socrates' courageous behaviour was perceived by Athenian law as 'criminal', even though his crime was 'his independence of thought', which 'served to prepare a new morality and faith which the Athenians needed, since the traditions by which they had lived then were no longer in harmony with the current conditions of life. Nor is the case of Socrates unique; it is reproduced periodically in history' (71–2). The recognition of the innovative significance of courageous behaviour is also evident in Durkheim's ([1915] 1973: 47) calling on intellectuals during the Dreyfus Affair to become publicly involved in this 'interest superior to the interests of individuals'. In such a crisis situation, 'courage is required to rebel against public opinion' (40) and scholars should 'leave their laboratories ... to draw nearer the masses, to involve themselves in life' (59). Finally, Durkheim ([1915] 1973: 34) also approaches the notion of civil courage while talking about the purpose served by 'a great man'. He proclaims 'a great man' to be 'the benefactor of humanity', because such a man, by revolting against injustice, 'defends the rights of the individual and defends at the same time the vital interests of society, for he prevents the criminal impoverishment of that last reserve of collective ideas and feelings which is the very soul of the nation' (53–4).

While Durkheim introduces examples of courage rather incidentally, Weber addresses the notion of civil courage in a more direct way. His writing suggests that the first individuals who stood up in defence of their convictions and/or civic values, even at the risk of paying a high price for this conviction, were people who rebelled or deviated from the religion of their society. Those who first showed civil courage were the prophets of the Old Testament who preached their messages in ancient Palestine. Nonetheless, Weber's contribution to our understanding of civil courage extends beyond the notion of the prophet who courageously defied public demands in order to impose his own message, and even more generally beyond the notion of charismatic authority that is 'of necessity revolutionary' (Shils 1968: 387). Weber's major input is connected both with his general argument that in most, if not all, actual cases the causes of social action are mixed and, more specifically, with his idea of 'value-rational' action. Weber investigates when and under what circumstances ideals become a powerful force in human action, and argues that culture influences action by shaping people's ends and the means they think will achieve them. While interests provide the motivating force or engine of action, ideas frequently determine 'the tracks along which action has been pushed by the dynamic of interest' (Weber [1915] 1946b: 280). It can be said that, whereas individuals are usually motivated by a combination of ideal and material interests, in the case of civil courage ideal interests clearly predominate. Weber's ([1914] 1968: 24–5) 'value-rational' action, one of his four types of action, describes courageous conduct well, since it is defined as the action that is inspired by 'a conscious belief in a value for its own sake' and as the action that it is carried out 'independently of its prospects of success'. Pure value-rational orientation always involves demands that, in the actor's opinion, are binding on him. It is only in cases in which human action is motivated by the fulfilment of such unconditional demands that it is called value-rational. Such an action is always performed in obedience to 'imperatives' or the fulfilment of 'claims' that the agent believes to be imposed on him (Weber [1914] 1968: 25). This type of action is determined by a conscious belief in the value for its own sake, for some ethical, aesthetic, religious or other forms of obligation, and examples include 'the actions of persons who, regardless of possible cost to themselves, act to put into practice their convictions of what seems to them to be required by duty, honor, the pursuit of beauty, a religious call, "personal loyalty", or the importance of some "cause" no matter in what it consists' (25).

Both value-rational social actions and acts of civil courage, like all actions inspired by ideal interests, are infrequent occurrences. Furthermore, 'value-rational' action is a 'limiting case' and a not very coherent type of action, because it refers to the rational achievement of ends that cannot themselves be chosen rationally. The ends of value-rational actions are socially learned and individually constructed; thus, by definition, no action can be wholly value-rational. When people submit to extreme pain and certain death in pursuit of some learned values, such as duty or honour, they act 'regardless of possible cost to themselves' (25). This type of action cannot therefore be defined in terms of efficiency but, rather, in terms of effectiveness, or 'in terms of weighing of consequences of different courses of action' (Turner and Factor 1994: 38). One example of value-rational action is Martin Luther's decision, despite being aware that ultimately he would be punished, to give a truthful account of his teaching, while facing the Emperor Charles V during his second hearing at Worms on 18 April 1521. Luther's famous words, 'Here I stand; I can do no other', are now proverbial in German. Interestingly, Weber ([1918] 1978: 224) quotes Luther's statement to illustrate what he means by the idea of a 'mature' intellectual who 'feels his responsibility for the consequences genuinely and with all his heart acts according to the ethics of responsibility'.

Weber's other concepts, such as the notions of 'conflict', 'convention' and a typology of social relationships, can also be of help in getting a better handle on civil courage as a sociological phenomenon. After including what these notions capture as an important aspect of courage, namely that it is behaviour regardless of the actor's lack of power to reach his or her goal, a Weberian perspective on courage can be summarised as defining civil courage as 'a form of value-rational social action; more precisely, it can be characterised as an action inspired by ideal interests, which is carried out irrespective of its chances of success, and which entails a conflict, typically by challenging a law or a conviction' (Swedberg 1999: 517). Seeing courage as nonconformist and inspired by ideal interest behaviour assumes that such action is a result not only of an individual's strength but also of her or his capacity for reflection on what is right. The requirements of reflection on rights and an orientation towards ideal interests make courage an essential aspect of democratic culture (Schwan 2004: 109). Noticing this affinity between civil society and civil courage, Swedberg (1999: 523) points out that civil courage is closely linked to many dimensions of civil society, such as freedom of expression, the rights of the individual, the right to form associations, and toleration. Although today's discussion of civil society 'never touches on the problem of civil courage and the difficulty of the individual to stand up to a hostile majority', the notion of civil courage 'could contribute to the development of the concept of civil society' (523).

These observations offer useful starting points for thinking about a typology of courageous actions associated with the values of civil society. The insight generated from our discussion so far suggests that, in order to develop such a typology, we should focus our attention on the nature of the interplay between courage and risk and on the nature of the relationship between allegiance to a group and nonconformity. Firstly, we should recall the importance in the explanation of courageous actions of such factors as people's capacity to overcome real difficulties in risky situations. The emphasis on risk, or the 'readiness to act despite perceived risk' (Oliner and Oliner 1988: 127), suggests that in the first

Table 3.1. *Forms of courage*

The perception of the situation	The nature of the system	
	Formalised	Informalised
Uncertainty	Challenging the rules	Challenging authority/ obligations/commitments
Frustration/risk	Breaking the rules	Breaking authority/ obligations/commitments

step towards a sociological approach to the courageous actions of public intellectuals we should discriminate between the levels of risk run by such individuals. Secondly, we should make the type of relationship and allegiance to the group a focal point of analysis. This means as a result that we should concentrate on the nature of social order, as embedded in the informality and formality of interactional practices, because it determines the amount of pressure put on people to conform (see chapter 2) These two axes, the type of situation (as described by the level of risk) and the nature of the relationship between formality and informality (seen as determining the scope of people's freedom to search for solutions to the situation), can serve as the basis for the construction of a matrix of forms of courageous actions. The same two axes have been used to build our table 2.1. Here, however, since we are interested in courageous actions (that is, actions in a situation perceived as risky), our table 3.1 does not include the previous table's first row (which describes the situation of 'ease/comfort') or its middle column (which refers to a balanced relationship between formal and informal relationships). Thus, our new table consists of only four forms of courageous conduct, seen as responses to challenges and problems in situations in which the levels of risk and uncertainty are more than comfortable and in which actions oriented towards change demand courage.

This matrix delineates the four basic types of courageous conduct demanded in different situations. The formal and informal systems of relations differ in terms of the nature of the pressure they put on their members, and therefore also in terms of the tactics and strategies that are mobilised in order to solve the perceived difficulties of the situation effectively. In the informalised system, in which members tend to belong to informal groups with relatively strong boundaries, so that they cannot escape scrutiny from and interaction with other group members, the pressure to conform is resisted by challenging authority and obligations, as well as by questioning the membership of and commitment to the group. In the formalised system, in which control is ensured in a distant, impersonal way through bureaucratic rules, the pressure to conform is resisted by challenging its more abstract rules, codes and roles. Furthermore, not only is the pressure to conform achieved in different ways but it is also associated with different costs. The lower level of risk under which 'challenging the rules' and 'challenging authority/obligations/ commitments' occur means that these forms of conduct require less extreme steps. Both forms of courage under the conditions of a high level of risk ('breaking the rules' and 'breaking authority/obligations/ commitments') demand more radical conduct. At the same time, the forms of courage in the same column, although characterised by different levels of risk, refer to a nonconformist stand under systems with a similar type of capacity to exert conformist pressure – or, in other words, with similar types of relations and rules, whether formal or informal.

The next chapter, in order to develop a general typology of intellectuals' public involvement, brings together various sociological approaches to creativity and civil courage, understood as being disinterested, motivated by the ideals of civil society, nonconformist and involving coping with difficulties and risky behaviour.

4   Typology of engagements

Intellectual marginality and creativity

The central aim of this chapter is to bring together the various sociological approaches to creativity and courage, and to propose a general typology of intellectuals' public involvement that, I hope, can advance our understanding of intellectuals' public practice. As we have already observed, the accounts of the social history of intellectuals in European and American political life often paint a contradictory picture. In some of them loneliness and marginalisation are seen as the prerequisites of creativity, while estrangement and alienation are presented as essential preconditions for intellectuals' progressive radicalism, and therefore trust in their courage. In other descriptions of intellectual life, however, intellectuals are shown as well-integrated members of vibrant communities, in which collaboration and gift-like exchanges flourish. My aim is to examine sociological approaches to intellectual creativity and intellectuals' stance vis-à-vis the public so as to suggest much-needed alternatives to both: to the stereotype of the creator as a marginalised genius and to the presentation of intellectuals as engaged radicals.

The image of the intellectual as a detached, estranged outsider owes much to the Romantic concept of creativity as being located in the atelier of the artist and as being an expression of artists' inner feelings. This model, further enhanced by Benda's powerful and even more idealistic formulation of the Romantic view of creativity, has established the myth of the importance of loneliness, solitude and alienation from the mundane problems and concerns of society as sources of universal truth and the creative power of intellectuals. The illusion of the marginalised intellectual, which claims that intellectuals' isolation is the necessary precondition of knowledge and impartiality, also owes much to Georg Simmel's concept of the stranger and Mannheim's association of intellectuals' unattachment with their interest in 'the whole', or their tendency, 'even though it is unconscious, towards a dynamic synthesis' (Mannheim 1949: 160).

In his classical sociological conceptualisation of the stranger, Georg Simmel (1950: 407) stresses that the stranger's ability to attain objectivity is a result of the more abstract nature of the relationship between her/him and the group, which is determined by the relative proportions of nearness and remoteness. Following Simmel's perspective, many scholars seem to view intellectuals, implicitly or explicitly, as strangers of a specific type, or as 'displaced persons' (Pels 1999: 67) who are capable of attaining objectivity. The association between knowledge, objectivity and home-lessness is elaborated in Mannheim's (1949: 154) notion of the relatively detached intellectual who is able to develop an outlook that is sensitive to 'the dynamic nature of society and its wholeness'. According to Man-nheim (1949: 157), the unanchored social position provides intellectuals with such a sensibility and understanding that 'the tendency towards a dynamic synthesis constantly reappears'. These 'free-floating' intellec-tuals, liberated from the compulsion of narrow commitments, are the 'bearers of syntheses', or the sole representatives of the 'total perspective', corresponding to 'their interest in the whole' (143–4).

Mannheim's view of the intellectual overestimates the diversity of social backgrounds among intellectuals, while at the same time over-stating their ability, despite their heterogeneous commitments, to attain universal truth. Even more problematic is Mannheim's equating of 'relative detachment from the economic interest of capitalists and pro-letarians with freedom from all forms of interested thought and conduct' (Ringer 1969: 292). In contrast to Mannheim's claim that intellectuals' 'uprootedness' is the guarantee of their impartiality, empirical studies demonstrate that intellectuals' free-floating status can provide 'fertile ground for radical antagonism to the existing order' – radicalism of either a leftist or a right-wing orientation (Karabel 1996: 212). In addition, the rhetoric of 'marginality and independence is quite capable of accompanying conformity' (Osborne 1996: xvi), as free-floating intellectuals' competence can be 'on loan and for sale to anyone' (Said 1994: 47). Finally, homelessness exposes intellectuals to failure and social instability, as Mannheim (1949: 159) noted himself. Thus, maybe Mannheim's thesis should be seen either as a utopian dream of intel-lectuals' objectivity, their freedom of ideological entanglement and therefore their ability to attain universal truth, or as 'a bid for power made on behalf of the knowledge class' (Bauman 1995: 232).

In spite of all critical evaluations of the thesis, the myth of the 'free-floating' intellectual has become the professional ideology of intellec-tuals (Bourdieu 1993: 43). This illusion is continually being reinforced; its latest re-formulation can be found in Said's (1994: 44) idea of 'the exilic intellectual', which stresses that being in exile carries with it some rewards and the possibility of developing a wider, more complex, less conventional understanding and 'even more universal idea of how to think'. His discussion of the conditions and significance of exile follows Theodor Adorno's ([1946] 1984) endorsement of the role of exile in enhancing the intellectual's creative and critical capacities. Said (1994: 47; emphasis in original) sees himself as 'the *exilic* intellectual who does not respond to the logic of the conventional but to the audacity of daring, and to representing change, to moving on, not standing still'. Exile, understood as a metaphorical condition, is one of the circumstances that enhances the intellectual's feeling of displacement and is therefore likely to be a source not of adjustment but of restlessness and criticism. Said's romantic presentation of the intellectual as a lonely creator who is also an engaged fighter in the name of solidarity with the oppressed, as we have already noted in chapter 1, does not address the tensions between lonely individuality and solidarity (Collini 2006: 428). Moreover, Posner (2001) and Fuller (2005) question Said's self-presentation as a marginal intellectual by pointing out that Said was well linked to various professional circles and social movements and that he enjoyed a high level of international recognition and status.

Very similar doubts about the role of marginality are articulated by Jacoby, who in his relatively recent book *The End of Utopia: Politics and Culture in an Age of Apathy* (1999) expresses his contempt for contemporary intellectuals' celebration of their marginality, which he sees as more 'a pose' of 'the self-defined outsiders' who 'are glad to be consummate insiders' (Jacoby 1999: 123). Posner (2001: 60) also suggests that, with the cost of exit from the public-intellectual market being very low for an academic, the modern public intellectual may be 'marginal' after all, 'but not in the dangerous sense in which Socrates found himself marginalised'. The role of marginality as the condition of intellectual production is also rejected by Bourdieu (1993: 43), who, contrary to Mannheim's vision of the detached intellectual, suggests that intellectuals 'are a (dominated) fraction of the dominant class'. Instead of the marginality, Bourdieu stresses the ambiguity of intellectuals' dominated/ dominating status, which explains a number of the stances that intellectuals adopt in politics.

The idea of the importance of marginality as the prerequisite of creativity is more directly criticised by the studies that stress the positive role of commitment and networks in the production of knowledge. These approaches do not focus on the relationship between marginality and proximity as the potential source of impartiality but, rather, emphasise dynamics and commonalities in the formation and development of scientific communities. For example, the notion of marginality is totally rejected by functionalist theory, organisation analysis and Mertonian scholars in the sociology of science, knowledge and culture; they have all made a strong case for seeing intellectual production and creativity as being linked positively to the resources and networks of established organisations, mainstream cultures and societal elites (Merton 1973; Cole and Cole 1973; Crane 1972). The concept that these perspectives have of the 'scientific community', seen as a group the members of which are united by a common objective culture (Hagstrom 1965), has established the tradition of empirical research on scholarly communities that assumes that core networks are essential for the development of intellectual creativity, argues that scientific research typically occurs in social networks of colleagues and analyses creativity in its own right (Collins 1974; Crane 1972; Goldgar 1995; de Solla Price 1963; Latour and Woolgar 1986). Such a sociological approach, in contrast to a more individualistic stand, which suggests that the notion of creativity is a matter of psychology, asserts that creativity is a collective phenomenon collaboratively created by individuals and that, as such, it is not reducible to explanations in terms of the individual. Describing exchanges that take place in the scientific field on the model of gift exchange, studies of this type stress the benefits of network centrality in the production of knowledge and propose that the density of networks of exchange is responsible for their participants' ability to cooperate for mutual benefit, because the norm of reciprocity that is built into these relations typically makes 'every participant better off' (Taylor 1982: 29).

More recently the importance of marginality in the constitution of the intellectual has been implicitly questioned by several studies, which exemplify how the collegial sociability of researchers involved in the informal exchange of information secures the distribution of rewards and prestige and facilitates innovations and new ideas. This type of investigation asserts that informal networks among scholars, in both the past and the present, attest to the importance of sociability in constructing the creative community. Historical and sociological reviews of the role of sociability in expanding the intellectual collaboration and creativity, such as Anne Goldgar's (1995) studies of the functioning of the Republic of Letters, Harry M. Collins' (1998) interaction ritual chains theory and Michael P. Farrell's (2001) notion of collaborative circles, directly address the issue of the relationship between marginality and intellectual creativity.

The Republic of Letters, which functioned from the fifteenth century, provides an exemplary illustration of the collegial sociability of researchers involved in scholarly exchange. It existed 'only in the minds of its members', it had 'no formal manifestation' and its rules were unwritten, while its 'regulation and even its membership were nebulous at best' (Goldgar 1995: 2). This informal community of scholars was based on informal interactions, which branched 'into an extensive network of connections available to provide information and help of all kinds' and which constructed the foundation for 'the invisible institutions of the Republic of Letters' (26). The Republic of Letters' social structure, which was based fundamentally on personal contacts, with sociability being a social technique to draw scholars closer together for self-protection and social cohesion, greatly enhanced its members' creative productivity.

Collins also (1998; 2004) follows the tradition of empirical research on scholarly communities that assumes that core networks are essential for the development of intellectual creativity, and argues that scientific research typically occurs in social networks of colleagues, analysing creativity in its own right. In his book *The Sociology of Philosophies* (1998) Collins aims at finding the explanation for global intellectual change, but, unlike Merton's (1973) analysis of simultaneous scientific discoveries, he stresses conflict. Collins' (2004: 4) interpretation of 'Durkheim through the eyes of Erving Goffman' allows him to introduce the notions of interaction ritual and emotional energy to argue that intellectual creativity is concentrated in chains of personal contacts and that the greatest concentration of creative emotional energy is to be found in face-to-face relationships at the centre of networks. He criticises most popular views on the nature of intellectual creativity (that ideas create ideas, individuals create ideas, culture creates ideas) and argues that it is the intellectual community that is paramount in producing ideas. Collins interprets rises and falls of ideas as the outcome of competition between rival intellectual networks, which can be based on either real relationships or imagined, symbolic ones. The networks pattern suggests that 'eminence breeds eminence' and that all creative individuals have relatively high degrees of emotional energy concentrated in their work (Collins 2004: 192).

Collins (1998: 31) asserts that creativity implies 'new ideas', but that these ideas cannot be 'too new', as, in order to be important and successful, they need to be recognisable, which means that they need to stand 'in relation to the ongoing conversation of the intellectual community'. The crucial features of creativity are the identification of unsolved problems and convincing others of the importance of solving them. Intellectual dynamics obeys the 'law of small numbers', in that at any period of history there are at least two, but usually no more than six, schools of thought in mutual contention, the numbers being dictated by the logic of what drives intellectual developments. If there are fewer than two schools this situation yields no conflict, whereas if there are more than six the result is an unstable squabble that soon resolves itself, via synthesis, into a more manageable number of contestants. Ideas are shaped not only by the combination and further development of ideas and techniques from prior networks but also 'by oppositions, formulating a stance in controversies that attract the most attention' (2004: 195).

What drives intellectual history in this view is conflicts within networks, as creative thinking is a process of making collations in the mind, positively as well as negatively. Creativity occurs in a situation of rivalry. 'Rival intellectual chains depend tacitly upon each other, and structure each other's direction of thought' (2004: 194). Collins' (1998: 875) theory of intellectual production maintains that 'conflict for attention space' is a fundamental fact about intellectuals, a fact entailed by the structure of the intellectual world, which allows only a limited number of positions to receive much attention at any one time. Faced with this situation, intellectuals necessarily 'thrive on disagreement, dividing the attention space into three to six factions, seeking lines of creativity by negating the chief tenets of their rivals, rearranging into alliances or fanning out into disagreement' (876). Intellectuals owe their success to their position in the networks of other intellectuals, as it is 'intellectuals' experience in the network of intellectuals that constitutes them as intellectuals and shapes the content of their thinking' (2004: 358). Collins (1998: 52) asserts that high degrees of intellectual creativity 'come from realistically invoking existing or prospective intellectual audiences, offering what the marketplace for ideas will find most in demand'. Although he recognises that creativity, as the property of intellectual networks, is shaped by the material bases of intellectual production (patronages, educational organisations, etc.), as changes in these material conditions destroy some networks' lineages and open opportunities for others, he does not pay much attention to the impact of the macrostructural conditions on individuals' or groups' identities, nor to their impact on the level and forms of creativity. Consequently, his theory does not provide explicit indications of the role of individual creativity and does not offer a clear vision of the relationship between individual and collective creative action.

The issue of the relationship between marginality and intellectual creativity has also been recently discussed in Farrell's *Collaborative Circles: Friendship Dynamics and Creative Work* (2001). Farrell (16–18) rejects conventional theories of creativity, which propose that creativity requires isolation and individuation, and argues that the creative person, embedded in a relationship 'with a selfobject, feels more cohesive and centered, more free to explore untried or even objectionable ideas'. By combining the findings of biographies, intellectual history and social science theory, Farrell presents case studies of five collaborative circles – that is, primary groups 'consisting of peers who share similar occupational goals and who, through long periods of dialogues and collaboration, negotiate a common vision that guides theory work' (11). Emphasising the commonalities in the formation and development of circles, Farrell asserts that collaborative circles that develop innovative visions are formed in a place that acts as a magnet, 'where the high-status masters are gathered, but within the valleys on the periphery of that network' (267) and flourish in turbulent cultural environments, 'where two or more visions of a discipline vie for centrality in a single place' (271). Successful collaborative circles usually form radical networks, in which members, as they are cut off from powerful mentors in their particular field, tend to synthesise elements of the old perspectives and to conceive an alternative vision of their own. Such a vision consists of 'a shared set of assumptions about their discipline, including what constitutes good work, how to work, what subjects are worth working on, and how to think about them' (11).

In the light of the evidence from Goldgar's, Collins' and Farrell's studies, the view of intellectual creativity that stresses loneliness and marginality, uprootedness and exile as the conditions of universal truth and creative power can be classified as a myth that does not really confront the reality of intellectual production. The reliance on an identity built around marginality not only represents a real impoverishment of intellectual creativity but can also aggravate the irrelevance of intellectual work for the general public. Thus, questioning the significance of the marginalisation thesis brings to our attention the issue of the intellectual's position within networks in the production of knowledge and the issue of the centrality of links between public intellectuals and audiences. Since in order to serve the well-being of society the intellectual needs a public, the relationship between intellectuals and their audiences, developed from a position of acknowledged achievement, should be the main focus of any study of intellectuals' public practice.

Intellectuals' links with their public these days are often presented as being accidental, redundant and not really meaningful (Bauman 1995). All the same, in contrast to a common assumption that intellectuals' public 'barely extends beyond the campus walls' (Robert S. Boynton, quoted in Collini 2006: 242), some intellectuals are successful in combining an academic standing with a genuine following among a non-academic audience. The most prominent among them are black writers and academics, such as Cornell West (1996: 134), who successfully speak 'for' as well as 'to' their audiences. In this role, the intellectual as 'critical organic catalyst' shares some identity and interest with a group on whose behalf he or she acts. For West (1996: 135), the issue of the intellectual has to do with 'the relation between those who have a deep commitment to the life of the mind and its impact on public life, of all sorts'. He sees himself as 'caught between an insolent American society and insouciant black community; the African-American who takes seriously the life of the mind inhabits an isolated and insulted world' (1999: 302). Here, the marginality is seen not as the issue of the intellectual's isolation/estrangement but, rather, as the problem of the nature of her or his ties with the audience. Thus, in contrast to Bauman's (1992a: 90) claim that today the intellectual, like everybody else, is the stranger who 'is universal because of having no home and no roots' and that this rootlessness 'revitalizes everything concrete and thus begets universality', West (1993) thinks that the intellectual is faced with the task of revitalising the old, or searching for new, publics.

In summary, in order to occupy the role of public intellectual successfully, writers, academics, artists and journalists need to reach a position of acknowledged achievement (made possible due to the intellectual's central position within networks in the production of knowledge) and need to establish links with publics that can legitimise their authority. Any further discussion of intellectuals' relations with non-specialist publics requires a clarification of what it takes to establish bonds with a general audience.

Intellectual engagement and courage

Just as popular as the idea of the intellectual being marginal and 'detached' from society are two other beliefs: the first, that being an intellectual means being deeply engaged in the issues of the day, and the second, that being an intellectual means adopting an oppositional stance towards power or the existing order. In other words, it is assumed that intellectuals are progressive radical thinkers who are engaged in politics. The first issue, the dilemma of detachment versus engagement, or whether intellectuals should put their knowledge and creative dispositions to social or political use, is widely discussed, with some voices suggesting that intellectuals ought to avoid engagement at all costs, while others encourage intellectuals to immerse themselves almost to the point of drowning.

For instance, Gramsci (1971: 9) argues that 'the intellectual could not but be political', thus conceptualising intellectuals as essentially political entities, and so dismissing the possibility of intellectual autonomy as utopian. In addition, Sartre (1974: 230), an influential supporter of full immersion, suggests that an atomic scientist is not an intellectual when working on the atomic bomb but becomes one when signing a letter of protest against nuclear arms. He argues that to be an intellectual is to be something other than a technician, an expert or even a scientist, as true intellectuals do not protest against the use of the bomb 'on the grounds of any technical defects it may have, but in the name of highly controversial systems of values that see human life as the supreme standard' (230–1). Yet Sartre did not recognise that his 'scientist-intellectual might just as easily be the pro-bomb Edward Teller as the anti-bomb Robert Oppenheimer' (Goldfarb 1998: 32). Even more importantly, such a definition also overlooks the possibility that a courageous and civic-minded scientist-intellectual can also move from being a Teller to being an Oppenheimer (see chapter 7 for a description of Sakharov's career, which illustrates his journey from involvement in and support for the nuclear programme to protesting against it).

In contrast to Gramsci or Sartre, other writers criticise committed intellectuals for being blinded by passion and guilty of treason or betrayal. Famously, Benda ([1927] 1980) demanded from intellectuals an anti-political, anti-ideological position and a search for joy only in the practice of an art or a science. Jürgen Habermas (1997) insists that the intellectual must not seek power but should offer instead to assist the public in making up its mind, particularly by undermining its immediate sense of what it ought to believe and do. Foucault (1977), who holds that the role of the intellectual is not to shape others' political will, advocates against engaging in political activities in the capacity of the intellectual, as it would means telling the masses what to think. Yet other commentators, notably Sartre's long-time friend and rival Aron (1957), suggest that the proper attitude for intellectuals is one of scepticism and moderation. Finally, some hold that disengagement would appear to be the fate of intellectuals because the development of science will, in some unforeseeable future, solve political problems in an objective way, or, more generally, that long-term processes will force intellectuals out of the political sphere (Eyerman 1994). Additionally, the issue of intellectuals' political commitment never arises in the same way in all countries. For example, German apolitical intellectuals discovered, with the outbreak of war in 1914 and then with Hitler's coming to power in 1933, that the principled 'unpolitical position' can carry great political meaning – in other words, that the issue was not the engagement of intellectuals but, rather, their political disengagement (Lassman 2000; Lilla 2001).

It seems that the core of the issue is neither engagement with, nor disengagement from, public matters, since, as Lewis Coser (1965: 360) has pointed out, detachment may at one and the same time be based on criticism of as well as 'a deeply felt commitment to the ideals and central values on which the society rests'. Walzer (2002: 140) goes even further and argues that detachment is the result of criticism, not the pre-condition of criticism. Lilla (2001: 207), who tends to scrutinise with suspicion the motivation of thinkers who engaged in politics, argues that both commitment and disengagement 'fail to take us to the heart of the matter'. What is really important is public intellectuals' contribution to societal well-being and their concern with matters of human significance. If what counts is their ability to fulfil these tasks, what is often required is the courage to defend their convictions and the courage to assume rather than to decline their civic responsibilities.

The second belief – that is, the assumption that intellectuals can be identified by their oppositional stance towards the status quo – still seems to be very popular. Today, as in the last century, when on the whole the typical intellectual was quite likely to assume that simply being dissident qualifies writers and academics as intellectuals (Nettl 1969), 'intellectuals like to think about themselves as liberators and progressive thinkers' (Bourdieu 1992: 18). The continuity of the image of the intellectual as having an 'anti-capitalist bias' (von Mises 1960: 368), being condemned for her/his 'hostility to capitalism' (Schumpeter 1947: 145–55) and thinking about her-/himself 'as the natural ally to the worker' (de Jouvenel 1960: 391) is sustained by many factors. Firstly, the myth of the intellectual as a progressive radical is supported by studies of public intellectuals that take a normative form and therefore reinforce the image of the intellectual as 'speaking the truth to power'. The persistence of this widespread image of the left-wing radical intellectual can also be attributed to the tradition inspired by Marxism and the centrality of Mannheim's theory. Another approach that helps to sustain the myth of intellectuals as progressive radicals is the elitist theory, which associates intellectual radicalism with the existence of an oversupply of intellectuals, who, as an 'intellectual proletariat', become the 'yeast of revolution' (Michels 1932: 122–3). According to yet another view, the radicalism of intellectuals can be explained by their fascination with utopian projects (Hayek 1960; Fuller 2005).

All the above approaches overstate the homogeneity of intellectuals' political affiliations as well as the social uniformity of intellectuals' social position, while underplaying the importance of contexts and personal choices. An appreciation of the variety of intellectuals' positions and the plurality of national circumstances can be found in more historically informed reflections on the characterisation of intellectuals. Such historical analyses of changes and continuities in the intellectual role demonstrate that, although it is true that intellectuals have often taken sides with the dominated, they have done so much less often than they could have done, and 'especially much less often than they believe' (Bourdieu 1992: 18). Since the nineteenth century there have been many examples in which intellectuals' engagement has involved a 'potential transformation into apologists' (Lipset 1963: 334), and many examples of intellectuals who served authoritarian regimes and used their knowledge in 'service of anti-intellectual values' (Lipset 1963: 333; Aron 1957; Deak 1968; Lasswell and Lerner 1965). There are also examples of anti-democratic gestures by intellectuals in democratic societies. For instance, the German 'mandarins, who helped to' destroy the Weimar Republic, not only 'abandoned intellectual responsibility' but 'wilfully cultivated an atmosphere in which any "national" movement could claim to be the "spiritual revival"' (Ringer 1969: 446). Among new sociological investigations that attempt to test the significance of the special appeal of leftist ideologies to intellectuals and that try to address a wider range of causes of the intellectual radicalism, we should mention Brym's (1980; 1988) search for explanation why intellectuals join leftist politics, Kurzman and Erin Leahey's (2004) review of intellectuals' associations with the processes of democratisation and Jerome Karabel's (1996) attempt to discover factors responsible for intellectuals' revolutionary stance.

According to Brym's (1980) structural theory of intellectual political affiliations, the social location and social identity of an intellectual depend on the relative power of her or his society's major classes and groups at any given point in time. His search for the mechanism that generates radicalism starts with questioning theories ascribing intellectuals' radicalism to their poor integration into the middle classes. Relying on historical evidence, Brym (1980; 1988) argues that intellectuals, in contrast to Mannheim's view, are not without ties; that they can be attached to different groups, with different degrees of power, and, therefore, only by analysing their shifting social ties can we see their political role. 'The character of intellectual politics cannot be adequately explained if we analyse intellectuals in isolation from their social context, groups, associations and communities' (1980: 72). Thus, the ideological diversity of intellectuals is seen as a consequence not of their relative classlessness or rootlessness but, rather, as a result of their complex networks of attachment (58). Seeing intellectuals as not hanging suspended between classes but instead tied, sometimes strongly, sometimes less strongly, to different strata, Brym (1988) argues that, when the ties binding intellectuals to workers were strong, intellectuals were relatively democratic in their thinking, while a lack of ties resulted in a more elitist ideology. This implies that the character of intellectual politics can be adequately explained only if we analyse the external networks that embedded intellectuals within the class system and the power of those groups to which they may become attached. Thus, it is intellectuals' embeddednees in social networks and their shifting ties to changing social groups, not their mal-integration, that has a major impact on their choice of political voice.

The link early in the last century between intellectuals and progressive politics is also a subject of Kurzman and Leahey's (2004) study, which analyses in detail the involvement of intellectuals in two waves of democratisation (1905–12 and 1989–96). While testing the pro-democracy stands of intellectuals, the authors, in contrast to Tocqueville, Bauman and Goldfarb, suggest that the relationship between democracy and the intellectual is time-specific. Their study shows that, prior to World War I, the intellectual identity was closely associated with one form of political activism: democratisation movements (938–9). At the beginning of the last century, when intellectuals' affiliation with democratic movements was a matter of pride and when such movements were relatively visible and well organised, intellectuals saw themselves as having an important role to play in the social and political life of democracy. In the inter-war period, however, when intellectuals were dispirited and disorganised, they turned more to anti-democratic movements (944). Kurzman and Leahey (973) find that intellectuals did play an important role in launching or facilitating democracy in the waves of democratisation of the last century, and that intellectuals 'provided hegemonic leadership and organizational infrastructure for the democracy movements of the early 20th century, while not in subsequent decades'. Nonetheless, their findings refer to the emergence of democracy, not to its preservation, and go no further than suggesting that, while there is 'elective affinity' between the overall size of the intellectual class and the likelihood of democratisation, this affinity may reveal itself only in very particular social and political circumstances. Thus, this affinity is time-specific, as the social basis of democratisation changes over time. Finally, according to this study, intellectuals were the prime beneficiaries of the successful democracy movements in the decade before World War I, but they were harmed by the subsequent failure of these new democracies (959, 974).

The recent disappointments of eastern European intellectuals with other new democracies offer a new twist to Kurzman and Leahey's argument that intellectuals are rewarded by the emergence of new democracies. The collapse of communism offered politically active intellectuals a wide range of opportunities, including the possibility of playing major roles in the processes of change, as writers of programmes, leaders of movements and parties and opinion-makers (Bozoki 1999; Kempny 1999). As this exceptional historical moment passed, however, the majority of intellectuals felt as if they were 'losers among the winners' (Bernik 1999: 113) and 'retired from the stage' (Kempny 1999: 151). These developments in the post-communist countries have further complicated the picture of the relationship between intellectuals and democracy, by suggesting that intellectuals 'are attracted to democracy as a concept, but their ardour tends to pall when it becomes a working political system' (Korosenyi 1999: 227).

In yet another attempt to clarify the nature of the intellectual's political affiliation, Karabel (1996) explains why intellectuals reach accommodations with the status quo and what it is that causes some of them, at certain historical moments, to rebel. According to him, intellectuals are influenced more by the social positions they occupy and the interests they strive to defend than by any ethical mission or responsibility that they may claim to have. Karabel identifies eight circumstances under which intellectuals are most likely to adopt a revolutionary, or at least an oppositional, stance towards the status quo. They include factors describing national differences in terms of their culture, political and social structure, social organisation, divisions and the strength of the main classes. Karabel's attempt to describe the conditions that make intellectuals more likely either to align with the status quo or to take up an oppositional stand captures the complexity of the differing national conditions. Hence, it can be argued that describing intellectuals' political affiliations demands a historical approach that aims to identify the conditions and processes shaping the actual political consciousness and actions of different groups of intellectuals.

All these findings of the studies under discussion can be generalised by pointing out that they stress that the best indicator of intellectuals' engagement – or, in other words, their move from the *via contemplativa* to the *via activa* – is the level of overall autonomy of the intellectual field. It is Bourdieu (1988) who suggests that it is the independence of the intellectual field from political and other interests that ensures that the intellectual's voice is heard. The autonomous field – that is, the field characterised by a low level of openness to outside influences and a high level of collective capital of accumulated resources – 'chooses' its own strategies, norms and controls on entry and 'obeys' its own logic of functioning (2004: 47). Nevertheless, while the level of autonomy of the field predicts the strength of the collective voice of intellectuals, the nature of an individual intellectual's political stance is not necessary explained by assuming that his or her endowment of capital describes his or her position in the field. For instance, not all small capital holders 'are necessarily revolutionaries' and not all big capital holders 'are auto-matically conservatives' (1992: 8). What accounts for differences in stances are differences in dispositions, which are linked, through social trajectory, to the values associated with the group of origin. These reactions to events are 'socially generated on the basis of situational properties, not as these properties are in fact given, but as they are perceived through the dispositions associated with a definite position and trajectory in the academic and social space' (1992: 11). According to Bourdieu (1992: 11), this explains why 'academics who occupy similar potions synchronically may take up quite different lines of political conduct'. Accounting for this paradox of his own life, Bourdieu (2004: 109) describes himself as an intellectual with a 'cleft habitus', and claims that his own experience confirms 'the social law that [one's origins and] social position play a decisive' part in one's intellectual practice. Hence, intellectuals tend to act either for the preservation or for the redistribution of capital, depending on their particular life and career trajectory.

To sum up, in order to construct a taxonomy of intellectuals' public engagement, we need to examine their life and career trajectories as well as the broader socio-political context.

Recurrent patterns of activity

The study of public intellectual authority, or the reputation for being likely to have important contributions to make to a society and for having the capacities and courage to do so, needs to be 'the study of the making of careers' (Collini 2006: 56). Thus, in the first step towards the construction of a taxonomy of public intellectuals' courageous actions, we need to identify recurrent patterns in their activity. Such a study of recurrent patterns of intellectuals' courageous activity, or types of intellectual engagement, assumes – following Bourdieu's (1992) sug-gestion – that in order to account for differences in the nature of intellectuals' public involvement we need to present an individual intellectual's social trajectory. In what follows we look at Philip Abrams' and Swedberg's approaches, as each of two perspectives treats the individual's stances and actions historically as the product of under-standing processes of becoming rather than states of being.

According to Abrams (1982), in order to develop our understand-ing of courageous action we should take notice of the sociology of delinquency, which can enhance our comprehension of heroes. Abrams, after bringing to our attention studies that view the deviant career as a process of becoming, seen as being embedded in particular conjunctions of life history and social history, develops his historical sociology of the moral career of an exceptional individual. While his explanations for becoming divergent are centred on the idea of temporally organised sequences, explanations of the processes that underlie becoming a hero focus, in a similar way, on the social organisation of a moral career. Such an approach allows us to articulate the conjunctions of life history and social history, a two-dimensional time frame, and to demonstrate contingencies in this type of career. In this way, becoming a revolutionary hero, for example, should be seen as a result of 'the process organised in terms of sequences of characteristics but not pre-determined interaction, probable but not prescribed episodes of action and response in which an individual moves or is moved from one status to another' (Abrams 1982: 272). Each heroic career is the dynamic realisation of a distinctive sequence of probabilities, produced through sequences of action, reaction and action in the setting of historically specific possibilities and opportunities and constraints. According to Abrams' (297) historical sociology of the moral career of an exceptional individual, the uniqueness of a hero is 'not a matter of some elusively private personal factors but of the diversity of movement available to historically located individuals within historically located social worlds'. Thus, the analysis of moral careers directs attention to the individuals' biographies, which reveal the chronology of interaction and the conditions that enable those who embark on them to succeed or cause them to fail.

Swedberg, like Abrams, who sees life histories of 'heroes and monsters' as being created by them and others through sequences of action, reaction and action in a historically specific setting and views individual moral careers as also being typical of collectivities, argues that there is a certain order to episodes of courage. Courageous people are those autonomous individuals who have freed themselves of the restrictions that their culture imposes and are capable either of creating entirely new alternatives or defending past values or of standing up to deviation from the current values. Swedberg (1999) analyses these stages of individual courage and shows that acts of civil courage are always embedded in a social context and involve going through various stages. The classification of the stages in episodes of courage, together with an account of the moral careers of rebels, suggest that, though people rebel and initiate innovations differently, there are not that many different ways of doing such things differently. At the same time, although people may find themselves in very different social situations, there are not that many different kinds of social situation to find oneself in.

The life and career trajectory can be fully comprehended only if it is situated within a broader historical and cultural context in which the role of the intellectual, as personal identity and social practice, takes shape. Even the autonomous intellectual field is influenced by the concerns and conflicts of the wider society. 'Logic itself is the social norm and it is exerted through the constraints (especially censorship) socially instituted in a given field' (Bourdieu 2004: 70). Following Eyerman's (1994) criticism of Bourdieu's idea of the field, we can adopt a more historical and dynamic study of the conditions of intellectual production, which sees the role of public intellectual as being constructed out of particular traditions and bounded by the rules and norms of specific contexts. The context of the formation of the intellectual consists of the historically formed institutions, including the established and emergent structures and the political, social and cultural movements that provide the framework of intellectuals' actions (Eyerman 1994: 94). Historical studies, such as Frank Jellinek's ([1937] 1965) exploration of the involvement of intellectuals in the Paris Commune of 1871, or Fritz Ringer's (1969) study of the German intelligentsia in 1890–1933, all illustrate the role of national contexts in shaping intellectuals' public and political positions. Investigations of Russian or eastern European radical intelligentsias, such as Berlin's (1979) description of the birth of the Russian intelligentsia, conceptualised them as 'the product of the cultural crisis which results from major structural transformations of a national society ... Under such crisis conditions, an intellectual's stratum may become a self-conscious, committed and coherent intelligentsia' (Turner 1994: 155).

More recent studies of the importance of historical contexts (Stapleton 2000; Lassman 2000) also show that intellectuals are rooted in cultural settings with distinctive national traditions, which, when they include well-established cultural repertoires of identity and action against authorities, could become breeding grounds for oppositional stances. The similar claim that a national framework constitutes the context for intellectuals, as each country 'offers markedly different paradigms of the relationship of the state to the nation and of the place of public culture' (Jennings 2000a: 785), has recently been elaborated by contributors to a special issue of *The European Legacy* (2000). All the articles in this issue testify that intellectuals until the second half of the twentieth century, while claiming to be the consciousness of nations, were, in turn, shaped by the national identities they helped to forge and were grounding their arguments in a widely shared conception of national identity (Jennings 2000a). The plurality of ways in which intellectuals have been interacting with their national publics, and the fact that the social practice of the role of public intellectual differs from society to society, further testify to the role of a specific cultural tradition and national context. So, despite the fact that the processes of European integration, multiculturalism and globalisation redefine national identities and therefore also the role of intellectuals, the conditions for an intellectual's entrance into the public domain still reflect the uniqueness of national traditions and the differing nature of nations' political systems.

A useful starting point for thinking about a typology of intellectuals' engagement is to focus on the specific aspect of a national context – that is, on a national civic context. Concentrating on the civic context is essential, firstly because of the affinity between civil society and civil courage (as discussed in chapter 3) and secondly because the civic context, since it determines the intellectual's access to an audience and links with networks in the production and acceptability of discoveries or inventions, affects the intellectual's contribution to the well-being of society. As the public intellectual must, by definition, 'build out from a relatively secure basis in one specialised activity and simultaneously cultivate the necessarily more contestable perspective of a non-specialist' (Collini 2006: 57), access to the networks, media or channels of expression through which the intellectual reaches her or his public is a necessary condition for the performance of the role. Since different types of civic context provide intellectuals with different opportunities to address non-specialised audiences on matters of general concern, in the construction of a typology we need to consider the socio-political characteristics of the different backgrounds in which intellectuals' interventions take place.

Generalising, we can say that, as structures of authorisation and justification evaluate what is acceptable and valuable, and what is to be suppressed and not allowed, public courageous actions are much tied up with the notion of civil liberty and the freedom of the individual. Civic contexts in non-democratic societies are characterised by low levels of accessibility for the channels, networks and media of communication as well as by a relatively high level of risk associated with entering the public domain. It means that, in such environments, successful fulfilment of the role of public intellectual comes with higher costs and risk. In contrast, in democratic societies, which offer a relatively high level of intellectual independence and relatively free access to various channels, networks, media and audiences, public intellectuals do not face such limitations on their access to a wider audience. In undemocratic societies, where the sphere of intellectual autonomy is limited, intellectuals in order to spread their message need to defy the formal networks and channels of communication and rely on informal networks and alternative channels. In other words, in the context of a formalised and high-risk system, in order to address non-specialised audiences on

Table 4.1. *Types of public intellectual engagement*

The perception of the situation	The nature of the system	
	Formalised	Informalised
Uncertainty	Charismatic inspiration	Rationalisation
	Challenging the rules	Challenging authority/
	Reliance on informal networks	obligations/commitments
	HEROES	Reaching beyond informal networks
		CHAMPIONS
Frustration/risk	Taming anxiety	Taming chance
	Breaking the rules	Breaking authority/
	Defiance of formal networks	obligations/commitments
	DISSIDENTS	Reliance on formal networks
		PIONEERS

matters of general concern, intellectuals have to reach beyond formal networks.

The importance of networks, broadly understood, is also connected with the fact that their nature and configuration explain the mechanisms and dynamics that enhance a specific practice. How the network is configured – how it influences the strength and centrality of individuals' involvement – facilitates or inhibits their pursuit of alternative and autonomous lines of interest. Moreover, social networks are not just instrumental ties enabling or constraining involvement, they are also 'networks of meaning' (White 1992: 67), which define and redefine identities through individuals' interactions with other actors and groups and the consequent shaping of their perceptions or preferences (Passy 2003). Such an approach allows us to identify intellectuals as members of an emergent 'category-in-a-network', and therefore to relate distinctive kinds of courageous conduct by intellectuals to their positions in differently structured networks and to different capacities for network building. By combining all the recurring features of the previous tables with our discussion of the significance of the civic context for shaping the availability and autonomy of networks and audiences, we arrive at our table 4.1.

Table 4.1, which is organised around the links between types of network and levels of risk on the one hand and the nature of intellectual and practical stances on the other, presents four ways in which public intellectuals engage in courageous action. This matrix locates four basic types of public intellectuals' courageous conduct, to which I have given the names of dissidents, heroes, champions and pioneers. By comparing types, or sociological abstractions created on the basis of conceptualised and theoretically determined categories, I aim to describe the differences between the various types of intellectual engagement. The category of 'dissidents' is defined by its location in a formalised system characterised by high levels of risk. Dissidents are radicalised intellectuals who display the exceptional courage demanded in societies in which the sphere of individual autonomy is minimal, which impose impersonal control, and in which the centre of power is remote and which, in consequence, enhance reliance on informal networks. The category of 'heroes' is defined by a combination of low risk and a formal system. Heroes are charismatic intellectuals who challenge the formal rules and who promote the good of the community. The category of 'champions' is characterised by its location in an informalised and low-risk system. Champions are public intellectuals who reach beyond their informal networks to advance a particular group interest or a specific cause. The category of 'pioneers' is located in the informalised system accompanied by rather high levels of frustration. Its members are courageous intellectuals who, in order to innovate and change, especially when the system's receptiveness to change declines, skilfully construct multiple network resources far beyond their informal ties.

Even though the construction of the typology of public intellectuals' actions has not been based on analyses of empirical incidences of creativity and courage, it has been informed by my familiarity with the lives, careers and actions of the selected laureates of the Nobel Peace Prize whose life and career trajectories will be used to illustrate and validate the four categories. The following chapters look at the ways in which the winners of this prestigious award represent the four positions created by combining kinds of networks with levels of risk.

Part II

Public intellectuals: the case of the
Nobel Peace Prize laureates

5   Intellectuals for peace

The Nobel Prize: its history and significance

In order to provide both an illustration and a validation of the typology of intellectuals' involvement in the public sphere, I rely on the sample of the public intellectuals who are the Nobel Peace Prize laureates. As I have already mentioned in the introduction, there are many reasons why I have employed this sample for the study of public intellectuals' contribution to the strengthening of the democratic values of their societies and the global community. One of the main reasons is that this prize, from its inception in 1901, has become an international institution, the strict rules of the selection process ensuring that it is now a well-known and highly respected peace prize. Since the Nobel Peace Prize's publicity and prestige also result from its association with other Nobel Prizes, in order to understand fully its function and meaning we need first to present the general ideas behind the Nobel Prize, its selection process and the main mechanisms by which it functions. This is followed by a closer look at the Nobel Peace Prize and by a general presentation of the sample, chosen as interesting examples of the four categories of intellectuals' engagement and as providing a significant confirmation of the typology.

We owe the establishment of this prestigious international award system to Alfred Nobel,[1] who stipulated in his will (signed 27 November 1895 in Paris) that the accumulated interest from the sale of all his assets was to be annually distributed in the form of prizes 'to those who, during the preceding year, shall have conferred the greatest benefit on mankind' (Alfred Nobel's will, in Sohlman 1983: 136). Nobel indicated that the prizes should be for specific achievements or breakthroughs in science rather than the lifetimes' work of outstanding scientists and that they should be given in five equal parts, three of which were to be awarded to individuals who had made the most important invention or discovery in the fields of physics, chemistry and medicine. The fourth award would go to the person 'who shall have produced in the field of literature the most outstanding work of an idealistic tendency' (136). The fifth award was to be for individuals who promote peace and work for peace movements and for the prevention of war, 'the horror of horrors, and the greatest of all crime' (136). The fact that the awards are the simultaneous endowment of prizes in several areas of human endeavour is one of the most original features of this reward system.[2]

Alfred Nobel in his will wrote that 'in awarding the prizes no consideration whatever shall be given to the nationality of the candidates, but that the most worthy shall receive the prize' (136). Thus, from the outset the aim of the Nobel Prizes has been to contribute to the internationalisation of science, literature and peace activities. Alfred Nobel also intended his prizes to encourage promising young 'dreamers', as they find it 'difficult to get on in life' (136). He also stipulated that the prizes in science and literature should be distributed by Swedish institutions, while the Norwegian parliament (Storting) should be responsible for the Peace Prize. After three years of negotiations over legal recognition of the will, the Nobel Foundation was established.[3] Also in 1900 the Swedish Academy of Sciences, the Karolinska Institute, the Swedish Academy and the Norwegian parliament agreed to accept the task of administering the prize. Following the establishment of five Nobel Committees, each consisting of three to five members, as the prize-awarding bodies in five different areas, on the fifth anniversary of Alfred Nobel's death – 10 December 1901 – the first prizes were awarded (Sohlman 1983: 134). From the beginning up to the 2005 awards, there have been altogether 890 prize-winners (Stenersen, Libaek and Sveen 2001: 292). The statutes of the Nobel Foundation, adopted in 1901, stipulate that the prize-awarding committees are to present each prize-winner with a diploma, a gold medal bearing the image of the testator and an appropriate inscription, and a cash award (see Lemmel 2001b).[4] The prestige, honour and distinction associated with the prizes mean that the laureates are celebrated as important contributors to human development and recognised as crucial markers of the major trends in their respective areas (Levinovitz and Ringertz 2001).

Except for the Peace Prize, which can be awarded to an institution, prizes are awarded only to individuals. Nobel prizes are either withheld or not awarded when no worthy candidate can be found and when the world situation prevents the gathering of the information required for reaching a decision. For instance, in the case of the Nobel Peace Prize, the prize has been withheld twenty times in peacetime and was not awarded ten times due to a situation of war (Abrams 1988: 258). An individual may not be nominated posthumously, but a prize proposed for a person alive at the time may be awarded posthumously (as with Dag Hammarskjold, the 1961 Nobel Peace laureate, and Erik A. Karlfedt, the 1931 Nobel Prize in Literature laureate). It has been known for prizes to be declined by their winners; for example, in 1964 Sartre refused to accept the Nobel Prize in Literature, arguing that a writer should avoid both being 'institutionalized' and giving any endorsement to the award system that symbolized an international division between the Western and Eastern blocs (Richmond 2005: 4). There have also been cases where governments have forbidden their citizens from accepting the prize; for instance, Boris Pasternak, who was awarded the Nobel Prize in Literature in 1958, was forced by the Soviet authorities to decline the honour. Moreover, governments can introduce a more general ban on acceptance of the prize, as happened in the case of Germany when Adolf Hitler, who was enraged by the award of the 1935 Nobel Peace Prize to the anti-Nazi journalist Carl von Ossietzky, forbade Germans in the future from accepting Nobel Prizes (Stenersen, Libaek and Sveen 2001: 123).

A statutory rule limits the number of people sharing the prize to three at most, while self-nomination automatically disqualifies the individual (Lemmel 2001b). According to the statutes of the Nobel Foundation, which aimed initially to protect the prestige of the prizes from adverse publicity, no part of the prize deliberations could be made public, nor could a prize decision be appealed. As the popularity of and interest in the Nobel Prizes grew, however, secrecy also proved to be useful in protecting the anonymity of the members of the prize-awarding committees (Crawford 1998). In 1974 the Nobel Foundation changed its statutes, and as a result material in the Nobel archives is now to become available to historians fifty years after an award was made.

In order to select potential and actual prize-winners, each year the respective Nobel Committees invite nominations from a wide range of informed individuals, including past prize-winners and professors in the given disciplines from around the world. Having reviewed the nominations and commissioned expert studies of the most prominent candidates, each Nobel Committee decides its final choice of up to three (in economics) laureates by a secret ballot. The annual presentation, presided over by the Swedish royal family, takes place in Stockholm and in Oslo (Peace) on 10 December, the anniversary of Alfred Nobel's death (Abrams 1988).

The Nobel Prizes are not without controversy and criticism. One of the most frequent comments concerns flaws in the selection mechanism, namely the role of more than purely scientific criteria in the processes of nominating individuals for, and awarding, the prize.

Elisabeth Crawford's (1984; 1992) studies, based on old documents released from the Nobel archives, have brought a new insight into the functioning of the system of selection and nomination and uncovered the role of politics and culture in this process. Her investigation provides evidence that one of the major factors determining where the nominations went was 'the phenomenon of informal networks, centering on research orientations and schools that linked the nominators, the candidates and their Swedish correspondents' (1984: 108). The follow-up examination of the nominations and nominees among physicists between 1901 and 1937 using network analysis discovered that, for getting a large number of nominations, it could very useful to be mobile and to know many physicists, particularly 'the right' ones – that is, ones with a high reputation and many contacts (Reichmann, Beidernikl and Fleck 2005). Other studies assert that trends or fashions determine what kind of scientific work is honoured, and that this explains why the ratio of the numbers of prizes awarded for experimental as opposed to theoretical discoveries changes with time and from one field to another (Crawford 1984; Karazijal and Momkauskait 2004). Despite Alfred Nobel's wish that nationality should not be taken into consideration in awarding the prizes, and the consequent aim of the Nobel Foundation to promote internationalisation, the nationality of a candidate has not been without significance. Nominators' tendency to propose candidates from their own country and a trend to having clusters of nominations from 'own' or other countries for a particular candidate mean that the country of origin of a candidate is not without importance (Crawford 1992; 1984).

The Nobel Prizes, as the only international prizes of the same importance as those in the Olympic Games (see britannnica.com/nobel/nobelprizes/html), can be seen as a contest between nations. Although the Nobel Prize's working rests on an international community of scientists and its honours are distributed throughout the world, it 'came to be used so extensively as the means whereby different nations took stock of their achievements' (Crawford 1984: 192). The common association of the Nobel Prizes with a contest among the nations has contributed to the prizes enhancing the 'winner-take-all' mentality which 'masks the realities of doing science in the late 20th century', creating myths about individuals who combine a range of attributes – scientist-achievers – and about the innocence of science (Crawford 1984: 189). At the same time, these illusions sustain the popularity of the prizes with the public, the media and scientific communities throughout the world.

From the beginning of the Nobel Prize, its laureates 'become the ultimate symbol of excellence for scientists and laymen alike, while the prizes in literature and peace, although more controversial than the others, also carry their share of international prestige' (Zuckerman 1977: xii). The prize has had enormous influence on the direction of research in many fields of science, on art, on the visibility of peace efforts and on the fate of international organisations (Feldman 2001). For most of its 100 plus years of existence the Nobel Prize has been regarded as the supreme reward for scientific achievement, as it 'carries the distinction of being the only award of its kind that is regularly used to indicate the importance of a scientist or a discovery, not only those honored by the prize but also the select group of scientists and works that are considered as being "of Nobel class"' (Crawford 1984: 3). The Nobel Prize also owes its highly respected status to the fact that it was created at the right time, and it has epitomised some of the principal historical transformations of the age (Bernhard 1987: xxxiii). The extraordinary success of the Nobel Prizes, seen as the most prestigious awards for intellectual achievement, has sustained the institution's broad popularity around the world. The celebration of the centenary of the first award ceremony in 2001, with the opening of both virtual and real Nobel museums, received a great deal of attention, with millions visiting the Nobel website (Stenersen, Libaek and Sveen 2001: 19). The highest level of popular and media interest is enjoyed, alongside the Nobel Prize in Literature, by the Nobel Peace Prize.

The Nobel Peace Prize: its aims and winners

The Nobel Peace Prize, administered by the Norwegian parliament, is for 'the person who shall have done the most or the best work for fraternity between nations, for the abolition or reduction of standing armies and for the holding and promotion of peace congresses' (Alfred Nobel's will, in Sohlman 1983: 136). The Storting elects five members to the prize-awarding Norwegian Nobel Committee, the composition of which reflects the strength of the political parties in the Norwegian parliament. 'Despite this arrangement, however, committee members are not expected to represent a political party or persuasion' (Abrams 1988: 13). Although nothing in the statutes prevents the Storting from naming international members (Lemmel 2001b), only Norwegians have ever been members of the committee. Moreover, until 1936 it was members of the Norwegian government who were elected to the Nobel Committee. As a result of controversy over the 1935 Peace Prize, it was decided that members of the Nobel Committee who became members of the government should be excluded from participation in the work of the committee. For the following decades many prominent politicians, though not members of the government, were selected by the Storting to serve on the Nobel Committee (Lundestad 1994). Further changes were introduced after the controversy caused by the 1973 awards. In 1977 an official rule was adopted prohibiting members of the government from serving on the Nobel Committee, and the name of the committee was changed from the Nobel Committee of the Norwegian Storting to its present name: the Norwegian Nobel Committee (Tonnesson 2005). From that year, although the formal rules for the appointment of committee members have not been changed, it has become the custom that members of the Storting should not be appointed to the committee. Nonetheless, the majority of members still continue to be former parliamentarians with a long record of political activity (Tonnesson 2005: 13). In the first seven decades of the Nobel Peace Prize it was customary for members of the committee, appointed for a six-year term, to continue being re-elected until they decided to step down voluntarily, but since the 1980s the tenure of both chairpersons and staff has become shorter (Abrams 1988: 13).

The process of selecting a winner of the Nobel Peace Prize starts in September, about a year before the prize announcement. The statutes give only a limited number of people the right to nominate individuals and organisations for the Nobel Peace Prize.[5] After the organisations and individuals qualified to nominate candidates send their proposals, which must reach the Committee before 1 February of the year for which the nomination is being made (for example, in 2005 the committee received the record number of 199 nominations; thirty-three were put forward by committee members, 163 were for individuals and thirty-six were for organisations; Henley 2005: 2), the Nobel Committee members convene for a meeting to decide on a shortlist of candidates (ten to twenty individuals and organisations). All the information about the shortlisted candidates is distributed among the Nobel Committee's specially appointed permanent advisers, whose task is to write detailed reports on each candidate. From February until August or September the committee of five meets once a month. In October the Norwegian Nobel Committee makes its choice, the prize-winners are contacted and during a press conference the announcement of the laureates' names takes place. The Peace Prize is awarded annually on 10 December in Oslo, and the laureate is expected to make a speech during the ceremony.

The Peace Prize differs from other Nobel Prizes in many respects. Unlike the committees for the Swedish prizes, the Norwegian Nobel Committee until as recently as the middle of the 1970s did not provide any official reason for its decisions. In order to improve the media coverage and reduce the criticism of the committee's choice, this practice was changed in 1975 (Abrams 1988: 16). Also, in contrast to the Prizes in science, the Peace Prize can be awarded to institutions as well as to people. Furthermore, in contrast to other Nobel Prizes, the Peace Prize is a political type of award, as to 'decide who has done the most to promote peace is a highly political matter, and scarcely a matter of cool scholarly judgement' (Tonnesson 2005: 11). Another important feature of the Nobel Peace Prize is that it is the world's most prestigious prize, enjoying the highest international standing, because 'almost everyone knows about the Nobel Peace Prize, while so few have heard of other respective prizes' (Lundestad 2001a: 8).

Not only is the Nobel Peace Prize the most prestigious peace award, and not only does it have the longest history and the most international character of all peace prizes, but it also distinguishes itself from the 300 or so other peace awards by employing a very broad definition of 'peace' (Lundestad 2001a: 8). This broad definition and the fact that the award has captured the most significant contributions to peace (with some exceptions) account for its high level of popularity. In other words, the existence around the world of huge public support for the aims of the Nobel Peace Prize is directly associated with this award's most distinctive feature – its moral and symbolic value. Both Nobel's will and the Nobel Committee's practice are founded on a moral concept of peace. 'The peace to be honoured is a peace that is rooted in hearts and minds; the work to be credited is work for fraternisation, tolerance, trust, and understanding' (Sejersted 2004: 9). As Ann T. Keene (1998: 7) notes, moral arguments provide a language with which to praise peacemakers and condemn conflicts. For example, the award in 1935 of the Nobel Peace Prize to Carl von Ossietzky, a German intellectual who was already under arrest, was viewed mainly as a sign of moral and symbolic approval of the struggle for peace. The prize also rewards 'efforts to establish institutional environments which help human beings to realise their better selves, or to "combat the evil principle in themselves", to return to Kant's formulation' (Sejersted 2004: 9). While some laureates' efforts have had more immediate results, as with Linus Pauling and the Test Ban Treaty and Martin Luther King's fight to improve the status of minorities, the importance of the Nobel Peace Prize cannot be measured by immediate political changes and responses.[6] It is, rather, a symbol of goodwill, as it contributes 'to turning history into a moral endeavour' (Elie Wiesel, quoted in Sejersted 2004: 9). In other words, the Nobel Peace Prize is not a 'magic wand' (Abrams 1994: 9). It serves only as a 'microphone in the hand of the laureate', insofar as 'voices that were barely heard before are suddenly listened to with great interest, quoted in the leading newspapers, and received by leading politicians' (Abrams 1994: 9). With the Nobel Peace Prize laureates attracting attention as 'symbols of goodwill', the prize is seen as a symbolic gesture aiming at creating and enhancing an atmosphere of trust, essential not just for creating but also for maintaining a peaceful society (Sejersted 2004: 9).

Taking into account this moral and symbolic nature of the Nobel Peace Prize, it is not surprising that the award has caused so many controversies. The level of controversy surrounding the prize is further increased by its high level of popularity and by its politicisation. Another fact that has clearly increased the criticism of the committee's choices and has put the prize at the centre of international public and media attention, with some laureates being publicly described in such terms as ' "the most notorious liar" and the most "shameless traitor" ' (Aaseng 1987: 7), has been the lack of an open exposition of the committee's criteria for the selection of winners. Consequently, the Peace Prize has been more frequently criticised than the science prizes (Kauffman 2001: 16). Additionally, in contrast to the prizes in science, where any protests have been carried out on behalf of the neglected individuals who were not awarded the prize, in the case of the Peace Prize the objections have been primarily against the award going to particular individuals.

The most controversial awards have been given to active politicians or statesmen, who frequently have been selected on the grounds of parti-cular actions they have taken, or in order to boost the chances for success of a specific peace process (Sejersted 2004). Among the awards that have been widely criticised has been the 1973 Peace Prize, awarded jointly to Henry Kissinger, the US National Security Advisor and Secretary of State, and Le Duc Tho, the chief North Vietnamese negotiator, for the Paris agreement intended to bring about a ceasefire in the Vietnam War and the withdrawal of US forces. On the other hand, the Norwegian Nobel Committee has been criticised for failing to award the prize to Mahatma Gandhi, the most famous pacifist of the twentieth century. Controversies have also been generated by the fact that the prize brings international or national conflicts to public atten-tion. As such, it can be seen by national governments, especially in the case of non-democratic authorities, as 'interference' in national matters. For example, the award of the 1935 Peace Prize to Carl von Ossietzky and that of the 1975 prize to Andrei Sakharov were both perceived by the respective governments as interfering in their national matters (Tonnesson 2005).

The Norwegian Nobel Committee has also been reproached for being too responsive to national political interests and for its alleged failure to follow Alfred Nobel's wishes to favour peace workers and peace activists rather than statesmen. When in 1906, one year after Norway's full independence, the Nobel Committee of the Norwegian parliament, chaired by Norway's first foreign minister, awarded the Peace Prize to Theodore Roosevelt, the president of the United States, questions were raised as to whether 'that decision was made primarily because it was politically useful for a small nation which had just become independent' (Tonnesson 2005: 11). As a result of this debate, for the next several years (from 1907 to 1913) the prizes were awarded to traditional peace activists.

Prior to the 1960s, peace meant the absence of war, specifically between nations. With the awards to Luthuli, the South African Zulu chief and president of the African National Congress, who was honoured for his opposition to apartheid and his fight for civil rights in 1960, and to Martin Luther King (1964), peace took on an additional meaning, and could be applied to the injustices within nations, such as the use of secret police or imprisonment, suppression of political freedoms, or censorship (Feldman 2001: 316). The Norwegian Nobel Committee has increasingly come to define itself as believing 'in humanitarian assistance to the weak and the poor, in arms control and disarmament, and more and more frequently in human rights generally' (Lundestad 2001b: 187). Its decisions in the last few years signal the emergence of a new criterion: 'It is about how we live together, share resources. ... about the earth' (Ole Danbolt Mjos, quoted in Henley 2005: 2). Thus, at present the aim of the Nobel Peace Prize is to support and honour organised peace movements, peace negotiations, policies of reconciliation, humanitarian work, world organisations, disarmament and non-violence and to honour the struggle for human rights, democracy and freedom.

The committee's ability to modify its criteria and expand its definition of peace in such a way as to make the prize more global and representative has contributed to the growing world approval of the decisions made by the Norwegian Committee, and consequently to the Peace Prize's international reputation. Although the committee still consists only of Norwegians, and therefore receives criticism for being marked by ethnocentrism and for being insufficiently autonomous, the high level of approval of its decisions can be seen as furnishing significant proof of the growing recognition of its political independence, international standing and objectivity (Lundestad 2001a). Many developments suggest that the committee has managed to avoid representing Norway's national interest; for example, to date only two Norwegians (the last in 1922, Fridtjof Nansen) have received the Nobel Peace Prize (Tonnesson 2005: 11). Moreover, the committee has consistently managed to speak with an international voice. The Ossietzky award (in 1935), the Sakharov award (in 1975) and the Dalai Lama award (in 1989), all of which could easily have jeopardised Norway's relationship with the laureates' respective countries, suggest that the committee has been capable of a high level of political autonomy (Tonnesson 2005: 11). Taking into account all the above changes, as well as the fact that it is rather difficult to envisage reforms that could create an independent committee, with the right qualifications to judge who were doing the most or the best work for peace, it can be argued that the Norwegian Committee has been relatively successful in its efforts to represent the international community (Tonnesson 2005).

To sum up, the publicity and prestige of the Nobel Peace Prize are a reflection of its extensive and generally successful history and of the growing identification of this prize with the voice of the international community. Attempts by the Peace Prize Committee to strike a balance between universal and culturally related factors have also been contributing to the growing approval of the Nobel Peace Prize as an honour in the 'peaceful contest' between nations (Crawford 1984: 204). Additionally, the publicity enjoyed by the Nobel Peace Prize has been enhanced by the media's growing interest in personalities and the celebrity culture (Holl and Kjelling 1994: 9). Nonetheless, the main factor sustaining and enhancing the relevance and prestige of the prize is the fact that it provides recognition and exposure for voices defending the values of peace, human rights, freedom and democracy.

Public intellectuals as the Nobel Peace Prize laureates

From its beginning up to 2005, 114 Nobel Peace Prizes were awarded to 93 individuals (81 men and 12 women) and 21 organisations. The spectrum of recipients of the Peace Prize varies from peace activists, politicians, diplomats, and priests to members of various international humanitarian organisations (for instance, Amnesty International, the Red Cross, Doctors without Borders, the United Nations). With the Norwegian Nobel Committee's criteria gradually evolving, the type of winner has also been changing. The Nobel Committee's broadened interpretation of 'peace' has given it the flexibility to adapt to new concerns and challenges and this consequently has changed the type of laureate.

During the first fourteen years (1901–14) the Norwegian Nobel Committee recognised members of the organised peace movement, with only two laureates (Jean Henri Dunant, the 1901 winner, and Theodore Roosevelt, the 1906 winner) falling outside this category and with nineteen prizes going to those who represented either the parliamentary and broader peace societies or the international legal tradition. During the First World War the Nobel Committee in neutral Norway did not award prizes, apart from in 1917, to the International Committee of the Red Cross (Lundestad 2001b: 169). The inter-war years (1919–39) reflected Norway's increasing involvement in international relations (Lundestad 2001b: 169). The Nobel Committee's selections during this period were shaped mainly by the formation of the League of Nations; at least eight of the twenty-one laureates had a clear connection with the League. In the Second World War no peace prize was awarded, as during the First World War, except to the International Committee of the Red Cross in 1944, in recognition of the work it performed during the war on behalf of humanity. The post-war 'Cold War' period, with Norway becoming a member of the United Nations and with the Norwegian Labour Party dominating national politics for two decades (1945–65), witnessed Norway's growing interest in human rights. This trend was reflected in the decisions of the Nobel Committee to honour many UN officials and departments. Statesmen and politicians continued to receive the Peace Prize after the Second World War, some for negotiating peace treaties, others for promoting reconciliation (Lundestad 2001b: 175–8). The 1964 Peace Prize awarded to Martin Luther King has become one of the most famous Peace Prizes, and this award also illustrates the committee's new policy of intervention (Feldman 2001: 317).

During the next period (1966–89) the committee continued to honour individuals and organisations that had worked to strengthen the ethical underpinnings of peace. The award also started to reflect the process of globalisation, with prizes going to Asia and the Middle East (five), eastern Europe and the Soviet Union (two) and Africa (one). In this period human rights represented the fastest-growing field of interest for the Norwegian Nobel Committee, which moved towards awarding human or civil rights activism – for example, honouring Amnesty International in 1977. Several awards (for instance, the 1979 prize to Mother Teresa) continued the humanitarian tradition, while the disarmament category was represented, for example, by the 1985 prize going to the International Physicians for the Prevention of Nuclear War. In contrast to the first half of the century, general advocates of peace did not figure as prominently in the Peace Prize list after the Second World War.

After the collapse of the Berlin Wall the Norwegian Nobel Committee's decision to award the prize to the president of the Soviet Union, Mikhail Gorbachev, in 1990 reflected the celebrations at the end of the Cold War. The Peace Prize was awarded in 1991 to Aung San Suu Kyi of Myanmar and a year later to Rigoberta Menchú Tum, the Indian campaigner for indigenous rights in Guatemala and the rest of Latin America. In 1993 the committee awarded the Peace Prize jointly to the leader of the African National Congress, Nelson Mandela, and the then president of South Africa, Frederik Willem de Klerk, for their work towards the peaceful termination of the apartheid regime, and for laying the foundations for a new democratic South Africa (Stenersen, Libaek and Sveen 2001: 26).

Awarding prizes to Asians, Africans and Latin Americans, a trend which started only in the 1970s, has continued in the recent period of 'pluralistic globalization' (Lundestad 2001b: 182). In line with this global approach, comparing the last three decades (1975–2005) with the first seven decades (1901–74) reveals that there were sizeable increases in the number of people rewarded from Asia (from two to fourteen), Africa (from one to seven) and Latin America (from one to five). Looking at the geographical distribution of Peace Prize nominees, until the mid-1970s, the majority came from western Europe: in the period 1901–25, 69 per cent; 1926–50, 54 per cent; and 1951–75, 37 per cent (Stenersen, Libaek and Sveen 2001: 292). In the period from 1976 to 1990 about 23 per cent of all laureates came from western Europe, with a similar level from the United States and Canada (Stenersen, Libaek and Sveen 2001: 292).

In the whole history of the Nobel Peace Prize twenty-eight prizes have been awarded to individuals and/or organisations associated with peace movements, sixteen to individuals and/or organisations associated with human rights, eleven to individuals and/or organisations associated with humanitarian work and nine to individuals and/or organisations associated with disarmament or non-violence (Stenersen, Libaek and Sveen 2001: 292; author's calculations). Human rights were not considered a criterion until about 1960, following the development of the United Nations charter and the declaration on human rights; only then did the Norwegian Nobel Committee include the struggle for human rights among the criteria for relevance to peace (Sejersted 2004: 6). Until the mid-1970s the most honoured category was statesmen, who altogether received thirty-four awards, but now the main three broad categories of winners are peace brokers, providers of aid and campaigners for human rights (Henley 2005: 1).The changes in the characteristics of the Nobel Peace Prize-winners, with the balance shifting to humanitarian causes, disarmament and the human rights category, as well as with the increased number of women (who won nine prizes between 1976 and 2005, while only three prizes were awarded to women in the entire period 1901–75), tend to reflect international values and the new political climate. Following the realisation 'that peace cannot be established without a full respect for freedom' (Abrams 1994: 24), the committee now gives awards to people and organisations involved in humanitarian work, disarmament, non-violence and the struggle for human rights, democracy and freedom.

My research on the different types of public intellectuals among the Nobel laureates involved the use of several books, which together served as a sort of *Who's Who?* of the Nobel Peace Prize (biographies, monographs and websites that deal with the Nobel Prize as a whole, biographical directories and encyclopaedias). For example: a work by Øivind Stenersen, Ivar Libaek and Asle Sveen, *The Nobel Peace Prize* (2001), provides bibliographical sketches of 107 individuals who received the prize between 1901 and 2001; a book edited by Tyler Wasson (*Nobel Peace Prize Winners*, 1987) gives a detailed account of all laureates between 1901 and 1986; Irwin Abrams' *The Nobel Peace Prize and the Laureates* (1988) covers practically the same period; Keene's book *Peacemakers: Winners of the Nobel Peace Prize* (1998) presents the Nobel Peace Prize laureates from 1901 to 1997 in terms of their education, occupation and major accomplishments; Nathan Aaseng's 1987 book *The Peace Seekers: The Nobel Peace Prize* paints portraits of many of the peace laureates; and the site of the Nobel e-museum contains an impressive amount of data on all the winners. The richness of the bibliographical material available has allowed me to select from the entire population of Nobel Peace laureates those individuals who fit the definition of public intellectuals. By scrutinising biographical characteristics of the prize-winners, I have constructed a sample consisting of twelve peace laureates who can all be defined as 'public intellectuals'.[7] They are laureates who were (or are) writers, journalists, academics or scientists and who spoke out about important social, political or cultural issues to the general public outside their professional roles. All twelve of these Nobel Peace Prize laureates, while working in academia or being freelance writers, artists or journalists, reflected on the social and intellectual conditions of their respective countries in the hope of changing them into more just and peaceful nations.

The sample of public intellectuals who received the Nobel Peace Prize consists of three women (out of twelve female recipients in all) and nine men. Five of the twelve come from the United States; this reflects the overrepresentation of American citizens in the population of prize-winners in general (there are twenty laureates from the United States from a total of 112). Two individuals in my sample come from the United Kingdom (twelve from the United Kingdom from the prize-winners as a whole), one comes from Sweden (five in total), one from Germany (four in total), one from Norway (two in total), one from the

Soviet Union (two in total) and one from Argentina (one in all, although there are five Nobel Peace Prize-winners from the whole of Latin America). These twelve public intellectuals who received the Peace Prize share many common characteristics. Five intellectuals in my sample are natural scientists (Fridtjof Nansen, the 1922 prize-winner; John Boyd Orr, 1949; Linus Carl Pauling, 1962; Norman Borlaug, 1970; and Andrei Sakharov, 1975), three are social scientists (Jane Addams, 1931; Emily Greene Balch, 1946; and Alva Myrdal, 1982), two are writers (Norman Angell, 1933; and Elie Wiesel, 1986), one is a journalist (Carl von Ossietzky, 1935) and one is an artist (Adolfo Pérez Esquivel, 1980). Some of them, moreover, combine many roles; for example Wiesel is a writer, journalist and professor of Judaic studies. Interestingly, all three women in my sample are social scientists.

The main common characteristics of the selected intellectuals are, by definition, creativity (as they are producers of ideas) and courage (as the Nobel Peace Prize is awarded for acts of brave and disinterested public involvement, and for the courage to work for, defend and spread civic values, human rights, peace and democracy). They have worked creatively in academia, journalism or cultural spheres, while also devoting themselves with great courage to attempting to change the social and intellectual conditions of their surroundings. In the lives of all the women and men who are a part of my sample, there have been incidences of both civil courage and creativity.

In order to identify and describe the four main types of engagement in public affairs, I have used as much biographical data on the twelve Nobel laureates, selected on the basis of their fitting the 'public intellectual' category, as possible. After further research into each chosen individual's life, career, achievements and publications, and by drawing upon a multiplicity of material on their careers and scientific, artistic or journalistic work, and autobiographical and biographical accounts of their lives (the data from biographies, monographs, diaries), I divided my sample into the four categories. By examining their imaginative ideas and programmes aimed at the expansion or defence of civic values and by analysing their efforts to realise those innovative aspirations, which frequently involved the risks of rejection, disapproval or even punishment, I have classified the selected group into pioneers, dissidents, heroes, and champions in the following way (see table 5.1).

The purpose of assigning each individual in the sample to one of the four categories is to present four group biographies illustrating, and – at least to some degree – verifying, the main categories of public intellectuals' involvement in the public sphere. My research has not resulted in a standard biography, as this type of study investigates in depth the life

Table 5.1. *Public intellectuals' engagement*

The perception of the situation	The nature of the system	
	Formalised	Informalised
Uncertainty	**HEROES** Jane Addams Fridtjof Nansen Elie Wiesel	**CHAMPIONS** Norman Angell Emily Greene Balch Alva Myrdal
Frustration/risk	**DISSIDENTS** Carl von Ossietzky Andrei Sakharov Adolfo Pérez Esquivel	**PIONEERS** John Boyd Orr Linus Carl Pauling Norman Borlaug

of one person. Nonetheless, although my research focuses on numerous individuals, it is not a conventional group biography either. Whereas conventional group biographies focus on individuals acting together, on their relations and mutual influences and their group's efforts and achievements, my version of the group biography provides a description of individuals who never met, and who were not connected, yet whose life stories display many similarities in terms of their creative and courageous achievements in their professional and public lives.

The presentation of public intellectuals' different types of engagement takes place in the following four chapters, dealing in turn with the main categories of intellectuals' involvement in the public sphere: heroes, dissidents, champions and pioneers.

Notes

1 Alfred Nobel (1833–96) was the inventor of dynamite, blasting gelatine and smokeless powder, industrialist, technological optimist, global enterpriser, world citizen.
2 Since 1968 a Nobel Prize has also been awarded in economics, its sixth field, as that year the Central Bank of Sweden, in connection with its tercentenary celebration, initiated a new award, the Central Bank of Sweden Prize in Economic Science in memory of Alfred Nobel (Breit and Hirsch 2004: vii).
3 The Nobel Foundation, set up in 1900, is a private institution that manages the assets made available through Nobel's will for the awarding of the prize. Its statutes provided for the establishment of the Nobel Committee and Nobel Institutes. The Nobel Foundation represents the Nobel institutions externally, and protects their interests, but it does not participate in the selection processes (Lemmel 2001a; Abrams 1988).

4 The monetary amount that the Nobel Prize gives to the laureates depends upon how well the Foundation has succeeded in managing its capital. In 1946 it was exempted from national income and wealth tax and local income tax. This tax-exempt status, followed by further liberalisation in 1953, has led to a gradual increase over time in the size of the Foundation's main fund; thus in 2000 it was valued at about $1 million, and in 2005 it stood at 10 million Swedish kronor – some £730,000, or about $1,282,400 (http://nobel.se/nobel/amounts.html).

5 Nominators can be either current or former members or advisers of the Nobel Committee, members of governments or national assemblies, members of the Inter-Parliamentary Union, members of the International Court of Justice and the International Court of Arbitration in The Hague, members of the International Peace Bureau or members of the Institute de Droit International. Also qualified are university professors of political science and law, history and philosophy as well as Peace Prize laureates (Tonnesson 2005). In recent years the Norwegian Nobel Committee has received over 140 nominations for each annual prize. About 1,000 people submit their nominations for each prize. This means that there are usually well over 100 nominees for each prize (www.britannnica.com/nobel/nobelprizes/html).

6 The prize often does not produce the hoped-for results. For example, the peace talks with North Korea initiated by Kim Dae-Jung, the 2000 laureate, are stalled, while the Dalai Lama is still in exile, despite winning the prize in 1989. The 1991 winner, Aung San Suu Kyi, the leader of the opposition against the military regime in Myanmar, received the award for her non-violent struggle for democracy and human rights, but she has not yet been released from house arrest and the military regime continues to hold power (http://nobelprize.org/nobel/).

7 My initial sample consisted of sixteen public intellectuals who had won the Nobel Peace Prize. After further reading and checking of all the available biographies and other materials, I reduced the size of my sample to twelve. I excluded from my final sample Joseph Rotblat (the 1995 Nobel Peace Prize laureate), who was a nuclear physicist and worked for peace. Joseph Rotblat shared his Nobel Peace Prize with the Pugwash Conferences on Science and World Affairs, a social movement that he himself created. He belongs to the category of the 'movement intellectual' (Eyerman 1994: 198) – i.e. a category that I am not concerned with for the purposes of this study. I also excluded from my sample two professors of law (Louis Renault, the prize-winner in 1907, and René Cassin, the winner in 1968), as both of them, while contributing to world peace, did so mainly in their professional capacities, and therefore their contact with non-specialised audiences (i.e. the public) was limited. I also eliminated from my sample Nicholas Murray Butler (the president of Columbia University, who was awarded the Nobel Peace Prize in 1931), because he was then one of the leading figures in the Republican Party, and therefore was perceived as a 'politician' rather than a public intellectual (Stenersen, Libaek and Sveen 2001: 113).

6   Heroes: legends in their own time

Realistic idealists

The notion of heroism, although frequently used, is rather ambiguous. This ambiguity is a result of the fact that different traditions emphasise different characteristics of a hero. In ancient Greece heroes were figures of divine descent, endowed with great physical and moral strength. For example, the heroes of Homer's *Iliad* and *Odyssey* were strong and beautiful aristocratic warriors, borne to the supreme heights of their deeds by a surge of power infused into them by the gods themselves. The Christian tradition altered this concept, replacing prowess and honour with spiritual purity. Now we think about heroes not as mythological figures or brave warriors but, rather, as men and women who exhibit great courage and exceptional qualities in pursuing noble causes.

This ambiguity regarding the notion of heroism allows it to be put to the service of various values and different causes, which, in turn, further complicates its meaning. Heroic virtues can, for example, be appropriated by propaganda and made to serve nationalistic interests. Thus, in authoritarian regimes 'heroism', basically, means a willingness to march in rank and be a soldier. Democracies, on the other hand, tend to have problems with heroes, as they cultivate suspicions about any worshipping of the kind of overwhelming brilliance displayed by great people. The complexity of the notion of heroism is also connected with the different levels of realism assigned to heroes' actions in terms of what our 'time says: [for] Don Quixote, the future will say "hero"' (Key, quoted in Swedberg 1999: 521). Nevertheless, what makes heroes legends in their own times is their unique combination of idealism and realism. While a mythical hero 'ventures forth from the world of common doings into a region of supernatural wonder' (Campbell 1949: 30), a modern hero's success depends upon her or his victorious passages through episodes of deliberation, action, sanction and diffusion (Swedberg 1999). What goes on at each stage and what kind of social context supports the actions in each phase determine whether a hero is seen as a Don Quixote – that is, as a 'quixotic or impractical idealist' (Walton 1986: 48) – or as a real 'hero' – that is, someone whose contribution to the well-being of the community, possible due to a sound combination of idealism and realism, is acknowledged.

Every country needs heroes, and they all tend to have their own lists of great people who are admired for performing exceptional roles in their history. National heroes are perceived as 'engines' or 'motors' of history, embodying the key virtues of their culture and capable of great achievements. In this spirit, Thomas Carlyle ([1840] 1924), who in the middle of the nineteenth century reinvented the classical version of the doctrine of heroic determinism, claimed that history is made by exceptional individuals. In his lectures on heroes he argued that each society, to prevent its civilisation from falling into moral chaos and destruction, needs great men. Hence, heroes are seen as those capable of exercising a great hold upon the imagination of their contemporaries, and their legacy is the inheritance of great examples of extraordinary beneficial deeds. Even today, in spite of the prevalent egalitarian and celebrity chat show culture, the idea of heroism still calls to mind countless images of daring and noble self-sacrifices. On the other hand, the popular media's romanticised stories of heroic achievements are often received with scepticism.

Here, the label 'hero' is used to describe the type of public intellectual who meets our criteria for inclusion in this category, as discussed in chapter 4. Public intellectuals included in this categorisation are charismatic figures who bring about change as a result of their ability to inspire and challenge the rules, while relying on informal networks. Heroes, embedded in a context defined by the combination of low risk and the predominance of formal structures, are public intellectuals who, while promoting the long-term interest of society, question the prevailing views and rules by their deeds and pronouncements. They show us how intellectuals, in order to perform a social role of exceptional value, may have to move beyond the dogmatism and radical optimism of their native ideologies. In our sample of public intellectuals whose national and international achievements were recognised and rewarded with the Nobel Peace Prize, there are three heroes, namely Jane Addams, Fridtjof Nansen and Elie Wiesel. Their accomplishments in their professional fields, as well as their successful public engagement in fighting for their ideas, made them legends in their times. We will start with Jane Addams, who was awarded the Nobel Peace Prize in 1931 for her work in the international pacifist women's movement.

Jane Addams: searching for democracy's middle ground

Jane Addams (1860–1935) was one of America's first public intellectuals: one of its most accomplished social reformers, one of its foremost social democrats and one of its most pragmatic ethicists. She was a social worker, social critic, suffragist, pacifist, sociologist and writer who promoted the virtues of peace and democracy and who challenged the gap between theory and practice.

Addams become a national figure by excelling in her three roles: as a founder and head of Hull House (a settlement in a Chicago immigrant neighbourhood), as a leader of reform and as a public intellectual. In the course of her life she moved from being 'the only saint America has produced' to being 'almost cast out of society' (Stenersen, Libaek and Sveen 2001: 108). Although she was a much-loved public figure, Addams' stand for international peace, when most Americans glorified war, transformed her into 'the symbol for everything anti-American, the betrayer of her country, the antithesis of what she had stood for so many years' (Davis 1973: 246). Today she is mainly admired as a social worker, original thinker and theorist (Bethke Elshtain 2002a; Deegan 1988; Lasch 1965), whose thousands of speeches, more than a dozen books and over 500 articles represent a coherent body of social and political theory addressing the issues of social justice, cooperation and democracy.[1] Addams was 'one of the first, and remains one of the most important, among a group of social thinkers committed to communicating to a general audience that we have come to call "public intellectuals"' (Bethke Elshtain 2002a: xxv).

Jane Addams, the daughter of an upper middle-class Protestant family, grew up in the wealth and comfort of the post-civil-war decades. Her life spanned both the gilded age and the progressive era, the periods characterised by technological innovation, the rapid expansion of industry, immigration and urbanisation, as well as the rise of populism, progressivism and socialism. After finishing at the Rockford Female College in 1882, Addams entered the Women's Medical College in Philadelphia, but her illness and depression after her father's death forced her to withdraw. Her recuperation over the next six years included two trips to Europe, where in London she visited Toynbee Hall, the first social settlement trying to educate the poor. Being a nineteenth-century woman, Addams had limited life choices, yet, being one of the first generation of college women who believed in knowledge and its application in the service of the nation, she searched for opportunities to be useful outside the domestic sphere. It was the visit to Toynbee Hall that gave her the idea for her future project, which would provide her with the ability to help others and would offer her an all-absorbing vocation.

In 1889 Addams, together with her friend Ellen Starr, moved to a poor section of Chicago, to a big house on Halsted Street, know as Hull House, which quickly grew into an entire city block of buildings, used every day by hundreds of migrants. The settlement was not a philanthropic effort but an enterprise undertaken out of 'the duties of good citizenship' (Addams [1893] 2002b: 45). It was also Addams' creative solution to the dilemma of how to 'be a respected and respectable single woman with engrossing, satisfying work, who could assert her authority' and, at the same time, capable of 'fulfilling her family's obligations and her friends' expectations' (Brown Bissell 2004: 110). The establishment of the settlement helped Addams to expand the boundaries of the domestic sphere and to redefine her role in the public sphere; thus, 'the subjective necessity for social settlement' was identical with the desire to 'give tangible expression to the democratic ideal' (Addams [1893] 2002b: 17). Nevertheless, at this time of the triumph of northern industrial capitalism and expanded migration, there were not only subjective needs but also objective reasons behind the founding of Hull House. For Addams, the settlement was 'an experimental effort to aid in the solution of the social and industrial problems which are engendered by the modern conditions of life in a great city' ([1893] 2002b: 16). Hull House, as a result of its pioneering services, became a thriving social, cultural and intellectual centre, and this achievement gave Addams and her co-workers 'a strong sense of being pioneers' and ensured her 'leadership in the national settlement movement' (Davis 1973: 93).

Addams' work with the ethnic communities in Hull House drew her into other areas of social reform. She established herself as a prominent advocate for immigrants at a time of national anti-immigration sentiments and as a promoter of compromise in the midst of waves of labour protests and strikes. Assisted by educated women like herself, Addams became practised in lobbying, collecting evidence and statistics and mobilising social support for labour legislation and labour mediation. Her and her colleagues' public campaigns resulted in many reforms, and she also served on and worked on many city and state projects.[2] Practically all the major reforms of the progressive era benefited to some degree from Jane Addams' support and involvement. By the end of the nineteenth century her role as the founder of Hull House and as a reformer, together with her increasingly important role in many local and national organisations and lecturing and numerous articles on topics related to Hull House, ethics, democracy, civic responsibility and social cooperation, had established her national reputation. She became 'a symbol of rectitude and reform' (Levine 1971: 81) and was perceived as 'the feminine consciousness of the nation' (Davis 1973: 134). As she became 'a celebrated public figure', Addams was proclaimed to be one of the greatest American woman (Bethke Elshtain 2002a: xxx) and was seen as 'an altruistic heroine who served society by bringing together all its best aspects' (Levine 1971: xi). Addams solidified her reputation in the country as 'the most admired woman' (Knight 2005: xvii) by publishing in 1910 a book about her experiences at Hull House. *Twenty Years at Hull House* immediately became a classic, and it is still recognised as one of the best examples of autobiography.

Hull House not only introduced Jane Addams to the reform movement but also initiated her relationship with a wider world of scholarship. The settlement house, which was a focal point of interest for many universities, helped to bridge the division between academia and the wider community. Through the regular lectures and public discussions it hosted, Hull House attracted 'many of the intellectuals of the Anglo-American world' (Phillips 1974: 55). This collaboration provided Addams with contacts with the intellectual elite; for example, she established a friendship with John Dewey, whom she met in 1894. Her relationship with the University of Chicago was mutually beneficial. Addams contributed to the creation of both sociology and social work as academic disciplines at the university, while many researchers adopted the settlement house as a social laboratory for urban sociology. Her career as a sociologist started her cooperation with Albion Small and many urban sociologists. In 1895, as a result of this collaboration, Addams and her colleagues in Hull House published *Hull House Maps and Papers*, the fundamental sociological survey of sweatshops, tenement housing and preventable diseases and ailments in the neighbourhood. With this publication, Addams 'came to think of herself as a scholar, even as a sociologist' (Davis 1973: 102), and she became an active and careful researcher.

Jane Addams liked to speak on college campuses, and she gave series of lectures at several universities (for example, in 1890 she lectured at the University of Chicago on social ethics) and for the American Sociological Society. While accepting many honorary degrees and awards from several universities, she resisted all attempts to make her a permanent member of any university faculty.[3] Addams remained an excellent 'interpreter of practical sociology' (Levine 1971: 90) who believed that only through the 'affective interpretation of others' needs and motives' could social justice be achieved (Addams, quoted in Brown Bissell 2004: 6). Her first book, *Democracy and Social Ethics* (1902), was already a good example of her interpretative social thinking and her ability to combine a powerful cultural and political critique with a constructive vision of American democracy.[4] Addams' ability to connect thought and action, scholarship and reform was appreciated by Albion Small, the first editor of the *American Journal of Sociology*, in the early volumes of which she published five articles and in which her books were positively reviewed (Hamilton 2003: 289). She also wrote for several other scholarly journals, while continuing to publish in popular magazines.

Addams, who achieved national and international success at a time where most professions were closed to women, had not compaigned for women's right to vote until almost the end of the nineteenth century. Later, however, she became an active and prominent supporter of voting rights for women. Her participation in the women's movement intensified with her engagement in international efforts for world peace. She always opposed what she called 'dogmatic nationalism' and was a committed pacifist who viewed conflict and violence as the natural enemies of social progress (Bethke Elshtain 2002a: 116). As early as 1907 she had published a book called *Newer Ideals of Peace*, in which, drawing on her experiences from living together with migrants from different countries in Hull House, she promoted the idea that all nationalities should cooperate at the international level for the common good. When, in 1915, women peace activists founded the Women's Peace Party, Addams, who viewed femininity as central to women's role as peacemakers, became its president and chaired the large peace conference it organised in The Hague in 1915 (Abrams 1988: 116). After the conference, she and other activists travelled to European capitals to meet national leaders in order to mobilise their support for a peace conference to be chaired by neutral countries. She unsuccessfully tried to persuade President Woodrow Wilson to call a conference to mediate a negotiated end to hostilities. When the United States entered the First World War in 1917 Addams did not change her pacifist stance, and virtually overnight she 'who had been an American heroine, representative of all the best of American democracy, was transformed into a villain by her opposition to the war' (Davis 1973: 251). For her uncompromising stance in the name of mediation, war enthusiasts labelled her as a traitor and denounced her as a dangerous and 'an unpatriotic subversive out to demasculinize the nation's sons' (Alonso 1994: 208). Addams was put under government surveillance, harassed, ostracised and vilified in the press (Stenersen, Libaek and Sveen 2001: 108). After the end of the war the delegates from The Hague met again in Zurich and formed a permanent organisation, the

Women's International League for Peace and Freedom (WILPF), with its headquarters in Geneva. Addams, in her role as the league's international president until 1929, and later as its honorary president, pursued pro-peace activity until the end of her life.

Until the mid-1920s Addams, who spoke out against the mistreatment of foreigners whom the government considered 'disloyal', was accused of being a dangerous and radical communist (Davis 1973: 252). She managed to rebuild her national reputation by engaging in relief work. Slowly the hostility towards her declined, especially when in 1931 she was awarded the Nobel Peace Prize for her work 'for peace and human brotherhood' (Koht [1931] 2005: 1). In the same year, a feature article in *The New York Times* presented her as a 'heroine' and as a 'saint' who was humble and respectful of others and who was 'an amazing example of the force of personality, of an obstinate idealism breaking a path though our mechanized and highly regimented civilization' (Alonso 1994: 215). By the time of her death, in 1935, she was again America's best-known and most widely hailed female public figure, praised for being 'a channel through which the moral life of her country flowed' (Spanish 2002: 5).

Jane Addams was a public intellectual who promoted democratic inclusiveness, pacifism, internationalism, feminism and a pluralistic society in which assimilation did not mean an elimination of differences (Levine 1971: 569). She believed that public intellectuals had a duty not only to criticise but also to affirm: 'They could not just tear down. They, too, had to build' (Addams, quoted in Bethke Elshtain 2002a: xxix). Addams also assumed that writers and public intellectuals had a duty to instil in 'the educated a sense of social responsibility' (Eyerman 1994: 118). She was one of the progressive era's most effective social critics, who never adopted a narrowly moralist approach and who wrote 'the most discerning studies of industrial society to be found in the literature of social criticism' (Lasch 1965: xiv). Although she was the public intellectual who 'helped make "progressivism" and "social justice" respectable causes to be taken seriously' (Levy and Young 1965: vii), by calling for cooperative relationships and by embracing altruism she distinguished herself from other progressive intellectuals (Davis 1973: 201). She, more than any other contemporary progressive American intellectual, insisted on the pre-eminence of kinship with 'the other half' of humanity (Lasch 1966: xv).

Addams, like other progressive intellectuals, attempted to operate in the middle ground by ensuring that the expanding urban middle class was aware of the importance of knowledge, cooperation and democracy. Her insistence that the secret of success in all social action is cooperation and the harmony of her language, with which she propagated the brotherhood of all and fought for social justice, were both rooted in her belief in the possibility of finding common ground and mutual interests in a common cause. According to Addams' idea of civic activism, for democracy to function the entire community had to take an affirmative role in securing the welfare of all so that every citizen could participate in political life. Her call for the overcoming of social division and her search for a balanced solution challenged the usual divide between liberal and conservative views. Exploring ways to close the gap between humanitarian theory and action, Addams promoted reforms through direct action, but also argued that action had to be preceded by thought; that 'the activities of life can be changed in no other way than by changing the current ideas upon which it is conducted' (Addams [1910] 1925: 243). Her ability to imagine and to bring into being 'the astonishing institution', without which many would be much worse off (Bethke Elshtain 2002b: 254), made her voice more respected, as 'people listened to her not because her words seemed right, but also because she had put words into action at Hull House' (Levine 1971: xi).

In addition to her enthusiasm for the ideal of a common culture and 'practical knowledge', Jane Addams was also 'able to stand back from what she was doing even as she was doing it' (Bethke Elshtain 2002b: xxix). She never became a dogmatic practioner of her ideology, and always tended to favour flexible arrangements and more informal solutions that allowed for higher levels of adaptability and modification so as to include and adjust to the continuous flow of new data and information. It was her preferred way of running Hull House's affairs. She learned there to keep herself in 'readiness to modify and adapt' her undertakings ([1910] 1925: 135). Consequently, she propagated a strategy that 'should never lose its flexibility, its power of adaptation, its readiness to change its methods as the environment may demand' (135). Addams preferred to work behind the scenes, avoiding party politics, and she always favoured 'an unofficial commission or conference which would act as "negotiators" between sides' (Davis 1973: 116 and 237). She also learned in Hull House that 'life cannot be distorted by definite rules and regulations; that wisdom to deal with a man's difficulties comes only through some knowledge of his life and habits as a whole; and that to treat an isolated episode is almost sure to invite blundering' (Addams [1910] 1925: 162).

Addams' success in fulfilling her ambitions to become involved in public issues was possible because of her creative redrawing of her household boundaries 'to encompass an entire city – her "civic housekeeping" – as an alternative to domesticity and as a sphere of action' (Bethke Elshtain 2002a: xxxv). Her achievements were a result of creative literary and rhetorical talents. A part of Addams' success, aside from her own personal appeal, charisma and self-discipline, was her courage to speak out on the main social issues. The courage of her conviction and the wholeness of her vision, which 'never mistook the part for the whole' (Tims 1961: 14), meant that she often defended unpopular causes and that 'she stoutly rebelled against any trend to orthodoxy and conformity' (Douglas 1960: xix). Her contemporaries were often 'shocked by her advocacy of strange, even radical causes, but they respected her courage' (Levy and Young 1965: vii). 'Even when her views were at odds with public opinion, she never gave in, and in the end she regained the place of honour she had before in the hearts of her people' (Koht [1931] 2005: 2). Hence, Addams, who described herself as a 'writer and lecturer', was admired not only for her creativity but also for her courage (Knight 1997: 96).

Addams' achievements also depended upon the fact that she was integrated into supportive networks. Her success 'must have come from her ability to pick gifted people and to strengthen their hands as they worked. She recognized the capacities of those around her, no matter who they were' (Hall 1960: 4). Addams had very close relationships with several women friends, while in her daily activities she was surrounded by 'adoring disciples' (Davis 1973: 94). Her informal network of colleagues and collaborators was very extensive, and she met and knew many influential people from academia and other spheres of life. Her accomplishment in running Hull House, and her achievements in terms of industrial, labour and education reforms, as well as her efforts for the women's and peace movements, would not have been possible without groups of collaborators, mainly well-educated women keen, like Addams herself, to 'put theory into action' (Addams [1893] 2002b: 22).

Jane Addams' advocacy of communitarian ethics and her efforts to correct injustice, despite her lifelong nonconformity, earned her respect and admiration from many. Her uniqueness grew out of her gift for understanding and interpreting the economic and political realities of industrialising Chicago, and for putting her ideas on the national agenda, and out of her ability to initiate national debates. Addams' significance was rooted in her ability to communicate to the American public the main problems and difficulties faced by the immigrants in the cities, and to convince the nation that 'the welfare ideology, and ultimately the welfare state, were both right and practical' (Levine 1971: x).

Fridtjof Nansen: expanding responsibility from the national to the international level

Fridtjof Nansen (1861–1930) was awarded the Nobel Peace Prize in 1922 for his international humanitarian work in three areas: the repatriation of prisoners of war after the First World War (1920–2); providing food aid during the famine in Soviet Russia (1921–3); and work for refugees. Nansen was also a pioneering scientist, a researcher, an explorer, a public intellectual and a statesman. His successes in these fields made him a legend in his own time, and established his reputation as one who 'helped to mould the age' (Huntford 1998: 1).

In the last decade of the nineteenth century Norway, the junior partner in the union with Sweden, aspired to an independent status and therefore needed heroes. Nansen's national and international fame, his numerous writings[5] and his devotion to both national and international causes well equipped him for this role. His first ever crossing of Greenland and his Arctic expedition (which made the greatest strides towards reaching the North Pole for nearly four decades) put his name into the history books and gave Norwegians a sense of pride. Even today Nansen's status in Norway remains unchallenged, and he is still seen and celebrated as a national hero.[6] In 1999 readers of one of Norway's leading newspapers elected Nansen 'Norwegian of the century' (Stenersen, Libaek and Sveen 2001: 91).

Nansen's respected presence on the Norwegian public scene, as well as his influence with the public abroad, can be seen as a result of his capacity to bring together all his gifts and achievements in various fields in the service of three further goals: helping his nation to achieve its independence, contributing to the construction of a new world order after the First World War and organising humanitarian relief efforts. Although Nansen was successful in advancing all three of these causes, he always took on public duties rather reluctantly. Even though he enjoyed being a public figure, Nansen's public involvement was only ever in response to the needs and demands of either the nation or the international community. Among his many accomplishments and talents, being a scientist was his primary vocation, which he had chosen very early in his life (Hoyer 1957: 19).

Fridtjof Nansen's research career started in 1882, when, having studied zoology at the University of Christiania in Oslo, he was appointed curator of zoology at the Bergen Museum. He devoted his time to research, and, as he himself said, 'For six years I lived in a microscope; it was an entirely new world' (Nansen, quoted in Reynolds 1949: 25). Nansen, a promising young scientist, published many scientific articles, one of which won him the Bergen Museum gold medal in 1885. In 1887 he obtained his doctoral degree for the treatise that established his reputation as a pioneer researcher into the structure of the central nervous system. But he still had – as he wrote to his father – 'a sneaking longing for further experiences, for travel ...' (quoted in Reynolds, 1949: 31). Nevertheless, since for him the pursuit of science came 'first and exploration second' (Bain 1897: 150), he did not overlook science, and consequently both his expeditions – the Greenland expedition (1888–9) and the attempt to reach the North Pole (1893–6) – were for scientific purposes; the observations made during his expeditions represented enormous advances for meteorology and oceanography. Moreover, Nansen's accomplishments as an explorer were largely due to the fact that, as a scientist, he was able to predict and evaluate the difficulties that might be encountered, and he was accustomed to the careful planning of each task, paying attention to details, and the independence of scientific opinion.

The success and the boldness of Nansen's Greenland expedition and the bravery and imagination of the voyage of the *Fram* were enthusiastically recognised by the public, in Norway and abroad.[7] The Arctic expedition was proclaimed as 'the most magnificent victory of science and a proof that a scientific training, no less than courage, perseverance, and physical endurance, is necessary in an arctic explorer' (Bain 1898: 441). Although Nansen never actually managed to stand on either pole, his status as a 'father of modern polar exploration' has never been questioned because, without his inspiration, his brilliance in designing a special ship (the *Fram*) and his pioneering pieces of equipment, Roald Amundsen probably would not have made it to the South Pole and North Pole. With the passing of the years Nansen's polar explorations continue to be known and admired, as he successfully 'became the incarnation of the explorer as hero' (Huntford 1998: 1).

Nansen's Greenland expedition resulted in two books and brought him fame and an offer of a research job at the University of Christiania. In 1896 Nansen was made professor of zoology, and this position's high prestige, and the resources attached to it, gave him the best conditions possible for carrying out oceanographic research and investigating the scientific results of the *Fram* expedition. The publication of the findings, in six large volumes between 1900 and 1906, broke new grounds in oceanic research and established his reputation as the originator of the modern study of the polar seas and the present-day theory of wind-driven currents, as well as one of the founders of modern meteorology. In other words, Nansen, 'having already become one of the founders of neurology, had made himself the same in oceanography'

(Huntford 1998: 390). From 1896 to 1917 Nansen devoted most of his time and energy to scientific work, with the years 1896–1905 being 'the richest ones for science' (Hoyer 1957: 164). The life of a university researcher suited him, and he initiated the work that was to lead to a classic study of the Norwegian Sea.

Nonetheless, in 1905, at a moment of national crisis, Fridtjof Nansen took it 'upon himself to exploit his reputation abroad in order to advance the drive to Norwegian independence' (Huntford 1998: 398). He traded on his authority as a great explorer and as a known scientist to awake the international public to his nation's aspirations for independence as well as to convince his countrymen that a peaceful dissolution of the union was the best way forward. Through articles, a book, letters to newspapers, interviews, speeches and contacts with influential people,[8] Nansen campaigned to ensure that the main European powers supported a dissolution of the union with Sweden and that Norwegian public opinion backed a diplomatic way of ending the union. In 1905, as the drive to independence entered a critical phase, Nansen left the university in order to take part in the negotiations with Sweden. With independence achieved, he was asked to serve, from 1906, as his country's first ambassador to the United Kingdom. His achievements in representing Norway's interest brought him several offers of high political positions, but, more interested in pursuing his research, he formally resigned from the diplomatic service in 1908. As his interest shifted to oceanography, Nansen was appointed the first professor of oceanography at the University of Oslo, and started work on making Norway an important centre for oceanographic research. In the first decade of the twentieth century, as part of his scientific work, he was on several maritime expeditions, making observations that led to the publication of numerous papers and a book on the Norwegian Sea (1909). This and many other lasting contributions to oceanography, as well as his work on the history of polar exploration, further enhanced his scientific credentials.

In October 1918 Fridtjof Nansen was elected rector of the University of Christiania, but he refused the honour. When the First World War was over Nansen got involved in helping to create a new international order by strongly promoting the idea of the League of Nations. Although he did not consider himself a diplomat or a politician, Nansen believed it was 'his duty as an enlightened European citizen to help the suffering' (quoted in Vogt 2005: 8). When in 1920 the Council of the League of Nations asked him to organise the repatriation of prisoners of war, he accepted the challenge. In the same year he became Norway's first delegate to the League of Nations. From that moment, Nansen was to remain on the international stage as a central figure until his death (Abrams 1988: 96). Although Nansen the scientist had become over-shadowed by Nansen the humanitarian, 'nevertheless a scientist he was – heart and soul' as he continued, wherever he went and whatever he was doing, to collect facts and information, 'anything that might help to increase his knowledge of the world, its peoples and the laws' (Hoyer 1957: 262).

In 1922, as the High Commissioner for Refugees of the League of Nations, Nansen finalised the transport of some 430,000 soldiers from camps in Soviet Russia back to western Europe. His accomplishment of this task provided the League with its sole tangible result – 'only one thing done by the League' (Huntford 1998: 498). This success led to new duties; already in the summer of 1921 he had been given respon-sibility for two more humanitarian tasks. The first was to find homes for 1.5 million refugees from the Russian Revolution (Stenersen, Libaek and Sveen 2001: 90). Under his aegis and with the help of the Red Cross, the status of refugees was regularised and stateless people were granted a special, so-called 'Nansen', passport. The second task, which was to provide help to victims of the 1921–3 famine in the Soviet Union, encountered obstructions, mainly on account of the Western powers' fears that a food relief programme would strengthen the communist regime. Moreover, Nansen himself was seen as being naive and manipulated by Lenin, while his book *Russia and Peace* was perceived as further evidence of Nansen's pro-Soviet orientation (Vogt 2005; Huntford 1998). All the same, despite the Russian Relief Committee being dissolved by the League and despite the unwillingness of the member states to finance the aid, Nansen's aid programme continued. Although he was unable to obtain loans from any government, and therefore had to work outside the League and rely on private charity, his relief mission still saved 20 million people. But Nansen 'always thought that another 7 millions had needlessly died' (Abrams 1988: 97), and – in protest – he resigned his post as the League's High Commissioner for Refugees (Patterson Meyer 1959: 99).

The following year Fridtjof Nansen was nominated for the Nobel Peace Prize for his humanitarian work. In his Nobel address, Nansen ([1922] 2005: 6) did not hesitate to criticise those whom he saw as being responsible for the unnecessary deaths of several millions of the victims of the Soviet famine: 'In all probability their motives were political. They epitomize sterile self-importance and the lack of will to understand people who think differently.' Nansen's public role did not end with the Nobel Peace Prize, as the League of Nations then asked him to solve a dispute between Greece and Turkey. He organised the resettlement of both populations; by the end of 1924 the exchange was complete. Nansen also took on the cause of Armenian refugees; he publicised their fate in many articles and in a book, and he also developed a plan for the establishment of a homeland for them (Abrams 1988: 97). In 1926 Nansen accepted the honorary position of Lord Rector of the University of St Andrews, in the United Kingdom. Until this death he continued to write and speak on important public issues, as well as carrying out his research and planning a new polar expedition. His state-sponsored funeral (17 May 1930) attracted a large crowd and was used as a great occasion for nation building (Vogt 2005: 11). The Norwegian state proclaimed him a national hero, while the League of Nations paid tribute to him by creating a refugee organisation in his name.

It would appear that Nansen's many public projects succeeded because he was skilful at exploiting his international fame as an explorer and scientist. He was helped by the fact that it was an age 'in which personality still counted in policy' (Huntford 1998: 404). Much could be achieved by the magic of a name, and Nansen's reputation, charisma, 'celebrated charm', heroic aura and power to inspire people to act enabled him to sail 'into the centres of power as if he had been some national leader and not an itinerant spokesman for a suspect cause' (Huntford 1998: 404). Secondly, many of Nansen's achievements would have been impossible without his links with influential people and without the cooperation of his associates, colleagues and co-workers, who helped him to carry out his research, expeditions and humanitarian work. Nansen had many friends among national politicians and also among international statesmen, mainly in the United Kingdom. In Norway Nansen was a member of the so-called 'Lysaker Circle' of intellectuals and artists, whose works and inspiration figured prominently in the creation of Norwegian nationhood. One of the artists from this circle used Nansen as a model for the medieval Norwegian heroes, which 'neatly symbolised Nansen's elevation to a national totem' (Huntford 1998: 386). Nevertheless, despite Nansen being seen as a symbol of a national cause, his devotion to the idea of nationalism declined when the union with Sweden was dissolved, and he even started to warn against nationalism (Hoyer 1957: 260). Consequently, he soon became a 'stranger in his own country' (Huntford 1998: 535).

This rather complex character of Fridtjof Nansen's involvement in public life did not start with the normalisation of Norwegian politics, when independence was achieved. It was present right from the beginning of his public engagement, and is most poignantly illustrated by the complexity of the relationship between his private and public personas. Initially Nansen acted as the self-appointed private advocate of Norwegian interests, as an independent public intellectual who took it upon himself to advance the Norwegian drive to independence through his writings and public speeches. At the same time, however, he was treated abroad as an 'agent for the Norwegian government' (Huntford 1998: 411). On later occasions he acted as a private emissary for the Norwegian government, and sometimes as a representative of the Norwegian authorities. Even when he was formally appointed as the Norwegian delegate to the League of Nations, Nansen's position continued to be anomalous, as not only did he not draw a salary for his work, he also did not consider it his duty to follow the governmental line (Huntford 1998: 539). Because of his personal conviction that Germany should be admitted to the League, and to the confusion of his own foreign ministry, Nansen negotiated with the authorities in Berlin on his own responsibility and without any instructions from the League.

Nansen was aware that formal organisations could restrict his scope for manoeuvre and therefore preferred to rely on innovative ways out of any impasse, which often involved challenging the established rules and authorities, as well as accepting risk. His preparedness to take risks and to subvert the formal rules in situations when he thought the cause demanded it can be illustrated by his decision, while on a mission to negotiate with the Americans for food provisions for Norway, to sign an agreement securing large amounts of supplies 'on his own responsibility' without waiting for his government's approval of the conditions (Hoyer 1957: 215). Nansen's 'fertile genius' for inspiring solutions (Reynolds 1949: 222) was especially helpful in the functioning of his relief and aid missions. Failures to achieve some of his goals – as, for example, with his unsuccessful attempt in 1905 to convince the German authorities to support the Norwegian cause – Nansen blamed on the rigidity of formal rules: 'My journey wasted, blocked by a *wall of formalism*. My time and trouble thrown away' (quoted in Huntford 1998: 402; emphasis added).

Fridtjof Nansen, unwilling to adopt the accepted view and avoiding partisan politics, always preferred to be his 'own master and stand alone, as it makes a person more independent and less likely to be turned aside on to wrong paths by others' (quoted in Hoyer 1957: 260). He was persistent in his efforts to ensure the success of his ideas and projects. For example, in the case of his relief mission for the victims of famine in the Soviet Union, he had to struggle to 'clear a path through all barriers which stand between the victims of misfortune and their rescuers', and time and time again he 'turned to the League of Nations for moral support in his demand. In a powerful speech, the words of which still ring in our ears, he argued before the League of Nations that the rescue of millions from death by starvation should not be impeded by political consideration' (Stang [1922] 2005: 5). Nansen would always express and defend his views, whatever the cost involved; for instance, in the case of Greenland, to the disappointment of his patriotic friends he supported the Eskimos' interests rather than Norwegians' aspirations. The same conviction enabled him, despite being labelled 'a mouthpiece of the Soviet regime' and a 'Russia-fancier' (Huntford 1998: 513), to render assistance to the victims of the Soviet famine and the Armenians.

Although on the world stage Nansen argued for international cooperation as the 'only other salvation for mankind', saying: '[N]o practical politics are conceivable in a civilised society expect based on brotherly love, reciprocity, helpfulness, confidence' (quoted in Huntford 1998: 520), he could be quite authoritarian and elitist in domestic matters. These conflicting views, unorthodox strategies and the complexity of Nansen's charismatic personality, rooted in the combined effects of his confidence in his own abilities and his devotion to wider causes, are responsible for the existence of contrasting images of Nansen. Some saw him as 'a high-minded world improver' (Huntford 1998: 514), 'the hero with the big heart', the saviour of the suffering or 'Europe's conscience' (Hoyer 1957: 220), while others identified him as an authoritarian, self-centred individualist (Vogt 2005), 'a diplomatic privateer' and 'the Assembly's enfant terrible' (Hoyer 1957: 220).

Fridtjof Nansen's creative contributions in many fields, including science and public life, consisted of making observations and knowing what questions to ask. 'His role was that of the enunciator of principles. He was one of the great simplifiers' (Huntford 1998: 1). He turned from a study of 'the microcosm to that of the macrocosm' (Harvey Cushing, a founder of neurosurgery, quoted in Huntford 1998: 456). Nansen's creativity and courage made him successful as a scientist, as a polar explorer and as a public figure on the domestic and international stages. He brought together all the powers that had led to his achievements in the scientific and other fields in order to serve important national and humanitarian causes. His nationalism was a part of a 'spirit of the times', yet his internationalism and concern with victims and marginalised groups was unique and inspirational.

Elie Wiesel: fighting against indifference

Eliezer Wiesel (1928–), commonly known as Elie, the Nobel Peace Prize laureate for 1986, is 'the world's most famous Holocaust writer' (Stenersen, Libaek and Sveen 2001: 239). A Holocaust survivor, philosopher, humanitarian, journalist and teacher, he has dedicated his life to recording the horrors of the Holocaust and defending human rights wherever they are threatened.

Wiesel has written forty books to date in a variety of literary modes: novels, plays, dialogues, portraits and legends, as well as Hasidic, Talmudic and Biblical essays and tales.[9] For his literary and human rights activities, he has collected numerous awards.[10] He is also a scholar who has received more than 100 honorary degrees from institutions of higher education and is a member of the American Academy of Arts and Letters. At present Wiesel is Andrew W. Mellon Professor in the Humanities and University Professor at Boston University.

Elie Wiesel was born in Sighet, a small Transylvanian town (now in Romania) into a Jewish middle-class family. As a young boy he received a religious education. In the spring of 1944 Wiesel, his parents and three sisters were deported by the Nazis to a work camp attached to the Auschwitz-Birkenau extermination camp. His father, mother and younger sister perished. Elie, however, was sent on to the Buchenwald concentration camp in 1945 as a slave labourer. After the American liberation he was brought to France by a relief organisation. In 1948 he enrolled in the Faculty of Letters at the Sorbonne, where until 1951 he studied philosophy, earning his living as a choir director, a teacher of the Bible and a journalist. After his time at the Sorbonne he became the chief foreign correspondent for a Tel Aviv newspaper. As a young journalist, Wiesel travelled widely to collect stories for Jewish, French and American newspapers (Wiesel 1996).

In 1958, having been persuaded by François Mauriac, the 1952 Nobel Prize in Literature winner, Wiesel wrote and published his first book, *La Nuit* (translated into English as *Night* in 1960). The book, a memoir about his experiences in the death camps, became an international best-seller, and since then has been translated into more than thirty languages. In 1956 Wiesel was assigned to New York as a correspondent reporting on United Nations affairs for a leading Israeli newspaper. In the same year he was seriously injured in a car accident, and during his long convalescence, when he was almost deported as a stateless person, he applied for US citizenship, which he obtained in 1963. He described himself then as 'bit by bit moving from professional journalism', which no longer satisfied his creative aspiration, and turning to writing and teaching instead (Wiesel 1999: 14).

Elie Wiesel has become a prolific writer, publishing seven books during the 1960s alone and another twelve in the following decade. He also started to be sought as a public speaker; he lectured in many colleges and cities on the Bible, the Talmud, Hasidism and Jewish tradition, as well as on the Holocaust and the fate of other persecuted groups.

In 1972 he was appointed Distinguished Professor of Judaic Studies at the City College of New York, from which position he resigned after three years. Subsequently he joined the faculty of Boston University, where he remains to this day and continues to teach in the departments of philosophy and religion. The growing interest in Wiesel's writings has found expression in many conferences devoted to his work (starting with a conference entitled 'The work of Elie Wiesel and the Holocaust universe' in 1976) and in a number of honorary doctorates (the first one he received was in 1967). Wiesel's fiction has come to be seen as a significant contribution to the literature of testimony, not only because of its subject matter but also 'because of the way in which his narrators unfold their stories with words suspended by silence in the text' (Berman 2002: 9). This 'crucial and innovative narrative device, – the use of silence as an artistic strategy – has been acknowledged as Wiesel's unique solution to questions about the Holocaust (des Peres 1978: 57).

Since the end of the 1970s Wiesel, as a witness for truth and justice and as a survivor, has been accorded a 'respect bordering on reverence' (des Peres 1978: 49). In 1978 President Jimmy Carter asked him to chair the commission charged with proposing the manner in which to erect a monument to the memory of the Holocaust victims. Initially Wiesel (1999: 182) did not accept the offer: 'I don't think this position is for me. I am not a political person, I have no desire to become one … all I want is time to write and study.' In his role as the chairman of the President's Commission on the Holocaust, Wiesel recommended the creation of a national day of remembrance and the US Holocaust Memorial Museum. From 1980 to 1986 he acted as the founding chairman of the United States Memorial Council.

In the 1980s Elie Wiesel continued to pursue a distinguished scholastic career, teaching classes in Boston University as well as lecturing extensively at universities throughout the world. Through his writings and actions he became an outspoken defender of human rights and supporter of oppressed peoples. The liberation of Soviet Jewry became his most urgent cause, but he was also concerned with the fate of refugees and victims of oppression around the world. He defended the causes of Nicaragua's Native Americans and Cambodian refugees and protested against South African apartheid (Wiesel 1999: 146). He also took part in actions organised by humanitarian organisations; for example, in 1980 he participated in a march for the survival of Cambodia. 'I believe that when human beings suffer I have no right to be elsewhere. How could I have refused to go to the place were the refugees from the Cambodian massacres were dying of hunger and diseases?' (1999: 90).

Wiesel's increasingly important role in the national and international humanitarian movement, together with his growing visibility in the printed and electronic media, established his reputation as America's 'moral leader' (Abrams 1988: 248). His appeal to President Ronald Reagan not to participate in a wreath-laying ceremony at a German military cemetery at Bitburg, on the grounds that such a gesture could suggest that the fallen German soldiers and the murdered Jews were both 'victims' of Nazi oppression, further solidified his reputation. That incident took place in 1985, when, in recognition of Wiesel's contribution to the nation's moral standards, Reagan was presenting him with the Congressional Gold Medal in a ceremony at the White House, transmitted live by all the main television stations. In front of millions of television viewers, Wiesel implored the president not to make a planned visit to the military cemetery at Bitburg. 'That place, Mr President', Wiesel pleaded, 'is not your place. Your place is with the victims of the SS' (Wiesel 1995: 173). Wiesel's courage in directly confronting the political leader was widely appreciated, and he received hundreds of letters of support. 'By standing up to the most powerful man in the world, the former refugee in me had in just a few minutes touched a thousand times more people than I had with all my previous writings and speeches' (Wiesel 1999: 240).

In 1986 the Norwegian Nobel Committee's press release ([1986] 2006: 1) announced that the Peace Prize for that year was going to Elie Wiesel as 'as one of the most important spiritual leaders and guides in an age when violence, repression and racism continue to characterise the world'. The committee further declared that Wiesel was 'a messenger to mankind; his message is one of peace, atonement and human dignity' and that – with his message and through his practical work in the cause of peace – he was 'a convincing spokesman for the view of mankind and for unlimited humanitarianism' (1). Egil Aarvik ([1986] 2006: 1), chairman of the Norwegian Nobel Committee, in his presentation speech further reinforced the view that Wiesel has become a powerful spokesman for all victims and for humanity in general. Pointing out that the fight for freedom and human dignity – whether in Latin America, Asia, Europe or South Africa – had become Wiesel's life's purpose, Aarvik (2) stressed the universalism of Wiesel's message and the significance of his roles as a 'spiritual leader and guide'. Wiesel dedicated his 1986 Nobel Peace Prize to his fellow survivors, who 'have tried to do something with their memory, with their silence, with their life ... they have given an example to humankind not to succumb to despair' (Wiesel [1986] 2006: 1). He explained that he writes because the world 'had been silent during the Holocaust – that is why I swore never to be silent whenever and wherever human beings endure suffering and humiliation' (1). He finished his speech by saying that we 'must remember the suffering of my people, as we must remember that of the Ethiopians, the Cambodians, the boat people, Palestinians, the Mesquite Indians, the Argentinean "desaparecidos" – the list seems endless' (13).

The Nobel Prize has endowed Wiesel with recognition, a wider audience and higher prestige. Acquiring a larger forum and serving on numerous boards of trustees and advisers have allowed Wiesel to become a very effective spokesman for human rights wherever they are threatened. For example, in the early 1990s he lobbied the US government on behalf of the victims of ethnic cleansing in Bosnia and voiced his support for the victims of famine and genocide in Africa. Through his speeches, actions and writings, Wiesel supports the goals of international humanitarian organisations. The universalism of his stance against injustice is rooted in his assertion that, by denying victims' humanity, 'we betray our own' (Wiesel [1999] 2006: 4). Wiesel sees respect for human dignity and life as a creative force; since the opposite of love is not hate but indifference, 'indifference is never creative' (4).

The Nobel Peace Prize has also provided Elie Wiesel with money to establish the Elie Wiesel Foundation for Humanity, which he runs with his wife and which aims to advance the cause of human rights and peace throughout the world. The Foundation's projects reflect Wiesel's tendency to challenge the rules and the boundaries and his rather informal manners and actions. In line with his belief that people with their moral visions can inspire the world, the Foundation has been organising Nobel laureate conferences with the aim of initiating change and action (Wiesel 1999: 369). Since Wiesel believes that only 'those who fought for an idea and an ideal that went beyond themselves' (1996: 162) can provide moral leadership, and since one of the main aims of the Foundation is 'to exercise moral authority in crisis situations around the world' (Abrams 1988: 249), the Foundation brings together Nobel laureates and world leaders to discuss the issues of peace, justice and education. The same informal and direct strategy can be seen in Wiesel's other actions. He is prepared to cut through bureaucracy and use unorthodox informal strategies to ensure that his voice is heard. For instance, he interrupted his speech at the inauguration of the Holocaust Museum, turned to President Bill Clinton and 'urged him to do something – anything – to stop the bloodshed in Bosnia' (Wiesel 1999: 394). He relishes 'personal meetings, discussions, conferences, the exchange of ideas and recollections. The role of soul matchmaker suits me' (Wiesel 1999: 220). Elie Wiesel (1995: 76) celebrates friendship as the most important part of life experience, as it is 'never anything but sharing', and relies on his informal network of very influential friends, which has included presidents and prime ministers (for example, Golda Meir, the Clintons and François Mitterrand, with whom he wrote a book: *Memoir in Two Voices*).

Wiesel, 'one of the most-known Jews in the United States' (Berman 2001: 17), is frequently criticised and attacked from both sides of the political spectrum, as well by Jews (both from Israel and from the Diaspora) and by non-Jews. Some of the very outspoken critics claim that Wiesel is concerned only with the Jewish victims of the Holocaust. In his response to this criticism Wiesel stresses that, even as he believes that 'not all the victims of the Holocaust were Jews but all the Jews were victims', he also acknowledges that one of the main questions is how to reconcile 'the purely Jewish aspects of the tragedy with its inevitable universal connotations' (Wiesel 1999: 180). While accepting that the dilemma of how to balance the victims who were specifically Jewish with the universality of all victims cannot easily be solved, Wiesel asserts that the universality of the Holocaust must be realised in its uniqueness. 'Remove the Jews from the Holocaust, and the event loses its mystery' (1995: 110). He understands the imperfection, the risks and the complexity of his stance, and that this makes him a 'target'; 'either as a symbol of something or as a witness whose testimony is troubling I have always rejected the notion of myself as a symbol' (1999: 6). In other words, he shows what Alfred Adler called 'the courage of imperfection', which exists in writers' willingness not to shy away from complex and ambiguous answers in their search for the truth (Adler, quoted in Cargas 1976: 98).

Elie Wiesel is also criticised for his silence on the Israeli–Arab conflict. It seems that his rather complex stand on this issue is a result of his devotion to Israel, on the one hand, and his conviction that indifference to human suffering 'makes the human being inhuman' ([1999] 2006: 4) on the other hand. Although he admits that he may be guilty of idealising Israel, he also declares that, as a Diaspora Jew, he cannot take a public stand on the Israeli–Arab conflict outside Israel because, 'since I do not live in Israel, it would irresponsible for me to do it' (1999: 128). Thus, 'when I feel that I must raise the voice, I do it in Israel' (134). Hence, Wiesel pays a double price: not only for not criticising Israel from outside but also for voicing his criticism from inside, within Israel. For example, when in 1974, after the Yom Kippur War, he expressed in the Israeli media his criticism of the hostilities, the Israeli prime minister, Golda Meir, asked him to 'take it back', while the Israeli press cried: 'How dare someone who lives in America tell us what to do' (1999: 60). More importantly, he does not want to be a neutral spectator to the suffering of the Palestinians. Wiesel recognises that the

Palestinian people has 'the right to fulfill its destiny' (1996: 310), and when Palestinians' human rights are violated, even when he knows that what he is saying will displease many in Israel, he voices his condemnation. For example, after the massacre of thirty Palestinians as they prayed in Hebron, he expressed his outrage in a speech given before the European Council in Strasbourg (1999: 135).

Another criticism of Wiesel's stance refers to his role in turning the Holocaust into 'the Holocaust industry'. Norman Finkelstein (2000) accuses Wiesel and the American Jewish establishment of using the Holocaust to enhance their own standing with American elites. But putting the blame on Wiesel for today's over-abundance of information about the Holocaust – the 'banalization of the Holocaust' and 'the marketization' of the Holocaust – overlooks Wiesel's own strong opposition to the process of memory commercialisation and trivialisation. He protests against the exploitation of the Holocaust by the media and business, fights against publishers' exploitation of the topic, and complains that there are too many Holocaust scholars and that 'we have come to the point where Jewish survivors no longer dare to speak out, [as] the others always know better' (1999: 122–3).

Elie Wiesel (1999: 389) sees his role above all as a writer, yet this vocation was not his choice but was thrust upon him as a survivor and a witness. He writes about the Holocaust because of his vow to keep the memory alive of those who did not survive. To forget nothing is 'the obsession of survivors; to plead for the dead, to defend their memory and honour' (1999: 380). For him, recollection is a powerful tool in the quest for understanding, justice and knowledge. Memory is a key element of his work, as it raises consciousness, restores dignity and gives life meaning. Since to 'forget constitutes a crime against memory, against justice', a writer is duty-bound to give meaning to his survival (Wiesel, interviewed in Berman 2001: 169). Thus, he does not believe in art for art's sake, and claims that 'literature must have an ethical dimension' (1999: 336). In his case, life and art are inseparable: his literature is a matter of his entire personality and his moral vision. It would 'be senseless' to separate Wiesel the man from Wiesel the artist, or his work from events in the world (des Peres 1978: 49). Wiesel (1999: 389) values the freedom and independence of his vocation, and stresses that he has never been attracted to any political ideology or party and that he does belong to any organisation or movement. 'When I take a stand, I commit to no one but myself. Sometimes I am right, often I am not. So what? I learn from my mistakes' (1999: 33). At the same time, however, the task of the writer, according to him, is 'not to appease or flatter, but to disturb, to warn. To question by questioning oneself'

(61). This leads him to ask himself which is more important, thought or action? In answering this question, Wiesel seems to accept the Jewish Masters' opinion: 'Study comes first, because study incites action' (47).

This inseparability of thought and action and the wholeness of life and art are two of the most fundamental characteristics of Wiesel's position that make him fit our category of hero. Furthermore, he, like other heroes, believes that one person can change the world, and that there may be times 'when we are powerless to prevent injustice, but there must never be a time when we fail to protest' (1995: 147). Our self-respect, writes Wiesel (1999: 220), demands that we choose danger over resignation. We should never stop yearning and fighting for justice: 'As long as one dissident is in prison, our freedom will not be true. As long as one child is hungry, our lives will be filled with anguish and shame. What all these victims need above all is to know that they are not alone' ([1986] 2006: 3).

Elie Wiesel's charismatic presence, his moral authority, his prolific writing and his role as a 'messenger to humanity' have ensured his international reputation as a 'witness for truth and justice' (Aarvik [1986] 2006: 1). Wiesel may oppose questioning the uniqueness of the Holocaust, but his message has a universal character. His work stands for the fight for freedom and human dignity and encompasses all who suffer, while at the same time reaffirming the principle that we have to remember past injustices.

The wholeness of life and work

Jane Addams, Fridtjof Nansen and Elie Wiesel are heroes because of their symbolic value for their respective communities. What makes their status outstanding has to do first with their unique position as, respectively, a creative thinker, a scientist and a writer and second with their civil courage in the public sphere, where they exhibited faith in the power of reason and belief in the potential for change in and the mutability of society. As well as expanding the boundaries of the private and the public, and combining realism with idealism, action with thought, they inspired others with their moral visions and showed people how to get things done by challenging the rules and by skilfully activating networks of informal contacts to achieve their aims. If we ask what further unites Addams, Nansen and Wiesel – or, in short, what the meaning is of our label 'hero' – an answer would be that, apart from their creative minds and the fact that they had the courage of their convictions, it is the wholeness of their life and their work. Their life and their work are interwoven to such a degree that it is almost impossible to tell them apart.

A thinker, a scientist and a writer, their interventions in national and international debates were almost invariably polemical, and occasionally catalytic. Addams, Nansen and Wiesel all had a unique base for their engagement with the public. They were charismatic people of many talents, aspirations and interests combined with confidence in their own abilities and their devotion to wider causes. Even more crucially, they knew how to bring all their powers together in the service of their important goals. They used their social and cultural capital accumulated in one area – to put it another way, their creative achievements earned in one field – to fight courageously for their causes in other areas. As heroes they never wavered in preferring their scientific, artistic or creative interests to a political career, resisting offers of political positions and avoiding partisan politics. Nonetheless, all three of our heroes were actively engaged in promoting the long-term interests of society, thereby performing a social role of exceptional value. Their success in questioning and challenging established rules and views came as a result of the connectedness of their thoughts and actions. They avoided a great many of the pitfalls that trap unrealistic idealists or extreme radicals because they did not believe in being dogmatic, following instead the path of compromise, mediation and searching for the middle ground, all of which allowed them to occupy centre stage in public debates. For example, Addams, unlike many social reformers who are strict followers of their own specific programmes, was capable of being very flexible and adopting a non-dogmatic stance (Bethke Elshtain 2002a: xxix). The heroes' courage, paraphrasing Aristotle, was rooted in their ability to find the middle ground between bravery and cowardice, or between conformity and rebellion. They were not too radical, as they were not attacking the vary bases of the system or the state; nonetheless, their attitudes towards the political process, expressed in their calls for change to many of its essential principles and rules, were more than those of moderate reformers. They can be described as realistic idealists.

Although each of these heroes lived in different societies, and although only Addams and Nansen shared the same historical time, there were nonetheless some similarities in their contexts. During the main part of their lives, for example, all three faced relatively well-structured formal systems with prescribed roles and clear boundaries – in the case of Addams and Nansen nineteenth-century society's restrictions and norms, in the case of Wiesel his religious context. Despite the temporal instability of their respective political, social and economic environments as a result of warfare (in the case of Addams and Nansen the First World War, while young Wiesel tragically experienced the Second World War), the dominant parts of their careers and lives played out in relatively secure and stable environments. They all registered a high level of social recognition and acceptance, which allowed them to undertake their unorthodox actions of expanding boundaries and challenging the formal rules.

The heroes' success was also due to their capacity to construct wide networks of friends and colleagues, which – in turn – enhanced the achievement of their goals. The configuration of Addams', Nansen's and Wiesel's networks facilitated the pursuit of their autonomous lines of interest because all three of them were gifted in constructing and maintaining strong informal ties, the strength of which positively influenced the outcome of their various actions. Even more importantly, the heroes' central location within a number of informal networks (for example, Addams' central position within her women's circle and her friendship with the University of Chicago professors) enabled them to bridge, bond or transfer resources (such as reputations, credentials, authorities, contacts) from one network to another (Lin 2001: 71). Taking into account the nature of their networks, and the nature of their contexts, it can be said that the cost of nonconformity for the heroes was relatively insignificant.

What is it that differentiates heroes from pioneers, champions and dissidents? Heroes, unlike dissidents, are not so much critics of power, although this does not mean that they always go along with the dominant views or attitudes. On the contrary, they question and challenge them when such a course of action is necessary to promote the long-term interests of society. Heroes, unlike dissidents, are not alienated or excluded from society; rather, they are integrated into it, and, moreover, they have authority and positions of influence within it. Heroes differ from champions, as their aspirations reach beyond one-sided views, and they exemplify excellence in generalised pursuits rather than in a narrow specialisation. For instance, Addams did not pursue or act in the name of any specific interest and insisted on being good not 'to people' but 'with people' (Brown Bissell 2004: 2). Heroes do have a lot in common with pioneers, as both types contribute to change. They also share a strong theme in breaking new ground. Nevertheless, heroes, in contrast to pioneers and dissidents, become famous, achieving a status as a public figure whose image as a 'hero' (Nansen), 'a benevolent saint' (Addams) or 'a messenger of humanity' (Wiesel) takes on a life of its own. The symbolic importance and the legacy of all three representatives of this category have given a sense of pride to their respective communities.

Furthermore, heroes exhibit a high degree of independence and autonomy, while at the same time enjoying authority and popularity within their respective communities. To sum up, a hero is someone who is recognised by the public as an intellectual leader with great sensitivity to collective problems and whose own image is supplanted by a legend.

Heroes are public intellectuals whose unconventional and courageous actions support and enhance their communities' well-being and moral outlook. The cases of these three heroes show the importance of civic activism as a way of enhancing social cooperation, inclusive democracy, universal human rights and political altruism, not as 'an agreeable ornament to social life' but as 'its fundamental basis' (Durkheim, quoted in Passy 2001: 3). Although civil courage and altruism are not identical notions, they can, under some conditions, overlap, mainly due to the fact that in some circumstances there is a need for courage in order to carry out altruistic actions. Civil courage is a necessary element in altruistic behaviour when the functioning of civil society is restricted. This is especially the case with dissidents, the subject of the next chapter.

Notes

1 Jane Addams wrote prolifically on a wide range of issues for scholarly journals and for mass-circulation magazines, such as *Ladies' Home Journal* ('a politically serious magazine at the time'), *McClure's* and *The American Magazine* (Bethke Elshtain 2002a: xxv). Some of her most important books are: *Democracy and Social Ethics* (1902), *Newer Ideals of Peace* (1907), *The Spirit of Youth and the City Streets* (1909), *Twenty Years at Hull House* (1910), *The Long Road of Woman's Memory* (1916) and *Peace and Bread in Time of War* (1922). Recently her writings have been collected in Jean Bethke Elshtain's book *The Jane Addams Reader* (2002), and they are also available in the collection edited by Emily Cooper Johnson, *Jane Addams: A Centennial Reader* (1960).

2 Addams' support resulted in many reforms, such as Illinois's first factory inspection act (1883), the establishment of its first juvenile court (1899), investigations into city sanitary and health conditions and laws to restrict child labour (Alonso 1994: 203). Addams used her influence to support legislation protecting female factory workers, ensuring compulsory school attendance and improving workers' conditions and industrial safety regulations. She was part of a wider network of organisations; for example, she was a leader in the Consumer League and served as the first women president of the National Conference of Charities and Correction, was a chairwoman of the Labor Committee of the General Federation of Women's Clubs and served on the Chicago School Board (Davis 1973).

3 Addams was the first woman to receive an honorary doctorate from Yale University (1910), and this was followed by numerous honorary degrees, including from Wisconsin University, Northwestern University, the University

of Chicago and the University of California. She was also awarded Bryn Mawr's M. Cary Thomas Prize (1931) and received the *Pictorial Review* award for 'the woman who in her special field has made the most distinguished contribution to American life' (Alonso 1994: 215).

4 In *Democracy and Social Ethics* (1902), Addams argued that a new social ethics was needed to solve social conflicts and to address the problems of urban life in industrial cities. She insisted that society should develop a higher type of collective social morality, in which the individual 'shall be willing to lose the sense of personal achievement, and shall be content to realize his activity only in connection with the activity of the many' (275, 206).

5 Fridtjof Nansen's scientific books, such as *The Norwegian North Pole Expedition 1893–1896: Scientific Results* (published in six volumes between 1900 and 1906) and *In Northern Mists* (published in 1910–11), are still classics and required reading. His *Norwegian Sea* (1909) remains 'an historical milestone from the beginning of oceanography and a classic of its kind' (Huntford 1998: 456). Nansen's books about his Greenland expeditions, *The First Crossing of Greenland* (published in two volumes in 1890) and *Eskimo Life* (1891), were very popular, engaging and uplifting tales of discovery. His other non-scientific books, such as *Norway and the Union with Sweden* (1905), *Russia and Peace* (1923) and *Armenia and the Near East* (1928), discussed the most important public issues of the day.

6 For example, the website of the Norwegian Ministry of Foreign Affairs (http://odin.dep.no/odin/engelsk/norway/history/032005-990458/index-dok000-b-n-a.html) presents Nansen as a national hero, one of the greatest Norwegian men. 'The Nansen heritage', based on Nansen's humanitarian activities in the 1920s, is actively used nowadays by politicians in Norway as a symbol for a Norwegian humanitarian tradition and to strengthen the country's images as a peace arbitrator (Vogt 2005).

7 Nansen's fame as an explorer brought him many scientific rewards, distinctions and honorary degrees (among others, from Oxford and Cambridge Universities) and invitations to become a member of various geographical and scientific societies. For example, in 1891 he received from the British Royal Geographical Society the Victoria Medal for 'all valuable and scientific results of his expedition' (Bain 1898: 44). In the spring of 1892 he delivered twenty-nine lectures in the United Kingdom, where he was known to every newspaper reader not only as the hero of the day but also as 'a man of science, a graduate from an institution of learning, a specialist in more than one branch of natural history, and a man who knew how to write' (Bain 1898: 106).

8 Nansen played an important role in ensuring the peaceful dissolution of Norway's union with Sweden, through his writing (for example, in his first book to address public issues, *Norway and the Union with Sweden*, published in 1905), public speaking, lecture tours and lobbying. His patriotic speeches during the public celebrations of his return from the polar expedition were followed by a succession of articles in Norwegian magazines and newspapers, which constituted his manifesto on the question of national sovereignty (Huntford 1998: 400, 420).

 9 The list of Elie Wiesel's books and articles is very long. Among others, it includes *Night* (1958), *Dawn* (1960), *The Accident* (1961), *The Town beyond the Wall* (1964), *The Jews of Silence* (1966), *The Gates of the Forest* (1966), *Legends of Our Time* (1968), *A Beggar in Jerusalem* (1970), *One Generation* (1970), *Souls on Fire* (1972), *Night Trilogy* (1972), *The Oath* (1973), *Ani Maamin* (1973), *Zalmen or the Madness of God* (1974), *Messengers of God* (1974), *A Jew Today* (1976), 'Why I write' (1978), *Four Hasidic Masters* (1978), *Images from the Bible* (1980), *From the Kingdom of Memory* (1995), *All Rivers Run to the Sea: Memoirs* vol. I, *1928–1969* (1996) and *And the Sea is Never Full: Memoirs* vol. II, *1969–* (1999).

10 Amongst the many literary honours bestowed on Wiesel are the Prix Rivarol (1964), the Prix Médicis and the Prix Livre Inter (1980), the Jewish Heritage Award (1966), the National Jewish Book Council's award and the Médaille de Vermeil. For his human rights activities, Wiesel has received the Congressional Gold Medal (1985), the Medal of Liberty Award and the rank of Grand-Croix in the French Légion d'honneur (Wiesel 1999).

7 Dissidents: peaceful rebels

Intellectuals becoming political

In Bertolt Brecht's play *The Land of Galileo*, a character says to the scientist who has denied his beliefs to avoid torture: 'Pity the land that has no heroes.' To which Galileo replies: 'Pity the land that needs heroes.' This exchange illustrates that, while the hero is the man or woman who lets no obstacle prevent him or her from pursuing the ideas he or she has chosen, it is the oppressive context that makes the scientist into the defender of the threatened values. It also helps us to understand why powers that do not encourage a variety of opinions are uneasy with heroic dissidents.

The first dissident, according to William Safire (1993), was the biblical Job, who questioned God's sense of justice, thus endorsing our rights to make demands on unjust authority and making us morally obliged to hold those in power accountable. Socrates, Jesus Christ and Galileo Galilei are frequently mentioned as ones who courageously defended their convictions. The British Enlightenment in the late eighteenth century, according to Roy Porter (2001), was characterised by a vibrant culture of dissent, with dissenting academics offering alternative ideas to the prevailing orthodoxies. The impact of dissidents such as Tom Paine and, later, intellectuals such as John Stuart Mill and R. II. Tawney was crucial in defining the core principles of public life, namely tolerance, diversity, pluralism and civic consciousness. In the American tradition, the justifications for dissent and arguments about its role are illustrated by Henry David Thoreau's *Resistance to Civil Government* ([1849] 2005) and Martin Luther King's *Letter from Birmingham Jail* (1963). According to Thoreau, citizens worthy of the name must withdraw their support of an unjust system. King, influenced by Thoreau and Gandhi, argued that non-violent dissenting citizens help publicise inequality and injustice (Sparks 1997: 88–90). Before the collapse of the Berlin Wall, Havel, Aleksandr Solzhenitsyn, Andrei Sakharov and Natan Sharansky were the best-known dissidents in terms of challenging the human rights record of their governments.

The significance of dissent is also reflected in common wisdom. Here the Hans Christian Andersen fable *The Emperor's New Clothes* is a good illustration of the importance of scepticism towards the conventional answers, refusing to take anything for granted and the freshness of clear vision. This tale offers us a broad definition of dissidents as people who 'reject the pressures imposed by others, [and] perform valuable social functions, frequently at their own expense' (Sustein 2003: v). Yet such a definition, by stressing the rejection of the views that most people hold, or nonconformity, fails to grasp the uniqueness of dissent. The majority of dictionary definitions make it clear that dissidents are more than nonconformists, in that they are people who actively oppose an established opinion, policy or structure, people who embark upon altering society and act on the strength of their convictions. They are contestants, objectors, protestors who confront and challenge the prevailing political and social values. The notion of dissident, in other words, encompasses 'the often creative oppositional practices of citizens who, either by choice or (much more commonly) by forced exclusion from the institutionalized means of opposition, contest current arrangements of power from the margins of the polity' (Sparks 1997: 76).

The term 'dissident', moreover, is most often used to refer to political dissidents, usually opposing non-democratic regimes, typically totalitarian or authoritarian. In such systems all opposition is potentially dangerous, as 'no distinction can be made between acceptable and unacceptable opposition, between loyal and disloyal opposition, between opposition that is protected and opposition that must be repressed' (Dahl 1973: 13). Consequently, if all forms of opposition are treated as dangerous and subject to repression, opposition that would be loyal, if it were tolerated, becomes disloyal because it is not tolerated. 'Since all opposition is likely to be disloyal, all opposition must be repressed' (Dahl 1973: 13). In terms of Hirschman's (1970) analysis of 'voice', 'exit' and 'loyalty', political dissent can be seen as the 'voice' of the criticism of the policies, values or structures of a government that does not tolerate criticism. Although, under official pressure, dissidents could be forced to 'exit', they tend not to leave freely as leaving, like silence, means failure to participate in collective political engagement. Neither do dissidents simply change their minds, or remain silent, even when they are prosecuted. 'Instead, to dissent is to maintain a principled oppositional stance against a more powerful group while remaining politically and publicly engaged' (Sparks 1997: 83).

When all opposition is treated as dangerous and is subject to repression, dissidents, unable to voice their opinion and under pressure of persecution, are likely to become radicalised. In other words, the difficulty of 'voice', which increases when the official policy of repression is accelerated, combined with outrage and despair, might prompt the further politicisation of dissenters and their search for alternative orders and solutions to their societies' problems. Nonetheless, dissidents, while expressing opposition in a system that does not allow for opposition, are constantly challenged by their own apparent futility. Thus, they do not see themselves as reformers acting in the real expectation of being able to influence policy and events. 'Instead, their inner compulsion is a moral one. An obligation to speak out against perceived injustice. It makes them optimists without concrete hope' (Friendly 1979: xv). This attitude also distinguishes dissidents' radical protest from calls for revolution or insurrection. They do not campaign for the replacement of political leaders or the destruction of the system; their protest is limited 'to articulating and dramatizing the "message" in ways that will appeal to the normative orientations of the intended receivers' (Biddulph 1975: 97).

In our typology, the category of dissidents is defined by its location in the formalised system characterised by a high level of risk for public intervention – or, in other words, by a high cost for nonconformity. Dissidents are public intellectuals who are defiant of formal rules in societies in which the centre of power is remote and the sphere of individual autonomy is limited. They are radicalised intellectuals who display the exceptional courage demanded in societies that, by imposing a high level of impersonal control and a high cost for dissent, encourage risk avoidance and enhance reliance on informal networks.

In our sample of the public intellectuals who received the Nobel Peace Prize there are three dissidents who defended and protected civic rights. They are Carl von Ossietzky, Andrei Sakharov and Adolfo Pérez Esquivel.

Carl von Ossietzky: a symbol for the 'other Germany'

Carl von Ossietzky (1889–1938), Nobel Peace Prize laureate for 1935, was a German public intellectual, journalist and writer who was editor-in-chief of the most influential journal of Weimar Germany's non-partisan leftist intellectuals, *Die Weltbühne* (The World Stage). Ossietzky wrote many articles on foreign policy and political and social issues as well as theatrical and literary reviews.[1] He 'was a first-class journalist and man of great courage', whose opposition to Nazism radicalised his stance (Deak 1968: 6). Ossietzky urged the Germans to create a progressive, democratic and just nation under civilian leadership, and worked for Germany's admission to the League of Nations and for the rebuilding of a peaceful Europe. For his stand against militarism and authoritarianism, Ossietzky was imprisoned in a concentration camp by the newly elected Nazi regime in 1933. Prevented from accepting the Nobel Peace Prize in person, Ossietzky died in 1938 as 'the most famous prisoner of the Third Reich and a rallying point in the fight against Nazism' (Stenersen, Libaek and Sveen 2001: 120).

Carl von Ossietzky was born in Hamburg, to which his parents had moved from Upper Silesia. His Catholic father died when Carl was two years old. His Lutheran mother's second husband, Gustav Walther, a sculptor and a social democrat, introduced him to liberal views and Hamburg's social democratic intellectual circle. With the help of his father's friends, Ossietzky was able to receive a very good education. Although he refused to enter university he was 'passionately interested in literature and history', and his aspiration was to become a writer (Frei 1971b: 13). Intellectually a self-made man, he became nonetheless 'remarkably erudite and cosmopolitan' (Deak 1968: 50).

He started to earn his living working as an assistant court clerk in Hamburg. By his early twenties Ossietzky had published poetry, book reviews and theoretical reviews in several periodicals (Abrams 1988: 108). In 1908 he joined the Democratic Association and in 1912 the German Peace Society, which were both 'progressive upper bourgeoisie organizations' (Deak 1968: 50). These movements formed Ossietzky's political convictions, and he remained 'faithful to the end to the philosophies of these movements: social justice, peace through international disarmament, free thought and militant anticlericalism' (Deak 1968: 51). From 1913 Ossietzky regularly sent articles about pacifist and social democratic movements to *Das Freie Volk* (The Free People), the voice of progressive writers and activists from social democratic circles. Here also Ossietzky published an article criticising German militarism, for which he was for the first time summoned to appear in court and charged with 'an insult to common good' and fined (Wasson 1987: 785). By this time Ossietzky had already gave up his job as a clerk and devoted himself to journalism, 'writing radical articles for little-known journals, and holding literary lectures for small groups' (Frei 1971b: 14). Even before the outbreak of the First World War the quality of his writing, developed as a result of his artistic and professional ambitions, had established him as a 'full-fledged left-wing intellectual for whom nothing seemed impossible' (Deak 1968: 51).

In 1913 Carl von Ossietzky married Maud Woods, an English nurse born in India who was a pacifist and a feminist, and whose education and money gave him 'the necessary impetus to a writing career'

(Deak 1968: 51). During the First World War, because of his poor health, Ossietzky was not called up for military service until 1916. His war experiences in the trenches in France confirmed his pacifist ideas and his feelings of responsibility for the future of Germany. On his return to Hamburg he became president of the local chapter of the German Peace Association and founded a short-lived periodical *Der Wegweiser* (The Signpost) (Wasson 1987: 786). Invited to act as the association's secretary, Ossietzky moved to Berlin in 1919.

After the war Ossietzky, through his writing and speeches, established his reputation as a supporter of social democracy, a pluralistic society, anti-militarism and pacifism. In 1920 he resigned from his secretarial duties because he could not combine them with his journalism. Still loyal to the pacifist cause, he added to his pacifist convictions a growing sympathy for socialism. Seeing the struggle for social justice as his ethical obligation meant that his articles from now on critically addressed not only the problems of German politics but also the issues of social justice. Between 1919 and 1924 he was a member of the staff of the *Berliner Volks-Zeitung* (Berlin People's Paper), a democratic, non-partisan and anti-war newspaper. Now 'a full-fledged Berlin journalist and no longer unknown', Ossietzky flourished there (Deak 1968: 55). In 1921 he became an editor of *Nie Wieder Krieg* (No More War), the Peace League's journal, and an active participant in its actions, mainly by delivering public speeches (Stenersen, Libaek and Sveen 2001).

In the early years of the Weimar Republic, between 1920 and 1924, Carl von Ossietzky, still full of hopes for the republic, wrote well-documented articles, moderate in tone, in which he called for the democratisation of the judiciary, social reforms and the removal of the old bureaucracy (Deak 1968: 57). In 1924 he joined the staff of *Das Tagebuch* (The Journal), a relatively moderate political weekly. For the next two years, as a responsible editor of the journal and a contributor, he carried out his campaign against German militarism, which he saw as the main enemy of democratic development in the country. From that time on he became 'more and more negative about the republican movement', as well as more sceptical about the 'wisdom of the masses' (Grossman 1963: 107). Gradually he developed a programme for action that was no longer in support of but against the Weimar Republic. By the late 1920s Ossietzky's resentment at the failure of the socialists to create a democratised Germany had reached such a level that he was writing articles calling on the leaders of the republic to combat the threats to democracy from both 'extremes of left and right' (Frei 1971b: 6), and to carry out reforms that would 'reconcile at least the Left extremists to the republic' (Deak 1968: 57).

From 1926 Ossietzky was affiliated to *Die Weltbühne*, the literary, non-partisan journal of leftist intellectuals who considered themselves the 'tribunes of the German people' (Deak 1968: 20). A year later, after the death of Siegfried Jacobsohn, the founder of the journal, Ossietzky was appointed editor-in-chief. Under him *Die Weltbühne* achieved world renown as 'one of the main forums of critical journalism in Germany' (Stenersen, Libaek and Sveen 2001: 121) as it gained in seriousness and universality and 'became more gracious and respectable, in the moral, if not in the political sense' (Deak 1968: 60). Ossietzky, already one of the best in his profession, wrote 'with elegance but also simply'; 'his sources of information were unimpeachable and above all, he had the courage of his convictions' (Deak 1968: 61). In the journal, in addition to theatrical and literary reviews, Ossietzky published well-informed critical political articles addressed to the educated public. He voiced serious concern over the fact that ultra-nationalist forces were strengthening their positions, and aimed to weaken the prestige of the army and keep up the pressure for the democratisation of the republic. His articles exposed the increasing power of the 'Black Reichswehr' (the paramilitary forces), which was becoming a 'state within the state'.

In October 1927 Carl von Ossietzky was charged with condemning the paramilitary organisations, tried for libel and sentenced to one month in prison, although the appeal hearing changed the verdict to a monetary fine (Fiedor 1986: 67). Undeterred, Ossietzky continued writing articles describing the secret training and recruitment carried out by the Reichswehr. He also wrote articles denouncing the judicial system and revealed the increasing number of sentences for 'betrayal of the nation' (Fiedor 1986: 80). In 1929, when *Die Weltbühne* published an article by Walter Kreiser, an aviation expert, that exposed the German aviation industry's rearmament in violation of the Treaty of Versailles, Ossietzky again came into conflict with the government. In 1931 both Ossietzky, as the editor, and Kreiser were indicted for 'espionage and treason' (Fiedor 1986: 68). During the trial Ossietzky's pacifist past was the main problem for the judges, who, being in favour of a strong army, considered the terms 'pacifism' and 'nation' to be mutually exclusive (Oppenheimer 2004: 359). Despite the fact that Ossietzky took upon himself complete responsibility, and despite his defence of Kreiser, they were both sentenced to eighteen months in prison for 'betrayal of military secrets', while the copies of *Die Weltbühne* were destroyed (Fiedor 1986: 68).

The harshness of the sentence can be attributed to several factors. Firstly, it reflected the political context in which 'the citizen is no longer asked how he feels toward the republic but whether or not he is zealous about bearing arms' (Ossietzky, quoted in Frei 1971a: 203). Secondly, it was due to the growing irritation of the Reichswehr Command with the anti-militaristic campaign of *Die Weltbühne*. Thirdly, 'Ossietzky was a victim of the reinvigorated administrative campaign against anti-militarism' (Deak 1968: 192). Ossietzky, unlike Kreiser, who shortly after his trial fled Germany, refused to leave the country. 'If you wish to fight effectively against rottenness in a nation, you must do it on the inside' (Ossietzky, quoted in Patterson Meyer 1978: 105). He was determined to turn the circumstances of his conviction into a major political issue. In 'Account rendered', an article published in *Die Weltbühne* on the day on which Ossietzky had to start his prison sentence, after defining himself as 'the dissenter' and pointing out the dilemma of subsequent German refugees, he explained that he preferred to become 'a living symbol of protest' and therefore an 'embarrassment to the government' (quoted in Frei 1971a: 89). He wrote that an 'oppositionist who goes abroad soon finds no echo in his own country', while one who 'wishes to fight effectively against the poisoned spirit of a country must share that country's general fate' (89). Ossietzky hoped that his arrest as the editor of a popular leftist, non-communist journal would help to create a broad anti-fascist front: 'However attractive and flattering to Kreiser and myself are all these expressions of sympathy, the issue should not rest here. Let us turn this movement of protest into a political campaign against the powerful forces of counterrevolution ... The time for individual action is over' (quoted in Frei 1971a: 93).

Analysing the motives and aims of his journalistic work, Ossietzky said that he acted from conviction and that political 'journalism is no life insurance; the risks involved are its best driving force' (quoted in Frei 1971a: 90). He confessed that he did not belong to any party and that his aim was to remain independent and to speak out as circumstances demanded. *Die Weltbühne*, which over the years had excelled in its critical analyses of German affairs and which, as a result, was attacked by both the right and the left, 'will maintain the courage to have its opinion in this country, which is shaking under the elephantine tread of fascism' (90). The majority of the leftist journalists and many prominent liberals, including Albert Einstein and Thomas Mann, joined in the campaign against Ossietzky's imprisonment and against the partisan judiciary. In November 1931 the first protest meeting of the German League for Human Rights, appealing to everyone with a sense of responsibility and justice, was attended by 3,000 people, and the appeal was signed by 33,999 people (Deak 1968: 192). On 10 May 1932 Ossietzky, accompanied by many friends, entered the military prison in Tegel.

After serving seven months of his sentence, Carl von Ossietzky was released as part of the December 1932 Christmas amnesty (Stenersen, Libaek and Sveen 2001: 121). He returned to his journal, and made even sharper accusations against militarisation, Germany's 'conservative revolution' and anti-Semitism. He warned that the deadly combination of all three already meant that '[t]oday there is blood in the air' (quoted in Frei 1971a: 246). Although there were many ominous signs, such as the burning of books – including Ossietzky's works – and an increasing number of imprisonments without charge, that left-wing intellectuals were increasingly in physical danger, Ossietzky continued to attack Nazism. During the last days of the Weimar Republic, in the article entitled 'The genie from the bottle', he wrote: 'Nobody dares any longer to question publicly the nature of the right of the Reichswehr to sole domination' (quoted in Frei 1971a: 147). Protesting against the fascisation of the republic, he noted that 'Germany accepts the censorship as a matter of course, democratic principles no longer count for anything' (147).

In February 1933, on the morning after the Reichstag fire and one month after Hitler had become chancellor of Germany, Ossietzky was again arrested, as an 'enemy of the state'. He was imprisoned for a while in Berlin, then later sent to concentration camps, first to Sonnenburg and in 1934 to Papenburg-Esterwegn (Patterson Meyer 1978: 10). His health, already weakened by a heart condition and tuberculosis, deteriorated under a regime of forced labour and mistreatment. An emissary of the International Red Cross, after seeing Ossietzky, wrote: 'A shaking, deadly-pale something, a being which appears to have lost all feeling, one eye swollen, his teeth apparently smashed, dragging a broken and badly mended leg' (Frei 1971b: 19). This testimony to Ossietzky's martyrdom moved many, and a compaign to save Ossietzky spread around the globe, attracting the support of many liberal Western newspapers and much liberal world opinion. On 23 January 1934 *The Times* in London published a letter from Wickham Steed, a British journalist, calling for support from the civilised world for the 'German Dreyfus' (Frei 1971b: 19).

As the support for the campaign to release Ossietzky grew stronger, his colleagues also started a letter-writing campaign to secure for him a nomination for the Nobel Peace Prize. Subsequently, the German ambassador to Norway warned the Norwegian government not to defy Germany by awarding the prize to a 'state criminal' and a 'traitor to our country' (Patterson Meyer 1978: 104). In the face of the growing controversy, the Nobel Prize Committee decided not to award the peace prize in 1935. As the petitions in favour of Ossietzky continued to arrive, however, the matter became even more urgent and difficult. In

November 1936, despite Berlin's counter-propaganda and some voices expressing concern that Ossietzky was too extreme in his warnings and revelations about the Nazis and that he was a communist, the Nobel Prize Committee retrospectively awarded the Peace Prize for 1935 to Carl von Ossietzky for his courage and his ability to tell of what he saw, for being 'an unafraid witness for truth and justice'.[2] The German press was forbidden to comment on Ossietzky's award and Hitler passed a decree forbidding Germans in future to accept Nobel Prizes. The committee played its hand carefully so as not to antagonise the Nazi government, emphasising Ossietzky's anti-militarist journalism and never mentioning his mistreatment in German camps. It was clear all the same that the prize was being awarded 'in response to the international campaign on his behalf organized by German exiles and joined by leading liberal and socialist intellectuals and politicians all over the world' (Abrams 1994: 32).

Ossietzky was transferred from a concentration camp to a prison hospital, where he received notification of the prize. Although the German government announced that Ossietzky was free to travel, he was not issued with a passport. In bestowing the award on Ossietzky *in absentia*, Fredrik Stang ([1936] 2006: 1), chairman of the Nobel Committee, said: 'Carl von Ossietzky is not only a symbol. He is something quite different and something more. He is a deed and he is a man.' Stressing that Ossietzky did not belong to any political party and that he was 'not a communist; he is not in any sense conservative', Stang (1) described Ossietzky as a liberal with a 'burning love for freedom of thought and expression; a firm belief in free competition in all spiritual fields; a broad international outlook, a respect for values created by other nations'. In 1936 Ossietzky was formally released and allowed to be moved to a private sanatorium in Berlin, where he died on 4 May 1938 (Abrams 1988: 128). In mourning Ossietzky, the world was 'remembering a man of heroic courage and devotion' who 'defied the Nazi power at its height and paid a bitter price' (Emily Greene Balch, quoted in Randall 1964: 420).

Carl von Ossietzky's life and work, as with all German leftist intellectuals, was deeply affected by the First World War, the Bolshevik Revolution and the polarisation of German politics in the 1920s. All these developments presented German leftist intellectuals with the dilemma of whether to support the moderate socialists and their newly created Weimar Republic or to work, by joining the German communists with their links to Moscow, to undermine Weimar's bourgeois compromise (Jay 1973; Laqueur 1974). The centrality of this dilemma marked all leftist writers, yet Ossietzky's solution to this problem, as his tragic fate exemplifies, distinguished him from the intellectuals who opted to support one side or the other on the spectrum of socialist politics, and from those who, like the Frankfurt School, chose a third course of action, namely the purity of its theory over affiliation and action (Jay 1973). Acting on the strength of his democratic convictions, he refused to be a bystander in the political process when democratic values were being threatened, and accordingly tried to transcend the differences between the leftist parties and to offer a viable alternative. In a speech to Berlin writers in 1933 he declared: 'My flag is no longer the black–red–gold banner of this degenerated republic, but the banner of the united anti-fascist movement' (quoted in Frei 1971a: 126). The 'revolution' which he initiated on the pages of *Die Weltbühne*, 'however imprecisely defined, was meant to revitalize both republicans and communists, and to begin together on a common platform of antifascist action' (Deak 1968: 5).

Ossietzky's radical attempt to bring together all the various anti-fascist forces was mistrusted and criticised as totally unrealistic by the forces on the left. At the same time, however, he was distrusted by the German conservatives, who regarded the left-wing intelligentsia as a subversive element engaged in the undermining of sacred German values (Laqueur 1974). Moreover, because of his pacifist beliefs and his claim that the militarism of the right was bound to lead to a new world war, the conservatives regarded his views as treason. Nevertheless, pacifism was also rejected by the communists, who regarded it as a petit bourgeois aberration (Laqueur 1974). Additionally, Ossietzky, while always loyal to pacifists, 'found them exasperating' (Deak 1968: 55). Unable to reconcile his longing for revolution with their pacifist convictions, Ossietzky claimed that, although the 'pacifists always had clean hands, and were often outstandingly courageous; but to be quite frank they were even more often outstandingly untalented' (quoted in Frei 1971a: 173).

In his political commentaries Carl von Ossietzky was always above all parties and critical of all parties. In the early years of the Weimar Republic, a supporter of democratic reforms, he wrote that 'for us collaboration with a political party is foreign and unthinkable' (quoted in Frei 1971a: 173). Even in 1933, when he rejected the republican cause, abandoned the idea of reform and recognised the necessity for commitment, he still stressed the need for detachment from, and the duty to be critical of, all parties. For example, even when writing in support of the anti-fascist front, he started with criticism, admitting that it 'is not easy to make a critical assessment of a movement which one would wish to see successful' (quoted in Frei 1971a: 125). Since he had 'received blows' from all parties (202–5), he knew better than anybody else that being a non-party intellectual was costly. He was doubly homeless, unwilling to identify himself with any party as well as unable to find a place within the pacifist movement, while at the same time being the target of the right. This isolation, although a close group of friends remained, together with the growing seriousness of the political situation, which he described as 'tragic', pushed him to opt for a radical solution: 'What is necessary now is not to be right; what is necessary is to save all parts of the organised socialist working class from destruction' (quoted in Frei 1971a: 206). Ossietzky called on all leftist parties to forget their past controversies and 'save us at the moment'. Failing that, 'there is a need for good mediators, non-party men' to do 'everything for socialism' (206).

Although his belief in the leading role of the intellectual, as one who would unify all progressive forces and carry out the revolution, was rather too optimistic, it was the pressure of the national emergency rather than his naivety that led him to call for the anti-fascist unity of the socialist intelligentsia. Ossietzky, who always envied the French intellectuals their unique status, aspired to enhance the role of public intellectuals in Germany. In his reformist stage, together with his calls for reforms to the judiciary and social reforms, he demanded the intellectualisation of political life and the politicisation of the intellectual (Deak 1968: 5). He wanted to restore the practice of open political debate in which intellectuals should play the role of 'the conscience of Germany'; they should wake up the nation, as Zola and other French intellectuals did during the Dreyfus Affair; they should 'inspire the opposition with an appeal to reason'; they should help Germany 'to find a way to decency' by awakening its conscience (quoted in Frei 1971a: 119, 55). Despite these calls, German intellectuals remained powerless and divided outsiders who received little respect, as social esteem was reserved for university professors (Laqueur 1973). It was this absence of space for left-leaning intellectuals in Weimar Germany, rather than Ossietzky's and his co-editors' ineffectiveness, that explains the failure of the *Weltbühne* programme. Although it is true that the *Weltbühne* journalists weakened their own position with their many inconsistencies and ambiguities (Laqueur 1974), they were nevertheless able to recognise the danger that militarisation posed to democracy.

Carl von Ossietzky proved that the left-wing intellectual can 'overcome the isolation traditionally imposed on the free publicist by thinking about himself as a better sort of German who belongs to "the other Germany"' (Deak 1968: 3). By aiming to transform Germany into a democratic state committed to the ideals of true peace and freedom, Ossietzky demonstrated that there are 'the other Germans in Germany'.

To prove the existence of another Germany was also the goal of those campaigning for his nomination to the Nobel Peace Prize. For them, the awarding of the prize to Ossietzky represented, as Thomas Mann wrote, 'a symbolic justice for millions of anxious contemporaries' (Mann, quoted in Wasson 1987: 787).

Andrei Sakharov: from Hero of Socialist Labour to state enemy no. 1

Andrei Sakharov (1921–89), the Nobel Peace Prize laureate for 1975, and one of the greatest physicists in the field of thermonuclear physics, later in his life engaged in a prolonged confrontation with the Soviet state over issues of nuclear responsibility and human rights. His courage and willingness to risk his career (as he was first demoted, then sacked from his scientific post) in the fight against nuclear tests and in making the Soviet state accountable to the world for its treatment of its citizens established his reputation as an irrepressible critic of the regime and an outspoken proponent of the values of freedom, human life and the principle of non-violence. Because of this oppositional stance in defence of human rights, Sakharov, the 'father of the Soviet hydrogen bomb', became 'state enemy no. 1', and he was condemned to internal exile. During the period of perestroika Sakharov became actively engaged in the process of democratising Russia. Sakharov's life, as is argued by Ernest Gellner, well exemplifies the life of the twentieth century, in which two 'great things happened': dramatic progress in physics and the dramatic demise of Marxism (Gellner, quoted in Lourie 2002: 1).

Andrei Sakharov was born into the Russian intelligentsia. His father was a teacher of physics who wrote popular scientific books. Andrei shared his father's passion for physics, which he studied in the physics department at Moscow University. After spending the war as an engineer in a mining factory, he continued with postgraduate study in the Physics Institute of the Academy of Sciences. Sakharov's interest in atomic physics reached its height during that period: 'I felt like the messenger of the gods' (Sakharov 1990: 84). Twice he rejected attempts to enlist him to work on the Soviet hydrogen bomb project, but 'the third time, in 1948, nobody bothered to ask' his consent (94). The work came with many privileges but also with isolation, as it was carried out in the seclusion of a nuclear research centre in the republic of Turkmenistan. Sakharov worked on the hydrogen bomb under the direction of the highly regarded Igor Tamm, a winner of the 1958 Nobel Prize in Physics, who came to play a very important role in his life as he influenced Sakharov's approach not only to science but also to social questions. 'What remain significant for me are the underlying principles by which Tamm was guided: absolute intellectual integrity and courage and willingness to re-examine his ideas for the sake of truth and readiness to take action' (Sakharov 1990: 122). In 1953 both Tamm and Sakharov received the titles of Hero of Socialist Labour and Stalin Prizes. The same year Sakharov, at the age of thirty-two, as the youngest ever member, was admitted to the Academy of Sciences. In 1956 he was awarded his second title of Hero of Socialist Labour (181).

At this stage, the nature of the weapon Sakharov and his colleagues were building did not present any moral dilemma to him or his co-workers. Their intellectual fascination, their patriotism and their country's recent history convinced them that their work was essential to prevent further threats to the homeland: 'I regarded myself as a soldier in this new scientific war' (Sakharov 1990: 157). Thirty years later, in an interview, Sakharov said that he and his colleagues considered their work to be absolutely imperative as a means of restoring the balance of power in the world (quoted in Bailey 1990: 420). By the late 1950s, however, Sakharov had 'become profoundly disturbed by the consequences of nuclear testing' (1990: 577). This new awareness of the human and moral implications of his work was a result of the confrontation with the terrifying consequences of the first test of a Russian hydrogen bomb in 1953, caused by several safety measures being overlooked. In 1957 he already felt 'responsible for the problems of radioactive contamination from nuclear explosion' (202).

In 1958 Andrei Sakharov called on the government to cancel a scheduled nuclear explosion and not to engage in any further testing, at least of the hydrogen bomb. In 1961 he personally lobbied Nikita Khrushchev, the first secretary of the Communist Party of the Soviet Union, against resuming the explosions. Although his persistent letter campaigns against tests and his pressure on the leadership to discontinue tests enraged Khrushchev, Sakharov's effort laid the groundwork for the 1963 Limited Test Ban Treaty, signed in Moscow. With hindsight, Sakharov was proud of his role in making this treaty, which bans nuclear weapons testing in the atmosphere, possible. Nevertheless, at that time, in the early 1960s, he felt 'an awful sense of powerlessness, [because] I could not stop something I knew was worrying and unnecessary. After that, I felt myself another man. I broke with my surroundings. It was a basic break. After that, I understood there was no point in arguing' (quoted in Dornan 1975: 362). For Sakharov, the atomic question 'was always half science, half politics, [it] was a natural path into political issues. What matters is that I left conformism' (quoted in Dornan 1975: 362). It was rejecting 'conformism and conformists' that started Sakharov's road to dissent: 'I developed a moral consciousness gradually in the 1950s. I suppose the turning point came when I sent a letter of protest to the Government against our atomic tests in 1958 – and again in 1961' (quoted in Bailey 1990: 235).

Andrei Sakharov's initial dissenting actions, which took the form of persuasion aimed at the Soviet political elite, coincided with the 'post-Stalin thaw'. His authority, rooted in his capacity as a top scientist, and the temporary openness of the political system provided him with a unique opportunity to voice his protest, connected with causes related to his work, directly to the people in power. In his next step on the road to dissent, Sakharov started to address general scientific and political matters. In the years 1965–7, despite being 'heavily involved in demanding scientific work', Sakharov (1990: 267) was actively engaged in protesting against any restrictions on intellectual freedom. 'The credo of progressive scientists and progressive intelligentsia the world over is the unconstrained discussion of all programmes, including the most pointed' (191). Motivated by his belief that where there is no freedom of discussion there is no freedom of thought, and that where there is no freedom of thought there is no freedom of enquiry, Sakharov joined in the campaign to free genetics and biology 'from the witch-doctoring of Stalin's favourite, Trofim Lysenko' (Friendly 1979: xiii). In the following years he protested against the official restrictions on freedom of opinion and the abuse of human rights. For instance, in 1966 he signed a collective letter to the party hierarchy warning against any rehabilitation of Stalin and wrote letters to the general secretary, Leonid Brezhnev, pleading for the rights of political prisoners and accusing the communist Party of being 'profoundly indifferent to violations of human rights, the interest of progress, the security and future of mankind' (Sakharov 1990: 416). Despite the fact that Sakharov kept his pleadings and protestations within the channels of the Soviet system, measures were taken to punish him: he lost his post as department head and his salary was reduced.

From the mid-1970s Sakharov, deprived of access to the public media and unable to rely on the Soviet authorities, increasingly had to use alternative channels for spreading information, such as informal networks, publishing abroad, contacts with Western reporters and foreign radio. His first step outside the official system was the publication of *Reflections on Progress, Peaceful Coexistence and Intellectual Freedom* in the United States in 1968, in which he put forward the 'somehow utopian' idea of a convergence of the two political systems, capitalism and communism (Sakharov 1990: 283). His outline of a global programme for mankind's future was rooted in two interdependent theses: the first to the effect that 'the division of mankind threatens it with destruction' and the second stating that intellectual freedom is essential to humanity. With the 18 million copies of *Reflections* sold in the West, Sakharov established his reputation abroad as a spokesman for the progressive, liberal Russian intelligentsia. The publication of the essay in the West, together with its circulation from hand to hand in the form of samizdat (self-published) manuscripts in the Union of Soviet Socialist Republics, brought repercussions. He was dismissed from the weapons laboratory and stripped of his security clearance, and within a year he was transferred to the Institute of Physics in Moscow, where he remained engaged in theoretical research in physics, until 1980. While still passionately interested in theoretical physics, he devoted more and more of his time to human rights and to studying a wider range of issues connected with war and peace and other global problems.

With the growing realisation that 'the technical, military, and economic problems are secondary, the fundamental issues are political and ethical', Andrei Sakharov decided to take 'an irrevocable step, a decisive break with the establishment' (Sakharov 1990: 267, 268). By launching the Human Rights Committee in 1970, the aims of which were to invesitigate and publicise violations of human rights in the Soviet Union, with a stated policy of acting openly and legally, Sakharov took the stand in the defence of the freedoms proclaimed in the Soviet constitution and slowly established himself as his country's most prominent dissident. His participation in activities of this type brought him into close contact with a new set of people. This new circle of friends, many of them artists, historians and literary people who were already involved in protests against the state's abuses of power, provided him with the resources and support for him to expand activities in defence of human rights (Bonner 1986).

Through the 1970s Sakharov became the country's best-known spokesman for Soviet human rights. His policy was to express his position openly and legally on various questions of public life, to oppose human rights violations and unjust governmental decisions, to defend the rights of ethnic and religious minorities and to write memorandums to the government and reform projects. He also went on hunger strike, twice, to call attention to the plight of political prisoners. In his articles and books, which were published in the West and circulating as samizdat manuscripts in the country, Sakharov exposed the reality of the Soviet system and argued for democracy and pluralist reforms, such as the development of a multi-party system, freedom of the press, freedom to strike, freedom of movement and information and an end to the privileges of the Communist Party.[3] He also warned the West that, before agreeing to détente, the Western powers should set minimal conditions. 'There is no doubt that Sakharov was risking his life in making such a statement when he warned against a rapprochement with an undemocratized Soviet Union' (Bailey 1990: 352).

Since public participation that was independent of party control was not permitted in the Soviet Union, and since the regime considered it a direct challenge to and fundamental criticism of the system, Andrei Sakharov's attempts to intervene in an open way were not tolerated for long. Moreover, as Sakharov consistently made his case visible to an international audience, the Soviet authorities increased their campaign against him. The anti-Sakharov operation aimed to paint him as 'a dangerous slanderous assault on Soviet society, … an enemy of détente' who defamed the Soviet state structures and distorted Soviet reality and appealed to reactionary imperialist circles (Sakharov 1990: 197). Newspapers, such as *Pravda*, accused Sakharov of 'calling on imperialistic states to take retaliatory steps against the Soviet Union' (Bailey 1990: 319). The Soviet authorities tried to intimidate Sakharov in various ways: he was put under secret police surveillance and his family was harassed. In building the case against Sakharov for 'anti-Soviet activities', open letters were published in many newspapers denouncing Sakharov as a 'traitor', some signed by members of the Soviet Academy, writers, artists and veterans, others by 'simple people'. Sakharov continued to answer the authorities' action with full publicity by talking to foreign journalists and organising press conferences, which became a 'transmission belt' to the larger world (Hollander 1975: 260).

In 1975 Andrei Sakharov was awarded the Nobel Peace Prize for his 'fearless personal commitment in upholding the fundamental principles for peace' and for emphasising that human rights 'provide the only safe foundation for genuine international cooperation and security' (Lionaes [1975] 2006: 1). Sakharov was presented as an 'uncompromising' fighter 'against the abuse of power and all forms of violation of human dignity', with the comment that 'he has fought no less courageously for the idea of government based on the rule of law' (Lionaes [1975] 2006: 1). In his Nobel lecture (delivered by his wife Elena Bonner – as the state authorities refused to let him travel to Norway), Sakharov declared that he shared it with prisoners of conscience and political prisoners. He observed that progress and human rights are indissolubly linked: it is impossible to achieve one of them if the others are ignored. With the official Soviet media totally condemning 'the imperialistic' Norwegian reward and its recipient, it was no surprise that Yury Andropov, the head of the KGB at that time, declared Sakharov 'public enemy no. 1' (Lourie 2002: 276). When in 1980 Sakharov publicly opposed the Soviet military intervention in Afghanistan, he was stripped of all his state awards and of his titles of Hero of Socialist Labour and exiled to Gorky. The exile was totally illegal, even according to Soviet law: there was no trial, and its main purpose was to break Sakharov's contact with the outside world, specifically with foreign correspondents. In Gorky Sakharov continued both his scientific work and his struggle for human rights. He devoted an increasing amount of his attention to individual victims of injustice, calling for an amnesty for all prisoners of conscience and the abolition of the death penalty. Protesting against his persecution and the persecution of his family, Sakharov went on two hunger strikes. He lived in exile until 1986, when Mikhail Gorbachev, the newly appointed general secretary of the Communist Party, personally called and invited him to return to Moscow and 'resume his patriotic work' – in effect, to become the regime's loyal opposition (Sakharov 1990: 615).

Understanding that Gorbachev's telephone call signalled that he was serious about changing the Soviet system, Andrei Sakharov became Gorbachev's supporter, without, however, giving up on his independence. Sakharov was, for example, an outspoken critic of Gorbachev's attempts to concentrate power in his own hands (Bailey 1990: 409). In the period of perestroika, Sakharov took on responsibilities as 'spokesman for the liberal intelligentsia' and got actively involved in the process of political change, hoping to foster the democratisation of the country (Kline 1990: xvi). In 1988 he was elected to the presidium of the Academy of Sciences, chosen as one of five directors of the Interregional Group of People's Deputies and made honorary chairman of Memorial, the society founded to preserve the memory of Stalin's victims. Only a few days before his death, Sakharov, as a leading voice of the movement for political reform in the Soviet Union, wrote a draft of a new democratic constitution. At his funeral tributes were paid to him as 'the incarnation of intellectual courage and conscience' (Kline 1990: xiv) and as 'a moral symbol for the West' (Kelly 2002: 13). Sakharov did not want to become just a symbol of a campaign for human rights, he wanted to implement them in his own direct political practice. Although his struggle for human rights during the Soviet period did not actually awaken the Russian people and did not make him popular with ordinary Russians (as only 1.5 per cent of them named him the 'man of the year' in 1989; Gussejnow 1994: 284), Sakharov did have a chance to contribute to the democratisation of his country during the period of perestroika.

Sakharov (1990: 476) disliked the role of 'opposition leader' into which he was thrust. He always preferred to describe himself as 'physicist' rather than 'dissident' (Kline 1990: xiv). Yet his ethical position in the context of the Soviet abuse of human rights led him to become a defender of human rights, which for him 'constitute the basis for fully human life and for international security and trust' (1990: 409). For Sakharov, the struggle, even if it was futile, needed to continue. 'Because for us it is not a political struggle … It is a moral struggle for all of us. We have to be true to ourselves' (quoted in Dornan 1975: 369). His ethical stand and his focus on human rights brought him into conflict not only with the Soviet authorities but also with other dissidents. His protest against the injustices done to anonymous people and his willingness to defend the right to emigrate were criticised by the Russian dissidents and intelligentsia generally, who, according to Sakharov (1990: 300), showed 'a totalitarian thinking' and a 'collectivist ethos' in their assumption that abandoning the homeland ran counter to civic duty. The most significant example of Sakharov's disagreement with dissidents is his conflict with Solzhenitsyn, who publicly accused Sakharov of 'playing the emigration tune' and therefore not being patriotic (Dornan 1975: 410).[4] The independence that Sakharov showed in this controversy reflects not only his rejection of the collectivist mentality but also his preference for 'the freedom of speaking out as an individual' (Sakharov 1990: 456). At the same time, though, he found the close network of friends and dissidents very supportive, essential to achieve his goals, and rewarding.

Andrei Sakharov was a humanistic liberal intellectual who believed that a genuine and long-lasting system of international cooperation can come about only if it is rooted in respect for individual rights. Despite numerous harassments and threats to him and his family, Sakharov never regretted his participation in the social struggle. Although Tamm often spoke of Sakharov's tragedy, 'that he had to sacrifice his great passion – elementary-particle physics – first to create an atomic and hydrogen bomb, then sacrifice it a second time in the struggle for social justice' (Sakharov 1990: 221), Sakharov argued that, in fact, 'the two was one, or at least in close symbiosis'; he could not be effective in human rights if he had not been the 'father of the H-bomb' (Lourie 2002: 22). While Sakharov preferred to think that 'he went from a Teller to an Oppenheimer' (Lourie 2002: x),[5] he is also compared to Gandhi, with whom he shared 'a mix of the moral and the political, defencelessness, a touch of sanctity, a quiet triumphancy' (Lourie 2002: 401), and to Galileo, with whom he shared 'the spirit of liberty that animated the growth of the new science' (Bailey 1990: 1). Although some of Sakharov's programmes were over-optimistic, his integrity and courage in speaking out on behalf of civil rights, peace and justice will be his lasting contribution to the democratisation of his country.

Adolfo Pérez Esquivel: a fighter for liberation

Adolfo Pérez Esquivel (1931–), the recipient of the 1980 Nobel Peace Prize for his notable work in defending human rights, is an Argentinian architect, sculptor, painter, teacher and activist. Pérez Esquivel, who for nearly twenty-five years was a professor of architecture and sculpture at the National Academy of Art in Buenos Aires, has devoted his life to promoting human rights, peace and justice not only in his country but in the whole of Latin America. His belief in and commitment to the principle of non-violence in the struggle for social and political liberty was fuelled by years of political and social instability, repression and human rights violation during the periods of military rule in Argentina. In the 1970s, inspired by Gandhi's philosophy of non-violence and by liberation theology, Pérez became one of the most prominent Latin American advocates of civil rights. He is a founder of Servicio Paz y Justicia (Service for Peace and Justice – SERPAJ), an international movement aiming to promote respect for human rights, including social and economic rights. For his resistance to and campaigning against the military repression, he suffered persecution in the 1970s. At present, Pérez Esquivel travels widely on behalf of the anti-war movement and is a member of many international bodies concerned with human rights and non-violence.[6]

Pérez has achieved great success as an artist and won several awards (Sanness [1980] 2006). As a sculptor he has worked in a variety of different media, and his sculptures have been widely displayed in Argentina's museums, galleries and public places (Stenersen, Libaek and Sveen 2001: 223). He is the author, for instance, of the 'Monument to the refugees' placed in the central headquarters of the United Nations High Commission for Refugees and a sculpture of Gandhi unveiled in Barcelona in 2000. As a painter, Pérez has worked in various media and has exhibited internationally. He produced iconic paintings, for example, to mark the 500th anniversary of the colonisation of the Americas by Europe: 'Latin America stations of the cross 1492–1992'. Pérez also writes on experiences of non-violence in Latin America and on many contemporary cultural, social and political issues.[7] He has received several awards and honorary titles,[8] and has never ceased his activities in the academic world.

Adolfo Pérez Esquivel was born in Buenos Aires. His mother died when he was three, so it was his father, a fisherman who had emigrated from Spain and who worked as a salesman for a coffee company, who took care of the family (Bacon 1999: 471). Despite his family's modest circumstances, he received a Catholic boarding school education. In 1956, after receiving a master's degree from the National Academy of Art in Buenos Aires, Pérez Esquivel became an art teacher and sculptor. Soon he had become a well-known architect and artist whose sculptures could be seen in various public places in Argentina (Sanness [1980] 2006: 2). In 1968 he was appointed professor of architecture and sculpture at the National Academy of Art in Buenos Aires. Pérez Esquivel's progress towards political activism was born out of Argentina's mounting political violence in the late 1960s and early 1970s. It developed gradually under the pressure of the political instability, growing oppression and social and economic problems in the country. Initially, while teaching in Buenos Aires, Pérez was involved 'peripherally with small organizations working for peace' (Bacon 1999: 471). He also helped with 'the Young Catholics organization, attending meetings, organizing events, and pitching in when he had time' (471).

Pérez became increasingly aware of the growing demands for change in society. He was especially influenced by the growing social and political problems and unrest, such as the workers' and students' uprising in Cordoba in 1966. Pérez's decision to get involved in public matters was also helped by liberation theology, which he got to know while working with popular organisations involved in the Christian non-violence movements in Latin America. Becoming increasingly influenced by its offer of a new 'language of opposition and this doctrine's carriers, namely the religiously inspired grass roots groups' (Levine 1986: 827), Pérez adopted liberation theology's focus on fighting for the dignity of the poor in Latin America. The theology's challenges to the existing order and its emphasis that people, in order to liberate themselves, must first develop a critical consciousness became a powerful motivating force for Pérez's art and public involvement, while its uniquely dense networks of informal contacts provided him with bases for his activism.

In the late 1960s, after a series of events, meetings and conferences with priests, protestors and lay volunteers across Latin America, Adolfo Pérez Esquivel began writing and publishing a small monthly journal, *Paz y Justicia* (Peace and Justice). The aim of this periodical was to document human rights abuses, educate its readers about the ideas and strategies of non-violent liberation and encourage people to work together for peace and justice (Bacon 1999: 471). In *Paz y Justicia*, as in his contacts with grass-roots groups, Pérez advocated ideas inspired by Gandhi and Martin Luther King as well as by liberation theology. In 1968 he attended a conference in Montevideo, Uruguay, that aimed to bring about change and development in Latin America through non-violent liberation. During this meeting the decision was made to set up a joint organisation covering all non-violent groups throughout Latin America, and Pérez's *Paz y Justicia* was made the official journal of the movement (Stenersen, Libaek and Sveen 2001: 222). Because of Pérez's calls for social justice and his criticism of military juntas, he was accused of 'playing into the hands of communism by criticizing the prevailing system. We reject this accusation' (Pérez 1983: 33). Claiming that his 'own work is much too humble and modest to attempt to resolve all these problems' (51), nonetheless in his writing and actions Pérez looked for an alternative: 'We want something besides capitalism or communism, something on the order of self-management and sharing. In fact, participation is the basic element we seek' (34).

As Pérez's life took a new turn, 'his sculptures and artwork began to reflect the sufferings around him' (Bacon 1999: 475). During the 1970s Pérez travelled across Latin American as the continent's chief promoter of a doctrine of non-violence and as a supporter of oppressed groups. He worked with isolated groups of rural and urban workers, indigenous populations and people concerned about missing family members. Pérez helped many peasant groups organise themselves, solidify and make their voices heard. For example, he campaigned in favour of rural communities evicted from their land in Ecuador, defended Christian communities in Paraguay and facilitated the writing of local economic development programmes in Brazil (Bacon 1999: 476). In 1975, because of his work with popular oppositional organisations involved in the non-violence movement, Pérez was detained by the Brazilian military police, and in 1976 he was imprisoned in Ecuador and deported back to Argentina. As he said himself: 'Personally I don't know how many times I've been arrested, say, for a day, after a demonstration' (Pérez 1983: 19). His prison experience 'became an integral part of his militancy, if only by way of corollary' (Antoine 1983: 6).

Despite the increased level of violence in Argentina, initiated by the military junta's policy of systematic repression following its seizure of power in 1976, Pérez continued to express his opposition to the terror and the violation of human rights. He strongly rejected the Argentina military regime's appeal to 'national security' as a justification for their fight against armed guerrillas as it implied that there was no real distinction between war and peace. Military rulers, starting with Carlos Ongania's dictatorship (1966–70), while fighting subversive movements, had 'deliberately sought to create a climate of fear in order to control the country economically, politically and socially' (Bacon 1999: 473). Much of Pérez's efforts went into supporting the families of the victims of the state terrorism and contributing to the formation and strengthening of ties between popular human rights organisations. Pérez nonetheless condemned the violence and terrorism of both sides. Not only did he denounce all the killings and the various kinds of repression committed by the authorities, he also 'denounced the killing of generals, colonels and innocent relatives of military officials' (Sanness [1980] 2006: 4). Although he was able 'to appreciate some of the motives that promote terrorism inspired by the left' (Sanness [1980] 2006: 4), Pérez (1983: 33), as a supporter of far-reaching social and political reforms, argued: 'Terrorism of the left and terrorism of the right only add up.' Hence, when Pérez went on a hunger strike in 1970–1, he did so as a protest against terrorism, both from the right and from the left.

The 1974 conference of Latin American non-violent organisations established a joint permanent human rights movement, Servicio de Paz y Justicia en América Latina. Adolfo Pérez Esquivel was elected secretary general of this newly established movement and his journal, *Paz y Justicia*, increased its circulation throughout Latin America. SERPAJ defines human rights in a broad sense, and not only protests against violence and terror but also 'looks at the case of the peasant who has no land and is dying of hunger' (Pérez, quoted in Sanness [1980] 2006: 4). Its chief task is to promote respect for human rights, a phrase intended to include social and economic rights (Bacon 1999: 472). What is unique about SERPAJ is that it is not a charity group but a movement dedicated to awakening a critical consciousness in grass-roots communities, so that people can develop their own solutions to the problems they face. 'Pérez was careful from the beginning not to make the group a movement but rather an iterative service that could grow and change as different needs arose' (Bacon 1999: 475).

The movement held frequent training courses in non-violent methods in many countries and its activists helped people to develop a critical awareness so that they could express their problems and organise themselves. Pérez, through his work with SERPAJ, provided support for various communities in their fight for their rights. Another example of Pérez's work is his support and help for the group of mothers who, every week, mourned in Buenos Aires' Plaza de Mayo the disappearance of their sons and daughters having been kidnapped and killed by the security forces. In 1976 Pérez began to assist the Mothers of the Plaza de Mayo (as they came to be called) in their efforts to formulate their demands and grievances to human rights organisations and the government, by organising and tutoring meetings that helped the women to write for themselves a list of objectives and a document stating the injustice committed (Bacon 1999: 473). He also initiated an international campaign aimed at persuading the United Nations to establish a Human Rights Commission to record breaches of human rights in Latin America.

In the context of growing terror and counter-terror and as the number of victims, due to successive governments' failure to solve the crisis, continued to increase, Adolfo Pérez Esquivel was forced to take a more active role and to accept a higher level of risk. In 1976, as the collision of grass-roots religious activism with Argentina's authorities led to further repression, Pérez, who by this stage had been forced to abandon his university position, travelled to Europe to gather support for his campaign for the establishment of a UN commission to document human rights violations (Abrams 1988). Argentina's ruling generals accused him of terrorism and he was arrested in Buenos Aires in April 1977. Imprisoned without trial for fourteen months, he was tortured psychologically and physically (Pérez 1983: 23). Even when he had, formally, been freed, due to international pressure, he remained under house arrest for the next year, subject to various restrictions, which lapsed only with the re-establishment of democratic rule in the country in 1983 (Antoine 1983: 6).

Free now of all limitations on his movements, Pérez resumed his job with *Paz y Justicia* as well as his artistic work (Stenersen, Libaek and Sveen 2001). In 1980 he was granted the Nobel Peace Prize for his activities for the poor and to promote non-violence, and because he offered 'an alternative to the solutions of the problems of a country, eradicating the use of force and violence to reinstate respect for Human Rights' (Sanness [1980] 2006: 1). Pérez's Nobel Peace Prize was an embarrassment to the general staff of the Buenos Aires junta, which quickly protested against the Nobel Committee's 'intolerable affront' to their national dignity (Antoine 1983: 6). Nevertheless, it took Argentina's government thirty-six hours from the Nobel Committee's announcement to draft 'an explanation of its past actions against Pérez Esquivel' (Bacon 1999: 471). In his acceptance speech, Pérez ([1980] 2006: 1) said that he would like to receive the award 'in the name of the people of Latin America' and 'in the name of my indigenous brothers and sisters'. After declaring that that there is 'no higher interest than the human being', he noted that, for him, 'a small voice for those who have no voice', the Nobel Peace Prize was 'the highest honour that I can receive; to be considered a servant of peace' (1).

Adolfo Pérez Esquivel took advantage of the publicity that came with the Nobel Peace Prize. He donated the prize money to SERPAJ and used his new visibility on the international stage to further his cause (Stenersen, Libaek and Sveen 2001). He visited the United States and Europe, where he spoke with Amnesty International, many leading international journalists, the UN secretary general and members of Congress. In addition, Pérez was awarded an honorary doctorate by

St Joseph's University in Philadelphia (Stenersen, Libaek and Sveen 2001: 223). SERPAJ continued to grow in the years after 1980, and Pérez remained its secretary general until 1985, since when he has been its honorary president. As secretary general, Pérez intervened in the most significant political trials related to the defence of human rights. In 1983 he embarked on a ten-day hunger strike in protest at the violation of human rights in Argentina. Later in the year he went on another ten-day hunger strike, protesting about the amnesty granted to members of Argentina's military accused of violating human rights. In 1990 Pérez again used the hunger strike strategy to protest at the closure of one of Argentina's independent newspapers. Today Pérez, while still developing his artistic interests, heads a project devoted to working with children in a situation of social risk. In addition, he continues to defend human rights, by writing petitions and articles and participating in conferences.

Pérez's success in building networks across all Latin America is not a result of his charisma (Antoine 1983: 8). According to all accounts, he is not a charismatic figure 'who can take charge of a popular movement and brand it with a spellbinding personality (Bacon 1999: 472). Neither is his impact a result of political affiliation or an orthodox stand on social and political issues. Pérez himself has declared: 'We have no connections with political parties of any sort, much less armed groups. We act by means of evangelical non-violence, which we see as a force for liberation' (quoted in Sanness [1980] 2006: 4). Pérez first established his reputation as an artist, while his development 'as a non-violent leader' (Bacon 1999: 472) was a result of his courageous efforts to help people. His achievements are connected with his ability to 'create channels of communication' among people and groups who often are 'not even consciously aware of being non-violent in a technical sense' (Antoine 1983: 8). He 'coordinates the activities of a variety of groups fighting for peace, justice and human rights' (Antoine 1983: 2). Pérez is an ethical dissenter whose efforts have been influential in getting Latin American non-violence movements under way. Seeing formal channels as relatively ineffective, Pérez tries to bring different people together and help them, through informal means, to establish cooperative relations (Antoine 1983: 8).

Adolfo Pérez Esquivel distinguishes his stance from that of liberation theology by explaining that he encourages people to go beyond this perspective to reach an understanding of the non-violent method of struggle. He has also gone beyond just protesting against violence and terror. Thus, it can be said that it is his principled, consistent and courageous stand against violations of human rights of all kinds that has earned him international respect. He also recognises the importance of human rights in terms of social justice. According to him, 'peace is only possible when it is the fruit of justice' (Pérez [1980] 2006: 3). Both in his writings and in his artistic work, Pérez promotes respect for people's rights and the dignity of human beings, and faith in the possibility of change based on justice and the importance of truth.

Pérez found expression for his ideas in the words of Argentina's poet, Jorge Luis Borges: 'My position on Argentina is purely an ethical one. I cannot ignore the serious moral problem which arose in my country with both terrorism and repression. In no way can I be silent in front of all those who disappeared, I do not approve of any action where the end justifies means. I am no politician' (quoted in Sanness [1980] 2006: 1). Because of his faith in liberation and non-violence as means of achieving peace and justice and because of his long campaign against the violation of human rights, Adolfo Pérez Esquivel, although unknown to the international media, occupies a position of great moral authority among the people of his continent who are devoted to peace and justice.

Challengers to political closure

In terms of our typology, dissidents are conceptualised as radicalised intellectuals who defy formal structures and who display the exceptional courage demanded in societies in which the sphere of individual autonomy is limited, in which impersonal control is imposed, in which the centre of power is remote and which, in consequence, enhance reliance on informal networks. As we have already seen, when comparing dissidents with heroes, in order to explain the underlying difference between these two categories we need to refer to the nature of their respective socio-political environments. The same is true with reference to the differences between dissidents and other categories of public intellectuals. In the broadest terms, in non-democratic polities it is those intellectuals who contest prevailing norms, decisions, laws and other arrangements of power who face higher levels of risk. In other words, while politics is always an inherently risky and uncertain enterprise (Arendt 1958), it is under conditions of political closure that dissenters' actions confront the highest level of risk and unpredictability. Courage is a critically important feature of being a challenger to political closure, as it enables and guides action in the presence of fear (Bickford 1996: 148–53). Thus, as dissidents' criticism and protest come the closest to civil disobedience, their courage is tested to a greater extent than the courage of heroes, pioneers or champions. If courage is understood 'as an active commitment to persistence and resolution in the face of risk, uncertainty, or fear' (Sparks 1997: 89), our dissidents provide a good illustration of this.

Although, in democratic systems, civil disobedience is the most widely recognised form that oppositional practices take, in non-democratic polities even the non-violent direct action of civil disobedience is defined by the political authorities as unacceptable and punished. According to Jürgen Habermas (2002: 375), who writes about constitutional democracy, civil disobedience, defined as the calculated breaking of rules, is actualised in civil society in crisis situations so as to defend the normative content of constitutional democracy 'against the systematic inertia of institutional politics'. Under political closure, however, there is no civil society capable of keeping intact the communication structures of the public sphere, and the government's laws and institutions do not accommodate free and open public discussion. As the public sphere is not allowed to reproduce itself through communicative actions, any attempt at criticism, opposition or protest that is public, principled and symbolic in character becomes an illegal act. In contrast to civil disobedience behaviour in democracies, which consist of deliberately illegal acts undertaken mainly by collective action, dissidents' actions are, by definition, illegal acts by individuals. Moreover, these acts of protest and criticism do not earn dissidents fame and recognition among their countrymen. While heroes enjoy a high status as they symbolise their nations' proudest achievements, dissidents remain unknown to the wider public at the time who are often suspicious of their motives (Feifer 1975). The contrast between Sakharov's low rates of popularity in his country with Nansen's status as Norway's national hero illustrates this point well.

There are many similarities between our three dissidents. Adolfo Pérez Esquivel ([1980] 2006) in his Nobel Peace Prize acceptance speech directly expressed his solidarity with Andrei Sakharov, who, from his exile in Gorky, sent him congratulations. They both stressed that the causes of human rights violations were the same in Argentina and the Soviet Union and that they understood 'the gravity and the tragedy of the problem' facing the two countries. Sakharov added that Pérez's struggle for justice was 'cherished by people who lived thousands of miles away, in another world' (quoted in Sanness [1980] 2006: 2). Pérez and Sakharov, as well as Carl von Ossietzky, despite the high cost of taking such a stand, did not ignore the problems that arose in their countries. They shared the same sense of purpose, which came not only from their shared positions vis-à-vis their respective regimes but also from a recognition of the importance of values such as respect for human rights, freedom of discussion and democracy. None of the three was a member of a political party and they all relied on a small network of friends and a few channels of communication through which to attempt to publicise their ideas.

Left-wing Weimar intellectuals and Soviet dissidents are often compared to the nineteenth-century eastern European or Russian intelligentsia, defined as 'the politically aware, critically thinking segment of the educated class' (Hollander 1975: 251). In political terms, our three dissidents' beliefs in the dignity of man and in the inherent goodness of man, as well as their aspirations to enhance human rights and democracy, were – like the Russian intelligentsia's ambitions to be 'modernizers' and 'tribunes of their people' (Berlin 1979) – often unachievable. But in all cases 'there was a need to tackle the impossible' (Deak 1968: 5), as there was time neither for compromise nor for moderation. All three dissidents demonstrated the need for intellectuals to become political and to seek to universalise their claims.

Although the importance and the forms of dissent vary from country to country, because of the dissidents' focus on universal values and morality the process of opposition 'may be regarded as a universal one, characteristic of all police systems' (Skilling 1973: 92). This tendency to universalise their claims and to take moral stands distinguishes dissidents from our next category of public intellectuals, namely champions.

Notes

1 An extensive bibliography of Carl von Ossietzky's publications can be found in Kurt R. Grossmann (1963: 553–70). Also Istvan Deak (1968: 295–7) compiled a list of Ossietzky's works. Among edited collections of Ossietzky's writings the most significant are: *Der Anmarsch der neuen Reformation* (The Advance of the New Reformation), Hamburg (1919); *The Stolen Republic: Selected Writings*, edited by Bruno Frei, London: Lawrence and Wishart (1971); *Schriften*, edited by Bruno Frei and Hans Leonard, two volumes, Berlin: Aufbau-Verlag (1966) and *Rechenschaft, Publizistik aus den Jahren 1913–1933*, edited by Bruno Frei, Berlin: Aufbau-Verlag (1984).

2 Ossietzky's Nobel Peace Prize 'was one of the most controversial ever made' (Aarvik [1986] 2006: 1). Although he was not awarded the prize in 1935, the following year the situation was resolved when two Nobel Committee members (H. Koht and J. L. Mowinckel) who held positions with the German government removed themselves from the committee's work (Stenersen, Libaek and Sveen 2001: 123). This, in the context of Germany's threats and the Norwegian government's desire not to be seen as being responsible for the prize, allowed the Committee to award the prize to Ossietzky in 1936.

3 Among Andrei Sakharov's books published in the West are: *Reflections on Progress, Peaceful Coexistence and Intellectual Freedom* (1968), *Memorandum* (1971), *Sakharov Speaks* (1974), *My Country and My World* (1975), *Alarm and Hope* (1979*)*, *Collected Scientific Works* (1982) and *Memoirs* (1990).

4 In his *Memoirs* Sakharov paid tribute to Solzhenitsyn, but also stressed their contrasting views on progress, nationalism, religion, the greatness of Russia

and human rights. Sakharov also (1990: 409) declared that he disagreed with Solzhenitsyn's idealisation of pre-Soviet Russia, that he did 'not share Solzhenitsyn's antipathy toward Progress' and that they also differed on the issue of civil rights. Sakharov further opposed Solzhenitsyn's nationalist and religious approach and did not accept Solzhenitsyn's revolutionary, utopian romanticisation of Slavophiles.

5 Initially, Sakharov was like Edward Teller, an American physicist who helped to develop the hydrogen bomb and who was proud to have persuaded political leaders of the necessity of building it. Yet, unlike Teller, Sakharov (1990: 100) did 'not have to go against the current in those years, nor was I threatened with ostracism by my colleagues'. Sakharov (1990: 99) observed striking parallels between his fate and Robert Oppenheimer's, especially when the 'father of the atomic bomb', after he had tried to apply brakes to the American hydrogen bomb programme, was declared by the US government to be a security risk. But, unlike Oppenheimer, Sakharov did not try to retain his standing with the authorities, and he did not feel physicists had 'sinned' by working on nuclear weapons (Bailey 1990: 4).

6 In addition to being honorary president of the Argentine chapter of SERPAJ and honorary president of its Latin American section, Adolfo Pérez Esquivel is president of the Commission for the Investigation of Attacks on the Press and Journalists in Argentina. He is president of the International League for the Rights and Liberation of Peoples and a member of the Permanent Peoples' Tribunal (Stenersen, Libaek and Sveen 2001).

7 Pérez has written several books and many articles, mainly on the topic of human rights and the socio-political situation in Latin America. Among Pérez's publications are *Christ in a Poncho: Witnesses to the Non-Violent Struggles in Latin America* (1983) and Walking Together with the People (1995). He also writes frequently in *Paz y Justicia* and other journals on the experiences of non-violence in Latin America and cultural, social and political issues of the day.

8 Pérez was awarded Pope John XXIII's Peace Memorial in 1977, a Citizen of the World prize by the Boston Center for the 21st Century and the Pax Christi International Award in 1974. He is doctor *honoris causa* at several universities, professor emeritus at the National University of San Cristóbal de Huamanga, Peru, and Principal at the University of la Pau, Barcelona. He was awarded an honorary doctorate by St Joseph's University in Philadelphia. Pérez is also Doctor of Public Service, *honoris causa*, at the University of Rockhurst, Missouri. For his role as a mediator between the Spanish government and the Basque terrorist organisation ETA in 1995, Pérez was granted the Anne Frank Award for the Culture of Peace in 1997 (Stenersen, Libaek and Sveen 2001: 223).

8   Champions: promoting the cause

Influencing public opinion and campaigning for reforms

A 'champion', in the most common understanding of the term, is either someone who has won first place in a competition or someone who fights for a cause. While the former stresses engagement in a contest and being a winner in competition, the latter puts the emphasis on engagement in acting or speaking on behalf of a specific reason or interest; on being a defender or a promoter of an idea, project or purpose. What these two definitions have in common is their indirect assumption that champions deserve our admiration as winners in challenging competitions or as achievers of noble goals.

Here, we employ the label 'champion' to describe a type of public intellectual who meets our criteria for inclusion in this category, as discussed in chapter 4. The category of champions, located in the informalised and low-risk sector, depicts public intellectuals who reach beyond their informal networks to advance a particular group interest or to support a specific cause. Champions are scholars, writers and journalists who, because of their devotion to a particular purpose, could be at odds with the official creed of their country, yet generally their relationships with the authorities, in contrast to dissidents, are not characterised by total hostility. Not only do champions benefit from a higher degree of social integration but, occasionally, they also have access to the wielders of power, and sometimes they even move in the circles of power themselves.

Champions, as public intellectuals engaged in the defence and enhancement of a sectarian interest, differ from Benda's *clercs* or ideal intellectuals, who are devoted to other-worldly pursuits and are not involved with the this-worldly passion of politics (see chapter 1). Champions, in contrast to *les clercs*, are engrossed in the issues of the day, participate in social movements and in debates in the public arena and reach out to the public on an issue that they define as important. They are public intellectuals who intervene in politics, engage with a specific audience and directly address topical issues of public and political affairs. Although they do not act in the name of a 'universal', champions, who believe that society should be founded on reason, do try to make science into an effective public weapon. Champions do not conform to the canon of academic disengagement, as they are not detached from practical affairs. They support and call for reforms to rationalise systems that they believe to be threatened by disorder and injustice. They are public intellectuals who act upon the outside world, influence public opinion and effect changes in the public sphere.

In our sample of public intellectuals whose national and international achievements have been recognised and rewarded with the Nobel Peace Prize, there are three champions. They are Norman Angell, Emily Greene Balch and Alva Myrdal.

Norman Angell: dispelling illusions about international politics

Norman Angell (1872–1967), born Ralph Norman Angell Lane, was the 1933 Nobel Peace laureate. He was a champion of liberal internationalism who wrote more then forty books and many articles on international politics, in which he argued for the need for 'a world philosophy and a world conscience'.[1] Angell was a journalist, philosopher, writer, progressive educationalist and organiser whose mission was to expose the fallacies about international politics by appealing to reason and common sense. He was the acknowledged authority on war and peace (Collini 2006: 309) who called for 'nothing less than the adoption of a new set of values which might ward off another major war' (Bisceglia 1982: 27). His writing commanded a wide readership and his readers' recognition gave weight to Angell's support for the cause of internationalism. His celebrated book *The Great Illusion* 'became a peace classic' (Abrams 1988: 121), and, although it was criticised for the failure of its predictions, since the 1970s social scientists have returned to Angell's questions (Berger 2000: 43) and his ideas about the futility of war now seem to have regained their validity (Fettweis 2003).

Angell was an intellectual whose public lecturing was always in demand and whose books reached a wide audience. Statesmen, journalists, scholars and educators all acknowledged debts to him. For example, Harold Macmillan admitted in the House of Commons that his political thinking had been influenced by Angell (Marrin 1979: 16). Angell's accomplishments were also praised by John Maynard Keynes (Marrin 1979: 16, 181). What distinguished Angell from other writers, according to Harold Laski, was 'the possession of a common sense which amounts to genius ... There is probably no man since Cobden who has been able to direct so general and widespread an attention to the problems of international politics' (Laski, quoted in Marrin 1979: 77). Angell, who believed that obstacles to peace lay in 'people's minds', made education 'a remedy of war' (Bisceglia 1982: 7) and aimed through his writing and lecturing, both in Europe and in the United States, to confine nationalism to rational channels. In the period between the wars Angell became an outspoken critic of the British policies of appeasement towards Nazi Germany, and urged the United Kingdom to open its doors to Jewish refugees. To his reputation and prestige as 'one of the oldest and most active internationalists' and as a 'prodigious lecturer and journalist' he added his accomplishments as a humanitarian (Bisceglia 1982: 5).

Norman Angell was born into the wealthy family of a landowner and tradesman in Lincolnshire. After elementary schooling in England he attended the Lycée de St Omer in France. At the age of fifteen he went to Geneva, where he edited a biweekly English-language newspaper and also attended lectures at the university. Despite his aspiration to be a radical, inspired by reading Herbert Spencer, Thomas Huxley, Voltaire, Charles Darwin and John Stuart Mill, contacts with Geneva's international revolutionary communities 'imbued him with antipathy to ideologies promising utopia as the outcome of violence' (Marrin 1979: 23). In 1881, without getting a degree, he left Switzerland and emigrated to the United States (Angell 1951: 2–31). In California he worked at various jobs: as a cowboy, a ditch digger, a vine planter, a farmhand, a settler, a mail carrier and a prospector. Finally, he became a reporter for the *St Louis Globe-Democrat*, the *San Francisco Chronicle* and other newspapers (Angell 1951: 32–91).

In 1898 Angell returned to Europe. After a short stay in England he moved to Paris, where he took up journalism and contributed articles to American newspapers on the Dreyfus Affair. In 1899 he became editor of the English-language *Daily Messenger*. In the early years of the twentieth century Angell gradually became committed to the goal of international cooperation (Keene 1998: 102). His observations on the Spanish-American War, the Dreyfus Affair and the Boer War instigated his first book, *Patriotism under Three Flags: A Plea for Rationalism in Politics* (1903). This volume was a warning against the disastrous consequences of liberal democracies' tendency to act in irrational and nationalistic ways. In 1905 Angell accepted the editorship of the Paris edition of the *Daily Mail*, a position that expanded his perspective on international affairs.

Although his editorial responsibilities gave him a certain status in Paris, Norman Angell devoted an increasing amount of his time to writing and lecturing, especially after he had become a well-known public figure. His fame was mainly due to the publication of *The Great Illusion* in 1910. The book originated from a relatively small (126-page) pamphlet entitled *Europe's Optical Illusion*, which he published at his own expense in 1909. The expanded work sold almost two million copies and was translated into more than twenty-five languages (Stenersen, Libaek and Sveen 2001: 116). In *The Great Illusion*, Angell argues that war is an inadequate method for solving international disputes. The subtitle of the book, *A Study of the Relation of Military Power in Nations to Their Economic and Social Advantage*, suggests the nature of 'the great illusion'. According to Angell, who followed the views of the nineteenth-century enthusiast for free trade, Richard Cobden, war was no longer profitable in an age of economic interdependence. No one really wins the war; even the victorious nation is harmed, not only in terms of human life but in markets, trade and general welfare. The book's preface holds that military and political power gives a nation no commercial advantage, that it is an economic impossibility for one nation to seize or destroy the wealth of another, or for one nation to enrich itself by subjugating another. Angell also argues that imposing reparation payments on defeated nations only plants the seeds for future conflicts. With physical force a constantly diminishing aspect in human affairs, the increasing factor, according to Angell, is cooperation. As closer relationships of people and nations make cooperation necessary, it is cooperation that brings prosperity and progress and peace.

Angell (1910) also warned, however, that wars would continue until people recognised their uselessness, thereby suggesting the importance of education in order to appeal to reason. *The Great Illusion* captured the public's imagination and provoked discussion all over Europe and America. In the context of the growing concern for peace, it was the right book in the right place at the right time. 'Possessing the simplicity and dogmatic clarity of Marxism, Norman Angellism appealed to the idealism and missionary zeal of undergraduates' (Marrin 1979: 118). The publication of *The Great Illusion* started a popular movement for international peace called 'Norman Angellism' and promoted the formation of many Norman Angell Leagues. The ideas of the new peace movement caught on particularly in English academic circles, while in the United States Angell's ideas were promoted by the Carnegie Endowment for International Peace (Abrams 1988: 121). During his lecture tours through the United Kingdom, the United States, Germany and France, Angell visited many leagues of 'Norman Angellism', which grew into a movement supported by the Garton Foundation (Angell 1951: 164).

The Great Illusion was also praised by many scholars and journalists as a secular theory of international relations and a scientific study of war, its causes and means of preventing it (Angell 1951; Marrin 1979). Its publishing success was a result of Norman Angell's ability to 'articulate and incorporate familiar ideas into a coherent system' (Marrin 1979: 118). Nonetheless, although many scientists and liberal journals, including *The Economist* and the *Economic Review*, applauded the book, 'Angell was not immune from abuse' (Marrin 1979: 166). He was criticised for a lack of originality and the claim was made that his ideas were not scholarly and were eclectic, while others misinterpreted his argument as a prophecy. For example, the leaders of the established peace societies claimed that Angell was not saying anything that they had not said before (Abrams 1988: 121), while the most common misreading of his argument was that Angell deduced from the trend towards financial interdependence not the irrationality but the impossibility of war. The public's belief that the book's message was that 'there could be no more war', lamented Angell (1951: 151), was the very opinion that the book aimed to destroy. According to its author, *The Great Illusion*, despite being a publishing success and despite giving rise to a theory and a movement, was a political failure, because 'it did not stop a war' (Angell 1951: 149).

In order to devote himself to writing and public lecturing in support of peace, Angell resigned from the *Daily Mail* in 1912. The following year several of Angell's friends established the periodical *War and Peace* as a forum for his views (Wasson 1987: 27). Angell also wrote extensively for American journals, especially the *New Republic*. His argument, that war is irrelevant to the end it has in view, introduced the distinction between older and newer pacifist conceptions. Angell's estrangement from the peace societies, which he dismissed as utopian, grew further with the publication of his next book, in which he challenged the old pacifist assumptions and the tenants of the diplomatic orthodoxy. *The Foundations of International Polity* (1914), the chapters of which had been delivered previously as lectures at various European universities, argues that the political ideas that shape the conduct of states 'are erroneous, despite their general acceptance as self-evident and axiomatic: they are the outcome of certain abstract theories at variance with the facts' (Angell 1914: x). While repeating his argument about interdependence and the decline in the effectiveness of physical force as a means of securing services in a cooperative process, Angell urges 'the political reformation' to ensure cooperation between nations (79). 'We do and must reason and talk about these things', as public opinion 'does not descend upon us from the outside, is not something outside our acts, and volition, but the reflection of those acts: it is not made for us, we make it' (80).

Norman Angell further discussed the issue of the importance of public opinion and the need to educate people in his 1926 book *The Public Mind: Its Disorders; Its Exploitation*. He warns that the errors of public opinion are more damaging than they used to be, both because they affect government more decisively and because society has become more vulnerable as it has become more complex (1926: ii). Adapting the political instruments of democracy to the changed conditions of the modern world requires, according to Angell (iii), educating the public more consciously for social judgement, 'for the art, that is, of thinking about common facts correctly'. Using education to develop a sense of social obligation and to rise above passions and nationalist fanaticisms relies on the existence of responsible cultural and political elites as well as on the press, which does not exploit human weakness; the press 'does not create evils like nationalism or race hatred', and does not 'intensify and fix more firmly the type of character and the state of mind out of which those evils grow and become more dangerous' (1926: 135, 138). Hence Angell's calls for press reforms that would institutionalise the cause of responsible journalism and establish the rule of reason (Bisceglia 1982: 68). Angell's contribution to *The Intelligent Man's Way to Prevent War* (1933), a book edited by Leonard Woolf, asserts that in the modern world war is a result of international anarchy and that the anarchy itself is not inevitable. Thus, the problem of preventing war is the problem of replacing anarchy with a system of international law and order. Ultimately, we need reforms rooted in reason, and thus education must play a role in creating the psychology of peace (Angell 1933: 59–62).

In the beginning of 1914 Angell toured the United States for the Carnegie Endowment for International Peace. In the same year he, together with some friends, founded the Union of Democratic Control, an organisation that sought to abolish covert diplomacy and that advocated greater public control over the government's foreign policy. When the First World War broke out he formed the Neutrality League, a nonpartisan movement voicing reservations about the United Kingdom's participation in the war. However, Angell's view on neutrality changed the following year. Nevertheless, his attempts to lecture against neutrality and isolationism in the United States were stopped short by the British government. As the *New Republic* of 1 September 1916 reported, 'The British government has refused to issue passports to Bertrand Russell and Norman Angell' in order to prevent them 'from fulfilling engagements in this country to lecture', because 'it was feared that they might talk about the war to Americans in unorthodox language' (quoted in

Angell 1951: 215). Not only was Angell denied a passport on the grounds of subversion but the chief censor also introduced an embargo on his journalistic works and correspondence. This caused a debate in the House of Commons, with speakers demanding an explanation from the government as to why Angell, 'an independent critic of government' and 'a very distinguished publicist', was not allowed to influence pacifist opinion in America (Angell 1951: 222–3). When he finally managed to visit the United States, Angell pronounced the doctrine of neutrality to be obsolete, attacked isolationism and called for the establishment of a new world organisation based on collective security (Stenersen, Libaek and Sveen 2001: 117). Through his lectures and articles in the United States, and later in the United Kingdom, Angell publicised his proposal for a permanent association of nations to protect international peace and security. This proposal for a new international organisation that would ensure world peace after the war had ended was read with interest by President Woodrow Wilson, who later incorporated some of Angell's ideas into his own vision of a League of Nations (Wasson 1987: 27).

Between 1914 and 1920 Norman Angell wrote six books elaborating the reforms necessary for ensuring security in a new international system and discussing the future position of the United States in international affairs.[2] In 1918 he was an observer during the deliberations of the Treaty of Versailles, which he found to run counter to his ideas as expressed in *The Great Illusion*. As he said in his *The Peace Treaty and the Economic Crisis of Europe* (1919), the Treaty of Versailles deserved to be condemned as it contained the seeds of another war. He positively valued the League of Nations, because it was based on the principle of collective security, and he urged the United States to join it. In 1919 Angell founded the Fight the Famine movement to provide food, medicine and clothing for the children from the regions of central Europe devastated by the First World War. During the 1920s he maintained his active involvement with war relief associations. At the same time, he continued to work as a journalist and to write books and articles, through which he upheld a constant commentary on world affairs. Between 1931 and 1935 Angell wrote five more books, in which he updated his basic conceptions, stated the case for cooperation as the basis for civilisation and analysed the implications of patriotism, nationalism and imperialism.[3]

Angell, who saw himself as a journalist and an author, 'never avidly sought public office' (Bisceglia 1982: 25, 80). Making a living from his books and journalism, he preferred acting outside politics in the role of educator-publicist, 'where I might hope to modify the climate of public opinion and make it easier for the politician to be relatively honest' (quoted in Marrin 1979: 185). After the First World War, however, Angell turned 'reluctantly' to politics (Marrin 1979: 185). In the 1920s, despite being 'a far too independent thinker to be trusted with responsible adherence to the party line', Angell decided to act directly upon government through political means (Bisceglia 1982: 6). In spite of his non-partisan appeal and the fact that his ideas were integral to liberalism, his attacks on isolationism and calls for the establishment of a new world organisation lost him his conservative connections and drew him into cooperation with Labour (Abrams 1988: 121). After joining the Labour Party in 1919 he took an active part in the debates on foreign policy, became an adviser to its leader, Ramsay MacDonald, and helped move the party to a position of favouring the League of Nations (Stenersen, Libaek and Sveen 2001: 117). In 1929 he won a parliamentary seat and became a member of the Consultative Committee of the Parliamentary Labour Party. 'Angell's task, his sole reason for involvement with Labour, was to influence its policy in favour of revising the Treaty of Versailles and in support of the League of Nations: all his potential actions must ultimately be seen against commitment to collective security' (Marrin 1979: 191).

His chief problem arose when it became obvious that his basically liberal philosophy began to run counter to his Labour economics (Bisceglia 1982: 6). In 1931 he gave up his seat in the House of Commons, arguing that 'he could accomplish more as a writer and speaker' (Wasson 1987: 28). The same year he was knighted in recognition of his public service. Initially he refused the honour, but later he rationalised his acceptance by saying that the knighthood gave him the means to influence public opinion even more effectively (Angell 1951: 320–2). Throughout the 1930s Angell concentrated his efforts as a lecturer, author and journalist on the task of educating the public on the League of Nations and on the principle of collective security (322–5).

In 1934 Norman Angell received the 1933 Nobel Peace Prize, which had been withheld in the absence of suitable candidates. In his Nobel presentation speech, Christian L. Lange ([1934] 2006: 3, 1), chairman of the Norwegian Nobel Committee, described Angell as 'a great writer and journalist' and as 'one of the educators, one of those who instruct public opinion, who pave the way for reforms which the statesmen attempt to carry out'. Pointing out Angell's numerous organisational initiatives and reform proposals, Lange praised Angell for having 'the courage of his convictions' (3). In his Nobel lecture, Angell ([1934] 2006: 15) asserted that to prevent wars it is essential to educate people so they have 'a clear understanding of the elementary, the rudimentary principles upon which all human society rests, by means of which alone it can be made to work'.

In the mid-1930s Angell's estrangement from the pacifist peace movement, which had started two decades before, heightened. Being a chairman of the League of Nations Union's publicity section, a member of the Council of the Royal Institute of International Affairs, an executive of the Comité Mondial Contre la Guerre et le Fascisme (World Committee Against War and Fascism) and a member of the Executive Committee of the League of Nations Union, Angell believed in rational pacifism. His insistence that pacifism and internationalism were harmonious antagonised many and led to numerous attacks on his position. 'The problems Angell encountered in his clashes with the pacifists seemed to have been derived from his own inveterate rationalism. What Angell was trying to do would seem to be impossible. He was trying to reason away conventions based upon a religious and ideological faith' (Bisceglia 1982: 186). Not only did he oppose basing peacemaking on intensifying the fear of war but he also became critical of the government's policy of appeasement. When Italy invaded Ethiopia Angell criticised the British government for refusing to intervene or impose sanctions. Later he became an outspoken critic of Neville Chamberlain's policy of appeasement towards Nazi Germany (Wasson 1987: 28). Increasingly afraid that Europe would come under Hitler's domination, he urged the United Kingdom to give shelter to Jewish refugees. Angell's concern for the refugees revealed 'the essential courage and decency of the man' (Marrin 1979: 228).

With the outbreak of the Second World War Norman Angell volunteered his services to the Ministry of Information, proposing to go to the United States to seek support for the British war effort. When he did not secure any official mission, he went 'entirely on his own as a private person' (Angell 1951: 335). By 1945 Angell's collective security ideas of the 1930s against fascism, based on the League of Nations, had become the basis for a new post-war collective security programme led by the United States and United Kingdom against the Soviet Union (Malcolm E. Jewell, quoted in Bisceglia 1982: xiv). He stayed in the United States until 1951, advocating a gradual move towards world government under the aegis of the United Nations, working on cementing Anglo-American relations and furthering international cooperation in general. He continued to write books and articles and to attend conferences; for example, in 1960 he lectured at a conference on the reduction of world tensions at the University of Chicago. In his last book, *Defence and the English-Speaking Role* (1958), Angell gave critical analyses of the expansion of the Soviet Union and the British Labour Party's policies towards the Stalinist Soviet Union. In 1967 he received an honorary doctorate from Ball State University, in Muncie, Indiana.

In order to champion reforms to reduce the anarchy of the international system, Angell actively engaged in the work of many organisations. This 'overcommitment' seemed necessary to Angell in order to spread his message; he was in need of the support and resources that only formal networks could provide (Marrin 1979: 51). Such support was essential, as Angell's internationalist ideas attempted to 'counter the threefold opposition to those ideas by nationalist, pacifist and lukewarm supporters of the League of Nations' (Bisceglia 1982: iv). It was also essential for the realisation of his aspiration to convert public opinion. Angell's determination to fight for the cause of international cooperation, to advocate a new structure of international order, rested on his faith in the benefits of education, because – as he noted in his Nobel lecture – it was only by the application of intelligence to the management of human relations that civilisation could be saved (Angell [1934] 2006: 15).

Norman Angell's theorising about the politics of open economies was undermined by the two world wars. Thus, until quite recently, his internationalist ideas were seen as an illustration of 'the creative function of the erroneous idea' (Marrin 1979: 7). Yet recent writings on the process of globalisation admit that Angell 'had already identified the very same factors that today are imagined to be the motors of globalization' (Berger 2000: 43). In addition, his ideas about the uselessness of war seem to 'have been taken to heart by policy' (Fettweis 2003: 109) and to be 'permeating American education', as they are 'in harmony with contemporary thinking in social studies education' (John D. B. Miller, quoted in Bisceglia 1982: xi). So, although until the 1980s Angell was seen as one of those intellectuals 'who have done more for science and humanity with their magnificent errors than others have done with their small truths' (Marrin 1979: 8), his lasting importance rests upon his efforts to lay bare illusions about international politics and express his ideas of liberal internationalism.

Angell's strong sense of mission, which he defined in his Nobel Lecture as aiming to expose the fallacies that prevented people from seeing clearly the true nature of the international system (Angell [1934] 2006), meant that, as many observed, he seemed to write the same book over and over again. Angell himself saw his life's efforts for peace as a failure: he claimed that the outstanding fact about his work was that it 'has not succeeded: it has failed all but completely: failed to affect in any discernible degree the course and policy towards war' (quoted in Marrin 1979: 15). While individual efforts could never prevent world wars,

Norman Angell's books, which spoke for liberal internationalism, pleaded for a 'community of nations' to replace competitive nationalism and promoted freedom and tolerance in international affairs and a world governed by reason and experience, have served the cause of peace.

Emily Greene Balch: awakening women's interest in peace and internationalism

Emily Greene Balch (1867–1961) was awarded the Nobel Peace Prize in 1946. She was only the third woman and the second American woman to receive the prize. Emily Balch was a social reformer, economist, sociologist, peace activist, writer and poet. Throughout her subsequent careers of social work, college teaching and working for peace she was an effective advocate for international cooperation and unity. Balch was professor of political economy and sociology at Wellesley College in Boston until 1918, during which time she wrote her major academic works as well as carrying out her social reform work.[4] The outbreak of the First World War started her thirty years of pioneering for peace. Balch was a co-founder and long-time executive of the Women's International League for Peace and Freedom and a member of many other peace organisations.[5] Her efforts to improve international relations included campaigns to promote international cooperation in non-political fields. Balch's imaginative proposals for working together through the international authorities for solving peacefully the world's problems earned her her reputation among American peace activists as one of their intellectual leaders (Bussey and Tims 1965).

Emily Greene Balch came from an upper middle-class family from New England. Her father was a distinguished Boston lawyer who was a secretary to Charles Summer, the senator, abolitionist and pacifist. Balch's education reflected the widening opportunities for higher education available to women in the late 1880s. In 1886 she entered a newly founded women's college, Bryn Mawr. Although initially she was attracted to literature and studied Latin and Greek, soon her interest shifted to the social sciences. On her graduation in 1889 she was awarded Bryn Mawr's highest honour, the European fellowship. Balch used the fellowship to study economics at the Sorbonne in Paris in 1890–1, where she carried out research on public relief for the poor. In 1893 the results of her investigation were published by the American Economic Association as *Public Assistance of the Poor in France* (Wasson 1987: 48).

On her return to Boston in 1891, Balch devoted her energies to 'the improvement of conditions of life through social reforms' (Jahn[1946]

2006: 1). She became a social worker with the Boston Children's Aid Society and, in the following year, she and several of her colleagues founded a settlement house in Boston (Wasson 1987: 48). While working as a head worker in the house and helping the poor and unemployed, Balch also came into contact with many members of the Boston sociological group, whose reforming activities influenced her enormously. Nonetheless, although freelancing as a social worker did not exhaust her aspirations, neither did it stimulate her enough. Despite her desire to be 'of use', Balch abandoned full-time social work to pursue an academic career. She hoped that as a college professor she would be able to exert greater influence by awakening 'the desire of women students to work for social betterment' (Randall 1964: 84).

To qualify herself as an academic teacher, Emily Greene Balch took a course in the Harvard Annex in 1893 and the following year in the University of Chicago (Stenersen, Libaek and Sveen 2001: 140). Finally, in 1895–6, she went to Berlin to study the German social welfare system and how a public employment exchange worked. In Berlin, as in Paris, Balch managed to enjoy complete independence and felt that she 'took her life in her hands' (Balch, quoted in Randall 1964: 74). In 1896, back in Boston, she accepted a teaching position in economics at Wellesley College, where for the next twenty-two years she taught courses on the theory of consumption, labour issues, socialism, the role of women in the economy and several practical subjects dealing with the issues of poverty, slums, crime and immigration. In 1900 she was asked to organise Wellesley's first course in sociology (Abrams 1988: 143), and she also offered the first college course on the subject of immigration. Her teaching was not only innovative and enthusiastic, it also had the advantage of a certain first-hand quality, as she used her experiences gained as a social reformer to expand her students' social imagination (Wasson 1987: 48). In addition to her academic carrier, Balch maintained an active interest in reform and trade union movements. She was often asked to serve on state and municipal commissions dealing with industrial relations and education, as well as performing arbitration duties. In 1913 she chaired the Massachusetts Minimum Wage Commission, which drafted the first minimum wage law (Abrams 1988: 143). Meanwhile, in 1902 Balch had taken part in the founding, and became president, of the Boston branch of the Women's Trade Union League (Stenersen, Libaek and Sveen 2001: 141).

In 1905–6, in order to carry out her research on Slav immigration to the United States, Balch took sabbatical leave from Wellesley College and travelled through eastern and central Europe. During this time she became increasingly convinced of the need for great social change in order to correct the competitive and unjust economic system. In 1906, back home from Europe, Balch informed the Wellesley College administration that she was a socialist. Although such a declaration placed her in a vulnerable position, her professional standing was such that her political persuasions had no consequence at that point (Stenersen, Libaek and Sveen 2001: 141). By this stage Balch's reputation as an excellent teacher and as a very imaginative productive social scientist was firmly established. Her writings on the economic role of women and various social problems were well received. The publication of her book *Our Slavic Fellow Citizens* in 1910 brought Balch much acclaim and praise for an original, comprehensive and well-researched analysis of an immigrant community. In 1913 she received a new five-year appointment as professor and chair in Wellesley's department of economics and sociology (Alonso 1994: 205). Not only did her job provide her with satisfaction and social recognition, it was also her only source of income, as after her father's death in 1898 she had given away her income from his estate (Randall 1964: 107).

The outbreak of the First World War had a powerful impact on Emily Greene Balch, not just because she saw it as 'a tragic break in the work' that, to her, appeared to be 'the real task of our time: to construct a more satisfying economic order' but also because it changed her own life (Balch, quoted in Jahn [1946] 2006: 2). From the very start of the war Balch, a pacifist since 1898, decided to devoted her energies to working for peace. She joined Jane Addams in her efforts to keep the United States out of the war and in her work for US mediation between the warring sides. In 1915 Balch obtained a leave of absence from Wellesley to participate in the International Congress of Women at The Hague. During the course of this women's peace conference she helped to prepare the mediation plan for ending the war (Patterson Meyer 1978: 113). Balch was chosen as one of the six envoys to visit European officials to urge upon them a concrete plan for attaining an early peace (Randall 1964: 153). Balch had talks with Scandinavian and Russian national leaders, as well as with President Woodrow Wilson, to try and convince them of the idea of peace through continuous mediation. Although Balch and the other activists saw the failure of their plans for a governmental conference of neutrals, they did not give up, and in 1916 they supported and participated in the Neutral Conference of Continuous Mediation set up by Henry Ford. Balch, in addition to presiding over many sessions and serving on the Mediation Committee, also wrote two studies, one of which was a proposal for the international administration of colonies that anticipated the later mandate system of the League of Nations (Jahn [1946] 2006: 3).

In order to work for peace and to participate in the women's peace movement, Emily Balch took another unpaid leave of absence from Wellesley in 1917–18. She moved to New York, where she was not only active in the Women's Peace Party but also participated in the activities of more adventurous peace groups, which advocated workers' rights and women's equality and also called for radical socio-political changes (Randall 1964: 218). Because of her contacts with radical and dissenting groups, Balch found herself in 'more politically radical waters than Addams' (Alonso 1994: 209). Consequently, in the context of the high pressure for conformity in support of the war, Balch was criticised, insulted and ridiculed by the press (Randall 1964: 239). Nevertheless, despite these public attacks, the war period was a very productive time for Balch. In cooperation with the American Union Against Militarism, she published in 1918 *Approaches to the Great Settlement*, a book that offered an objective account of the various peace proposals, parties, issues and methods. Furthermore, throughout the war years, as a result of her writing, activism and contributions to many international gatherings, Balch had acquired within national and international peace movements alike a reputation as 'a figure of wisdom and common sense' (Alonso 1994: 209).[6]

While attending the International Congress of Women in Zurich in 1919, Emily Greene Balch learned that Wellesley College had decided not to renew her appointment. Although the news was not a surprise and although, in her own words, she had 'overstrained the habitual liberty of Wellesley College', she felt the loss of her teaching job deeply (Randall 1972: 79). The dismissal from Wellesley's faculty for her anti-war views left her, at the age of fifty-two, without an income, with her 'professional life cut off short and no particular prospect' (79). She accepted an invitation to join the editorial staff of *The Nation*, a weekly, in which she soon began publishing articles in support of the struggle for peace (79). With the ending of the war she ceased to call herself a socialist, not because she had moved to the right in her social politics but because the word seemed to her to have moved more definitely to connote the Marxist doctrine and because she felt a growing distaste for labels that suited 'only simple situations' (Randall 1964: 125). Moreover, she turned her emphasis towards women's international pacifism as she discovered that this movement provided the most integrated framework for the expression of her beliefs (Wasson 1987: 49). During the 1919 conference in Zurich Balch took part in founding WILPF and became its secretary and treasurer (1919–22), while Jane Addams was elected president. Balch worked for WILPF for the rest of her life, serving in various capacities.

In the years 1919–22, during which she was secretary and treasurer of the International Executive Committee of WILPF, Balch set up the headquarters of the association in Geneva, organised its office finances, developed branches in more than fifty countries and served as the association's chief representative at the League of Nations (Abrams 1988; Stenersen, Libaek and Sveen 2001). She wrote reports and draft resolutions, planned agendas, served on various committees and helped to initiate international summer schools to promote peace, which enjoyed great success and which had Bertrand Russell and Romain Rolland among their speakers. Balch also put much hard work into establishing and formalising links with various bodies, especially with the League of Nations. On behalf of WILPF she worked with League delegates and members of the secretariat. Balch's scholarly knowledge and her ability to reconcile divergent opinions and forge a working consensus helped to make WILPF's objectives heard loud and clear on the international stage (Abrams 1888: 144; Wasson 1987: 48–9).

From 1922 on Emily Greene Balch divided her work between the international WILPF and its US Section, holding important offices on both sides of the Atlantic. In 1928–33 she served as president of WILPF's US Section, while in 1929–32 she was one of three chairwomen of the WILPF International Executive Committee. In the mid-1920s she travelled for WILPF to North Africa, the Middle East and central Europe, where she tried to inspire women's interest in peace and internationalism (Stenersen, Libaek and Sveen 2001). In 1925 Haitian members of WILPF requested the International Executive Committee to look into conditions in Haiti, which had been occupied by the American Marines since 1915 (Randall 1964: 303). Balch, with five other members of the mission, spent three weeks on the island examining the effects of the US military presence on the condition of Haiti's population. The mission's findings were published in the book *Occupied Haiti* (1927), edited and largely written by Balch. Following her subsequent campaign and struggle to get the solutions accepted, the US government carried out almost all the mission's recommendations (Wasson 1987: 49).

In 1928, after some weeks of campaigning and lecturing in England, Ireland and Wales for the renunciation of war, Balch returned to Geneva, where she worked on proposals for the internationalisation of two fields that by their very nature transcend national frontiers: the sea and the air. She saw reforms leading to the internationalisation of aviation and the internationalisation of the waterways as the first steps towards a world government, which, according to her, could only be developed gradually, by expanding legislatures in one area after another (Randall 1972: 162–6). Balch wrote many other specific proposals in which she expressed her 'planetary concerns', her idea of setting up different supranational authorities for reaching agreements on different matters. In 1932 she presented to the Council of the League of Nations WILPF's concerns over arms trafficking in the form of a well-developed proposal under the title 'Disarmament' (Alonso 1994). She urged the League of Nations to recognise the need to reform, revise treaties and address not just diplomatic but economic questions as well.

In 1934 Emily Greene Balch acted again, this time without receiving payment, as the international secretary of WILPF International in Geneva. In 1935, on her return to the United States, Wellesley college invited her to give the formal Armistice Day address. Her satisfaction from the reconciliation with her college 'revealed how deep the wound had been when Wellesley failed to reengage her' (Randall 1964: 326). At the same time, Balch's criticism of American isolationism and American neutrality legislation placed her for the first time in opposition to the US branch of the Women's League (Jahn [1946] 2006: 4). During the 1930s in the United States she helped many European refugees to resettle there. Her book *Refugees as Assets* (1930) was an argument for the US acceptance of refugees from Nazi Germany for economic, cultural and humanitarian reasons (Wasson 1987). In 1937 she was elected honorary president of WILPF International, the position in which she continued to serve until her death.

The Second World War represented a difficult challenge for Balch as it forced her to re-evaluate her pacifist views: 'I went through a long and painful mental struggle, and never felt that I had reached a clear and consistent conclusion' (quoted in Randall 1964: 340). When the United States entered the war, in 1941, Balch concluded that defensive war could be sanctioned, and wrote guidance for all the branches of WILPF to reaffirm their loyalty to the country and government (Randall 1964: 344). While Balch's reluctant approval of the American war effort was seen by many as a sign of her realism, it also cost her a loss of status among many 'absolutist pacifist' members of WILPF (Stenersen, Libaek and Sveen 2001).

In 1942 the US branch of WILPF gave a public luncheon in Emily Greene Balch's honour, during which she delivered a speech entitled 'Towards a planetary civilization'. Believing that education alone was insufficient to change people's attitudes towards international organisations, Balch declared that what was really needed was new international organisational structures, enhancing functional cooperation on specific social, economic and cultural problems. In her presentation, Balch stressed the need to rationalise the world's relations in order to reduce the negative consequences of the existing 'national anarchies'.

'I see no chance of social progress apart from fundamental changes on both the economic and the political side, replacing national anarchy by organized cooperation of all peoples to further their common interests and replacing economic anarchy, based on the search for personal profit by a great development of the cooperative spirit' (quoted in Randall 1972: 1963). Balch believed in the development of international unity through a gradual process of establishing a world government that would take charge of interests that concern all peoples. According to her, an international administration, guided by the spirit of cooperation, should consist of 'a complex inter-weaving of functional arrangements for common interests' (quoted in Randall 1972: 166).

During the Second World War, despite her age, Balch worked hard to provide support and help for moral and conscientious objectors and refugees from Europe. She criticised the US government's policy towards Japanese-American citizens and helped to relocate Japanese-Americans who had been forcibly interned by the US authorities in camps (Randall 1964: 348; Abrams 1988: 144). All her work during the war, although it did nothing to improve her standing with the government, earned her the reputation of being someone who in a time of distress could be both 'good and intelligent' (Randall 1964: 368). Even more importantly, 'her independence and intrepid behaviour earned her many admirers' (Stenersen, Libaek and Sveen 2001: 141). In 1946 friends in university circles set up a 'Committee to Sponsor Emily Greene Balch for the Nobel Peace Prize'. Interestingly, she was recommended for the award by the president of Wellesley College, and among many scholars supporting her candidature was John Dewey (Keene 1998: 127). In his Nobel Peace Prize presentation speech, Gunnar Jahn ([1946] 2006: 1), chairman of the Norwegian Nobel Committee, said that Balch had been awarded the prize for her persistent fight for peace and the unfailing courage of her efforts in promoting international cooperation. Praising the realism and pragmatism of her proposals and reforms, he ended by saying that Balch 'has taught us that the reality we seek must be earned by hard and unrelenting toil in the world in which we live, but she has taught us more: that exhaustion is unknown and defeat only gives new, fresh courage to the man whose soul is fired by the sacred flame' (5).

Emily Balch was an accomplished researcher and academic. Her preoccupation with the ideas of peace, liberty and freedom did not remain purely academic, however, as she turned readily from theory to practice, from thought to action. She was a 'brilliant woman intellectual who bore the indefiniteness of her life with grace of stamina' (Palmieri 1996: 187) and who had a real talent for constructing and restructuring organisational networks. Her imaginative proposals for a gradual international coming together through functional cooperation and the rationalisation of non-political matters are remarkable, because her key conceptions and methods were rooted in reason and her scholarly knowledge. She found a way to capitalise upon her knowledge by devising ways in which people could become interested in international affairs and in finding solutions to such problems. 'Though she never held any high public office and made her contributions largely outside governmental agencies, she managed through her tireless work of writing, travel, organisation, and more uniquely by effective and continued letter writing, to achieve a wide hearing and influence' (Randall 1964: 326). Without waiting for governmental action, she relied on the formal networks of various peace and women's organisations to propose and carry out the required reforms. A typical example of her achievements is her successful work to address the issue of the American military presence in Haiti. Although a public figure, Balch was most admired by 'the small group of educated, politically active women' who regarded her as their intellectual leader (Alonso 1994: 221). All her work can be seen as realistic, detailed and based on scholarly research, leading to proposals of the reforms that would be needed to enhance the rational organisation of international affairs.

Emily Greene Balch, a practical scholar of the international peace movement, continued her efforts for peace until the end of her life, when she wrote: 'Certainly my life, like other little lives, has not visibly affected the course of events but I do not believe that any good effort is wasted' (quoted in Randall 1964: 289). Her legacy rests upon her creative and courageous promoting of 'planetary civilisation' as the great venture beyond nationalism.

Alva Myrdal: endorsing women's rights and peace

Alva Myrdal (1902–86), the 1982 Nobel Peace Prize laureate, was one of the most influential Swedish public intellectuals of the twentieth century, anticipating the centrality of gender issues in the development of the welfare state. She was a social scientist, educator and social reformer, one of the founders of the Swedish welfare state, a diplomat and a disarmament negotiator. Myrdal, as 'the most influential intellectual in the Swedish women's movement' (Ekerwald 2000: 345), was a symbol of the fight to achieve progress for women towards greater equality in all spheres of public life. Her lasting legacy rests upon her contributions to the reform of family planning, housing and education. Her writings and activities also provided powerful arguments in support of the peace movement in Sweden and internationally. Myrdal published many books and hundreds of articles, gave numerous lectures and speeches and directed large research programmes.[7] Through her writings and in her distinguished career she was an important source of inspiration, exercised enormous power over public opinion and managed to place on the international political agenda many topics that had previously been excluded. Her persistent advocacy forced such issues as gender, development issues, peace research and the problem of poverty and hunger in the world to the top of the political agenda in Sweden, and elsewhere. Myrdal received more than a dozen awards for her peace and humanitarian work.[8]

Although initially most of Myrdal's writings and organisational work 'were on a part-time and voluntary basis with women teachers and reformers' (Ekerwald 2000: 342) and although she did not hold any important position until she was in her forties, her later career included many prominent jobs, provided her with a high-profile international reputation and took her to many countries. She worked for many governmental commissions and was Sweden's second woman ambassador, the highest-ranking woman in the UN Secretariat, chairman of the United Nations Educational, Scientific, and Cultural Organization's (UNESCO's) social science section and one of the first female ministers in Sweden. After 1949, when she headed the United Nations' section dealing with welfare policy, Myrdal's concerns for equality, social justice and public welfare became international in scope. Her work as Sweden's chief delegate at the Geneva disarmament conference 1962–6 established her reputation as a symbol of the achievements and the ordeals of the nuclear disarmament process.

Alva Myrdal (born Reimer), the daughter of a building contractor who was a member of the Social Democratic Party and active in the Cooperative movement, grew up in the little town of Eskilstuna (Abram 1988: 234–5). Determined to continue her education having left school, after two years' work in the local tax office and offering private tutoring for girls in a local high school she entered Stockholm University, to study the history of religion, languages and literature. She received her BA degree in 1924, and the same year she married Gunnar Myrdal.[9] In the following years they pursued advanced studies in Stockholm, London, Leipzig, Geneva and the United States, where Alva studied psychology. She also travelled with her husband to the United States on Rockefeller Foundation scholarships in 1929–30 and studied in Geneva from 1930 to 1931. After their return to Sweden in 1932 Alva did graduate work in philosophy and pedagogy, and earned a combined master's degree from Uppsala University in 1934. By the end of the

1930s her primary academic interest was in child welfare, the family and the role of women, on which topics she published many articles.

During the 1930s Alva Myrdal, who joined the Social Democratic Party in 1932, was involved in the struggle for equal rights for women and served on a number of commissions initiated by the Social Democratic government. Having gained power in 1932, the reformist party undertook an ambitious programme of modernising industry and rationalising education and family life. 'It was a period of the expansion of and intervention by the state into both economy and society, also a period when academically trained experts, armed with scientific rationality and their particular expertise, began to seek inroads into the ruling circles of society' (Eyerman 1994: 151). Constructing the basis for the development of social democracy through processes of dynamic state planning and reforms gave a key role to social science. In this context, Myrdal's attempts to overcome traditional ways of thinking about the family structure, education and the role of women were met with interest.

In 1934 the Myrdals published *The Crisis in the Population Question*, a book which had an important influence on social policies throughout Scandinavia and contributed to Gunnar's and Alva's growing reputations in the field of population problems. In the context of the Swedish population crisis in the 1930s, when birth rates were declining, the Myrdals, with the help of the new functionalist social science, made the family an object of scientific investigation and administration and asserted that 'the family structure as well as moral and ethical values were a function of social development' (Eyerman 1994: 158). The book, seen as 'a manifesto of the Swedish Welfare' (Ekerwald 2001: 542), publicised and politicised the role of expert-intellectuals (Eyerman 1994: 158). The Myrdals' 'proposed reforms were radical' (Ekerwald 2001: 548), and designed to improve conditions for the poor, women and children and to counteract segregation and to promote equality of opportunity. But the book also caused a scandal because of its open discussion of contraceptives and sex education, and its call for radical reforms such as housing subsidies for families with children, free health care and a law forbidding employers to fire women who become pregnant was seen as posing a threat to culture and morals. As Alva Myrdal travelled around Sweden 'carrying her book's message, more than one irate listener stood up to scold her for not being at home with her new baby. Merely to take up sexual matters was daring: for a woman to co-author a book on such topics defiled her in the eyes of many' (Bok 1991: 115). Although the Myrdals' population policy now faced new criticism, the positive value of their radical proposals, which directly influenced the government's decision to assume responsibility for the well-being of all children, regardless of the financial situation of their parents, and prompted reforms in the fields of family, housing and population policy, cannot be underestimated.[10]

The publication of *The Crisis in the Population Question* led not only to the passage of social welfare legislation but also to Alva Myrdal's participation in government commissions on population and housing. As the study's co-author and a recognised authority in the field, she was appointed to the Government Committee in 1935. In 1936 Myrdal founded the Training College for Nursery and Kindergarten Teachers and directed its work until 1948, gaining reputation as an expert in early childhood education (Abrams 1988: 235–6). During the 1930s and 1940s she also played a leading role in the movement for the political and economic equality of women. As chief secretary of the state Commission on Women's Work from 1935 to 1938, she edited a monthly magazine for women members of the Social Democratic Party. As the vice-chairwoman of the Stockholm Organisation of Business and Professional Women in 1935–6, she sought to achieve feminist goals through the market place rather than through political power or psychological change. From 1938 to 1947 she served as vice-president of the International Federation of Business and Professional Women. In all her activities, Myrdal's basic aim was to design and facilitate democratic social policies consistent with a feminist conception of women's rights. Through her activities and writings she managed to put feminism on the public agenda and raised the aspirations of her contemporaries about what modern and emancipated women should and could achieve, both at work and in the home. Her slogan, 'The Working Woman's Right to Children and Marriage', had an impact not only on the women's movement but on the whole of society (Frangeur 2002).

From the beginning of the Second World War, in which Sweden remained neutral, Myrdal became concerned with the plight of refugees. She was vice-chairwoman of the Joint Committee of Swedish Civic Organisations for Cultural Relief in Europe. For her war work she was decorated in Finland and in Norway (Abrams 1988: 235). During the war she also lectured and wrote books, as well as columns for one of Stockholm's afternoon newspapers. In *Contact with America* (1941), which she co-authored with her husband, their attempts to 'arouse their fellow Swedes to guard their freedom more forcefully contributed to a greater awareness of democracy' (Bok 1991: 147). Recognising that the time was right for people to have the courage to speak out critically, the Myrdals also encouraged individuals to protect their democratic ideals and resist all who were trying to undermine them. In her own book on population issues, *Nation and Family* (published in Sweden in 1941, in

English in 1945), Alva Myrdal addressed many dilemmas connected with the relationship between the social rights of citizens and women's rights, and provided a feminist account of the national welfare state. She showed that issues of class and gender are both integral and proved that a feminist perspective is a necessary ingredient in any adequate theory of the national welfare state (Holmwood 2000: 35). While analysing procreation in modern societies, Myrdal (1941: 49–55) focused on sexuality, identity and social conditions and pointed out that it is impossible to separate the personal from the economic motives behind having a child. She asked what the principles ought to be underlying a responsible family policy and looked at the measures that society should take in order not to only counter poverty and suffering but also to promote a way of life that people could aspire to. While stressing the democratic nature of the Swedish efforts to shape a family policy, Myrdal (1941: 12–31) noted that only the population policy of a democratic state can create 'a new stronghold for married women's fight for their right to work'.

Myrdal's writings and activities made her the most famous public figure in Sweden (Ekerwald 2005: 3). In 1946, as an advocate of progressive educational methods, she was appointed to the Royal Commission on Educational Reform and named chairwoman of the World Council for Early Childhood Education. Three years later Myrdal, who was known as an active supporter of the UN, was appointed director of the United Nations Department of Social Affairs. During her stay in New York she 'was not only a civil servant in a big organisation but also, obviously, a public intellectual, known at least by other public intellectuals although perhaps not by the broad masses' (Ekerwald 2005: 3). In her new role, she enjoyed a degree of intellectual independence, as working for the United Nations in the 1940s was 'something like working for an NGO today' (3). In this role she coordinated projects involving such issues as human rights, freedom of information, the status of women, drug abuse and population growth. Myrdal not only gave talks and interviews to the media but also had intellectual debates with colleagues around the world and became 'important in wide circles in the progressive world top layer for formulating a social policy for the world through the politics of the United Nations' (4). In 1951 she moved to UNESCO in Paris as the director of the Department of Social Sciences, where she coordinated a major research project on racism and was responsible for re-establishing scientific institutions destroyed during the war and creating new research structures and universities in the newly formed independent states (Bok 1991: 215).

In 1955 Alva Myrdal was appointed Sweden's ambassador to India, where she served for six years, during which time her work contributed to the promotion of international connections, tolerance and mutual knowledge. For her efforts and goodwill she received the Nehru Award for international understanding. During this period she was also helping Gunnar with his book *Asian Drama: An Inquiry into the Poverty of Nations* (finally published in 1968), to which she contributed much research and the preliminary writing of some chapters (Bok 1991: 261). On her return to Sweden in 1961, she initiated a campaign for European aid for the developing countries. Through her lectures, her participation in conferences and her writings she contributed to the development of a new internationalism that stressed the West's obligations to Third World nations. 'Her persistent advocacy forced the issues of poverty and hunger abroad and of Swedish foreign aid to the top of the political agenda' (Bok 1991: 278). In the book *Our Responsibility for the Poor People* (1961) and in many speeches, such as 'Responsible citizenship in the world' and 'A scientific approach to international social welfare', she urged people and governments to think globally, to lower trade barriers and introduce other much-needed reforms to reduce the gap between the nations.

In 1961 Myrdal was elected to the Swedish parliament and joined the Cabinet, first without portfolio and then from 1966 to 1973 as the first Swedish minister for disarmament (Bok 1991: 294). In 1962 she was nominated Sweden's representative to the Geneva disarmament conference. During the negotiations there she played a very active role, becoming the leader of the group of non-aligned countries, on behalf of which she initiated a proposal for a nuclear ban. Representing eight non-alliance nations, she worked hard and proved to be a resilient negotiator who knew how to influence public opinion successfully (Herman 1993). Because of her humanistic pacifism, which was practical rather than radical, and because of her confidence that the road to world peace lay in both nuclear disarmament and social development for all nations, Myrdal was called the 'conscience of the disarmament movement' (Theorin 2001: 7). She became increasingly critical of the superpowers and their unwillingness to disarm, and attacked both the United States and the Soviet Union for increasing the probability of war. Nevertheless, when denouncing both world powers for their failure in the arms negotiations, Myrdal, a great believer in democracy, made it clear that she did not regard their political systems as equivalent. Her courage to speak up and to criticise world leaders and her practical work as a reformer gained her 'respect not only in her own camp but also among her adversaries' (Theorin 2001: 1). Although she did not manage to achieve her goal of a complete ban on nuclear testing, she did succeed in securing a partial ban. Her influence also contributed to Sweden's unilateral renunciation of nuclear weapons in 1968, and later of all chemical and biological means of warfare.

Until her resignation from all her government positions in 1973, Myrdal maintained her interest in disarmament issues. 'Alva Myrdal became a one-woman crusade on behalf of disarmament' (Keene 1998: 238). She gave many speeches, wrote numerous articles and published an influential book, *The Game of Disarmament* (1976), which provided powerful arguments in support of the peace movement. In the book, while showing her remarkable mastery of scientific and technical detail and her powers of analysis, she again expressed her criticism of the superpowers as being chiefly responsible for the failure of the disarmament efforts. Recognising the need for professional insight into the disarmament debate, she helped to establish the Stockholm International Peace Research Institute. Her crusade for disarmament won her several awards, including the Nobel Peace Prize. In the Nobel presentation speech, Aarvik ([1982] 2006: 1) stressed her work for nuclear disarmament and women's liberation as well as her contribution to the building of the Swedish welfare state. He noted that, because of her advocacy concerning the global issues of poverty, human rights, refugees and disarmament, she belonged to 'the world community' while at the same time being 'firmly rooted in Nordic constitutional principles and its democratic ideals' (2). In her Nobel Peace lecture, Myrdal ([1982] 2006: 5) demonstrated that, despite her idealism and her Enlightenment values, she was neither an uncritical modeniser nor a naive believer in progress. She pointed out that the progress of technology, which is a driving force of our civilisation, can be exploited for various means. While admitting that 'we human beings do not seem to have succeeded to make a choice quite consciously, nor how to steer the considerable consequences' (5), she argued that an attempt to modernise any society must respect and educate its people, and that we can and must be both practical and moral.

Alva Myrdal was 'a true intellectual, continuously exchanging views with scientists and leading politicians, who provided her with inspiration for policy work' (Theorin 2001: 2). Although she did not identify herself as a sociologist (Ekerwald 2000: 344), Myrdal made significant contributions to sociology. Moreover, the Myrdals, both jointly and separately, not only 'introduced and established American sociology in Sweden', but also 'influenced 20th-century social thought, socio-economic methodology, and public policy' (Lyon 2001: 515). Alva herself is probably best known among sociologists for the book she co-authored with Klein, *Women's Two Roles* (published in 1956), which was praised for its important contribution to developing conceptions of modern womanhood, making gender issues central to the development of democratic politics and opening debates on how to harmonise women's two lives – home and work. The authors, pointing to many studies and relying on comparative statistics, advocated various measures and reforms to enhance women's aspirations to combine family and work.

Myrdal was a very innovative and creative thinker and writer, who believed in the democratic form of government and the role of civil society as the essential element of democracy. Her main frame of reference was organised movements and the ruling Social Democratic Party and she always courageously spoke up when democratic values or processes were under threat. Being an active feminist during her time and having experience of the state bureaucracy, Myrdal 'was not afraid to point out employers or politicians' who were preventing women from participating fully in social and political life (Frangeur 2001: 11). Although many of her projects were met with strong opposition, she was never stopped by difficulties: 'I have never, never allowed myself to give up' (quoted in Stenersen, Libaek and Sveen 2001: 225). Her preparedness to struggle and not to surrender to difficulties, her reliance on a solid foundation of scientific facts and her 'very personal way of concretising general ideas' all contributed to her success in influencing public opinion, and established her image as a 'creator of public opinion' (Theorin 2001: 1–3). Myrdal proved herself to be one of the most influential reformers and moulders of public opinion associated with the ideology and praxis of social democracy in Sweden, and consequently one of the most important contributors to the development of democratic social policy worldwide.

In the context of the building of the Swedish welfare state, her role as the expert creator of public opinion was not unusual, as Swedish reformers of that time tended to combine the roles of expert-intellectuals and agitators – 'to become what can be called rationalizing intellectuals' (Eyerman 1994: 151). 'Rationalisation' in the social democratic vocabulary meant 'bringing order to a disordered world, to a world ruled by custom, rather than science, by power rather than reasoning' (152). It promised, through state intervention, stabilisation, steady growth, modernisation and social democracy. In this context, the idea of rationalisation and social science 'were given a key role' (154). Alva Myrdal's work exemplified this idea, although she added to it her concern for 'the underdog', as all her life, in her own words, she had 'been championing the underdog. I have worked for the equality of children with adults, of women with men, of the poor with the rich, of poor countries with rich countries and of lesser with strong nations' (quoted in Coughlin 1986: 45).

Trusting the positive power of reason and communication

Norman Angell, Emily Greene Balch and Alva Myrdal can all be classified as champions, because their consciousness-raising critique of various aspects of their societies was not an expression of protest or resignation but a manifestation of their trust in the positive power of reason and communication. They were more knowledgeable about the realities of power than, for instance, heroes, and they were less convinced that voicing mere ideas was sufficient to trigger desirable changes, and the outcome of these two realisations was their attempts to educate wider audiences and speak to power in support of a specific cause or interest.

The important part of all three champions' creative lives took place in the inter-war period. In the 1930s, according to many authorities on the history of intellectuals, in many Western countries the emphasis was on 'the oppositional, bohemian, or "alienated" position of the intellectual' (Collini 2006: 148). The inter-war intellectuals were 'alienated' and 'ideological rebels', who, while rejecting the bourgeois culture, 'could not find anything to substitute for it except Bohemianism and an utterly spurious proletarianism' (Shils 1955: 11). In contrast to oppositional or bohemian intellectuals, who only either protested against or rejected reality, champions' reaction to the ambivalence and uncertainties of the inter-war situation was to consider what ought to be done. They took more direct steps to realise their aspirations to humanise and rationalise the workings of societies and communities of which they felt themselves to be an integral part. In addition, as all three champions lived and worked in many countries and as they combined patriotism with internationalism, they promoted the global perspective and called for a cooperative, stable and orderly international system.

The term 'champion', as used here, presupposes the existence of a political system seen as having the potential to benefit from some processes of formalisation and rationalisation. It also assumes that the system would be a liberal democracy, in which the consequences for open criticism are not so dire as in others. Additionally, all three champions increased their scope of freedom and independence by often working abroad, mainly for international organisations – which, moreover, tended to be in the relatively early stages of formation and therefore not yet totally formalised and centralised. All the champions' reformist efforts were endorsed and initiated through their formal connections with various organisations, movements and political authorities. In their search for responsive audiences, the champions were constructing and revitalising various formal networks, and the configuration of these networks enhanced their reformist programmes. All three intellectuals in this category constructed and maintained robust formal ties, the strength of which positively affected the success of their instrumental action. It can be said, following Nan Lin's (2001: 67) proposition, that the strength of champions' organisational ties facilitated their 'access to better social capital for instrumental action'. Moreover, their multiple roles and memberships, by 'bridging' or 'linking' various movements and networks together, consolidated and strengthened their opportunity to access sources and the bases of their public authority (67–70).

The champions' relationship with power, although it constituted only one aspect of their larger networks, also allowed them to reach out to the public. While Sakharov and other dissidents were faced with state prosecution, the champions' ideas were incorporated into the state's policies. For example, Alva Myrdal, who was a champion for women's rights and for disarmament, became a political insider, an MP, a Cabinet member and even a minister, while many of her projects have been incorporated by the Swedish welfare state. Her theoretical work and her reformist activities provided support for the welfare state, a new role for women, changes in family policy, the expansion of children's welfare and the peace movement, internationally as well as in Sweden. Her involvement in the process of reforming the status and welfare of women and children permits us to say that she was the champion who established the link between scientific circles and a non-specialist public.

While heroes believe that one person can change the world, champions stress the need for dispelling old attitudes and awakening people to and informing them about alternatives to such 'truths'. Whereas heroes offer their contemporaries moral guidance on important issues, champions act upon the outside world, effecting changes in the public sphere. The difference between heroes and champions is well illustrated by the comparison of Jane Addams' high profile and Emily Greene Balch's low visibility on the American public stage. Addams' charismatic personality, her absorption in 'great things' and her work in the settlement house movement, commonly perceived as 'an extension of the domestic sphere and traditionally occupied by women' (Alonso 1994: 210), were widely admired. Balch's concentration on a more specific cause, pursing a professional career and entering the world of international affairs, 'a sphere traditionally closed to women' (Alonso 1994: 210), made her name familiar only to a select group of people. Furthermore, while Addams relied on an informal network of friends, Balch operated more on the international stage and worked with politically oriented international women's movements and other international organisations.

Champions are public intellectuals who are committed modernisers and who assume multiple roles as educators, moulders of public opinion and experts. Being very much bound up in the political realities of the day, they voice powerful arguments – based on knowledge – in favour of reforms, which they also help to advocate, promote and implement. Champions come with novel ideas but their messages, unlike pioneers' projects, are less 'revolutionary'. Our champions' attempts to rationalise the international or national order were rooted in their arguments for reason, planning and cooperation. For example, both Norman Angell's and Balch's proposals of reform were attempts at the rationalisation of the anarchy of the international system, while Myrdal voiced and supported proposals of reforms aiming to rationalise and improve the state's functions and services. In other words, what makes champions different from pioneers, who will be the subject of our next chapter, has to do with their practicality, their involvement in institutional settings, their lobbying skills and the gradualism of their proposed reforms.

Notes

1 Among Norman Angell's many books, the most important are: *The Great Illusion: A Study of the Relation of Military Power in Nations to Their Economic and Social Advantage* (1910), *The Great Illusion: 1933* (1933), *The Great Illusion – Now* (1938), *America and the New World-State: A Plea for American Leadership in International Organization* (1915), *America's Dilemma: Alone or Allied?* (1940), *Arms and Industry: A Study of the Foundations of International Policy* (1914), *For What Do We Fight?* (1939), *From Chaos to Control* (1933), *Let the People Know* (1943), *The Menace to Our National Defence: London* (1934), *The Money Game: How to Play It* (1928), *Patriotism under Three Flags: A Plea for Rationalism in Politics* (1903), *Peace with the Dictators? A Symposium and Some Conclusions* (1938), *The Public Mind: Its Disorders; Its Exploitation* (1926), *The Steep Places: An Examination of Political Tendencies* (1947), *This Have and Have-Not Business: Political Fantasy and Economic Fact* (1936) and *The Unseen Assassins* (1932).
2 *The Dangers of Half-Preparedness: A Plea for a Declaration of American Policy* (1916), *The World's Highway* (1915), *The Political Conditions of Allied Success* (1918), *The British Revolution and the American Democracy* (1919), *War Aims: A Plea for a Parliament of the Allies* (1917) and *The Peace Treaty and the Economic Chaos of Europe* (1919).
3 *The Unseen Assassins* (1932), *The Great Illusion: 1933* (1933), *The Menace to Our National Defence* (1934), *From Chaos to Control* (1933) and *Preface to Peace: A Guide for the Plain Man* (1935).
4 Among Emily Greene Balch's most important publications are *Public Assistance of the Poor in France* (1893), *Approaches to the Great Settlement* (1918), *Our Slavic Fellow Citizens* (1910), *Women at The Hague* (with J. Addams and A. Hamilton)

(1915), *Occupied Haiti* (1927), *Refugees as Assets* (1930), *The Miracle of Living* (poems) (1941), *Vignettes in Prose* (1952) and *Beyond Nationalism: The Social Thought of Emily Greene Balch* (ed. by M. M. Randall) (1972). For a full list of Emily Greene Balch's publication, see Mercedes M. Randall (1972), which includes a collection of documents, published and unpublished, and a comprehensive list of her publications. Also see Swarthmore College Peace Collection's website.

5 Balch joined many organisations campaigning against US entry into the First World War. She was a member of the Collegiate Anti-Militarism League, the Fellowship of Reconciliation American Neutral Committee, the People's Council of America, the Liberty Defence Union, the Women's Peace Party, the American Union Against Militarism, the Women's International League for Peace and Freedom and the Intercollegiate Socialist Society (Jahn [1946] 2006; Randall 1964).

6 Balch's articles, such as 'A double alignment', 'The war in its relations to democracy and world order' and 'A time to make peace', were regarded by many as some of the most statesmanlike propositions on the settlement of the European war that had appeared in any periodical (Randall 1964: 259).

7 Alva Myrdal's publications include books written with her husband Gunnar Myrdal, such as *The Crisis in the Population Question* (1934) and *Contact with America* (1941), and her own works, such as *Nation and Family* (1941), *Women's Two Roles* (with Viola Klein; 1956) and *The Game of Disarmament: How the United States and Russia Run the Arms Race* (1976).

8 These include prizes from West Germany, the Netherlands, India, the Food and Agriculture Organization of the United Nations (FAO), the Swedish Royal Academy of Sciences, the first Albert Einstein Peace Prize (1980) and in 1982 the Norwegian People's Peace Prize (Abrams 1988: 234). In 1981 Myrdal was awarded an honorary doctorate by the University of Oslo (Stenersen, Libaek and Sveen 2001: 226).

9 Gunnar Myrdal was a great scholar, winning the Nobel Memorial Prize in Economics in 1974. Together with Alva he played an important role in the shaping of the Swedish welfare state. Their book *The Crisis in the Population Question* (1934) led to the passage of social welfare legislation in Sweden and several other Scandinavian countries.

10 Recently Alva Myrdal's work was criticised for supporting the Swedish sterilisation policy. Yet, as Hedvig Ekerwald (2000: 345) notes, portraying Alva as 'a eugenic utopian is "a false image"'. Moreover, her work needs to be seen in historical context. Furthermore, in her 1941 book *Nation and Family* Myrdal herself stresses the difference between Swedish efforts to shape family policy, presented as being democratic, and the Nazis' pro-natalist and racist family propaganda.

9   Pioneers: bringing science to politics

Visionary ways of shaping uncharted territories

Searching for definitions of 'pioneer' in dictionaries or on the Web, it
soon becomes clear that the main meaning of this term refers to a person
who originates or helps open up a new line of thought, art, research or
technology – an innovator who initiates or participates in new developments. Using this conception of the term, we describe the achievements of leading scientists by stressing that they are pioneers – such as a
pioneer of artificial intelligence or a pioneer in aviation. The second
meaning of the notion refers to a pioneer as a person who first enters a
new field or settles a new region, opening it up for others; in other
words, pioneers are the first colonists or settlers in a new territory. These
two definitions can overlap when pioneering refers to a situation in
which both actions take place simultaneously, when both activities – the
developing of something new and the exploring of uncharted areas –
occur at the same time. For example, with reference to the surgeons who
pioneered organ transplants, we suggest both they participated in the
creation of something new and that they went into a previously unex-
plored field of medical practice.

Our definition of 'pioneer', as developed in chapter 4, puts the
emphasis on this double meaning of the term. The category of pioneers
is located in the informalised system underwritten by a relatively high
level of frustration. Its members are scientists whose breakthrough discoveries have earned them a reputation in the scientific community,
while their courageous acts in the interests of their community and
humanity in general testify to their sense of responsibility as scientists.
They are inventors of tools, products and theories, and at the same time,
as a moral force, they provide new insights into problems. Pioneers go
out of their way to have the community recognise the value of their ideas
and projects no matter what the resistance – and this both in the scientific and in the political sphere. Their passion for solving nature's
puzzles, together with their ethical responsibility for the knowledge they

create, make them courageous public intellectuals whose creative actions are invoked at the frontiers of knowledge and experiment.

Pioneers, believing that the discoveries of scientists should benefit mankind, aim to ensure the absorption of their inventions into the day-to-day functioning of society. When introducing their new methods, products or ideas, they rely on skilfully constructed multiple network resources that reach far beyond their informal ties. Despite the fact that they live in modern, democratic societies that are open to change, pioneers often run risks in defence of their projects. When they are successful, the process of routinisation follows, which entrenches the new actions, methods or uses of the new products. Their pioneering actions tend not to be embedded in encompassing and closed networks as the implementation of innovative ideas demands broader social reforms, for which reliance on wider, and thereby less intimate, networks is necessary. Pioneers, in contrast to champions, who are tireless advocates of a specific cause, are more instrumental and incremental in their approach. Firstly they are instrumental in the growth of their invention, especially in its early stages, and then – by linking the consequences of that invention to general principles – they get engaged in the fight for those general principles.

As the backdrop to their initiatives for change is a system that is less centralised and formalised than in the case of dissidents, pioneers are more successful in overcoming obstacles to that change than dissidents. At the same time, in contrast to heroes, whose life has an epic quality, they are not bestowed with instant recognition and lifelong celebrity status. All the same, pioneers' creative achievements grant them high professional authority and public standing within the communities that benefit from their innovations. While a hero is someone who is recognised by the public as an intellectual leader with a great sensitivity to collective problems and whose image is supplanted by the legend, pioneers are mainly scientists, who, despite the fact that their discoveries contribute to the well-being of all, are not always well known and remembered.

In our sample of public intellectuals who have won the Nobel Peace Prize are three scientists: John Boyd Orr, Linus Pauling and Norman E. Borlaug.

John Boyd Orr: freeing mankind from want

John Boyd Orr (Baron Boyd Orr of Brechin; 1880–1971), a Scottish farmer, doctor, nutritionist, biologist, soldier, politician, professor, chancellor of the University of Glasgow, banker, Member of Parliament and the 1949 Nobel Peace Prize laureate, was the first scientist to win the Nobel Peace Prize not for his scientific discoveries but for the way they were employed to promote cooperation between nations (Abrams 1988: 151). Boyd Orr was the creator of the world-famous scientific organisation the Rowett Institute, in which he established a programme of research on human and animal nutrition. His research had a significant impact on British health policy and food policy during the Second World War. He published an impressive number of original research papers and ten books.[1] Believing that, in order to solve the problem of hunger and subsequently to create the basis for a peaceful international order, agricultural and nutritional policies should be coordinated, Boyd Orr propagated and fought for a new approach to agricultural and nutritional problems on a world scale. As the first director general of the Food and Agriculture Organization and a founder of the International Emergency Food Council, not only was he interested in increasing agricultural production but he also tried to ensure an equitable distribution of the food products among the nations. Boyd Orr received more than a dozen honorary degrees from universities at home and abroad, was knighted in 1935 and elevated to the peerage in 1948.[2]

John Boyd Orr was born in Kilmaurs, Ayrshire, as a son of a quarry owner. He was educated at the village school, in which he later worked for four years as a pupil-teacher (Keene 1998: 136). Between 1899 and 1902, after winning a Queen's scholarship, he attended Glasgow University for some classes and the teachers' training college for others, but the university education was 'the most important' (Boyd Orr 1966: 40). Because of the scholarship he was expected to go back to teaching, so after graduating in 1902 he took a job as a teacher in Glasgow's poor district. After three years of teaching, Boyd Orr re-entered Glasgow University in 1905 to study science and medicine. He then worked as a GP for a short period, but when he was offered a two-year Carnegie research fellowship he accepted and went to carry out research in Glasgow University, and later in a newly created Nutrition Institute in Aberdeen. During the First World War he volunteered for the army and served as a military doctor for both the British army and the Royal Navy, firstly in active duty and later as a researcher into military diet.

After the armistice Boyd Orr returned to the Nutrition Institute in Aberdeen, from which he had had a leave of absence for the war. As the first director of the institute, his task was to build it up from scratch, establish its reputation and provide a vision for its expansion. All the institute's facilities were built as a result of Boyd Orr's efforts, imagination, organisational skills and talent for raising money. Although he worked with great enthusiasm, in his autobiography he says: 'I still look back with bitter resentment at having to spend half of my time in the humiliating job of hunting for money for the Institute' (1966: 94). By 1927 the Rowett Research Institute, as it became known, had attained an international reputation as a research centre. The status and profile of the institute were further elevated by Boyd Orr's decision to publish a journal, *Nutrition Abstracts and Reviews* (Wasson 1987: 133). In 1932 he was elected a fellow of the Royal Society, an honour which, while acknowledging his achievements as a scientist, also testified to the fact that the institute was recognised as 'one of the great research centres', which 'set the seal of success on the long struggle to establish it' (Boyd Orr 1966: 101).

From his first days in the Rowett Institute, John Boyd Orr was engaged in research, despite his various administrative duties. During his early years there he carried out a study into the role of proteins and mineral metabolism in farm and dairy animals. This investigation, which led to the publication of his influential work *Minerals in Pastures and Their Relation to Animal Nutrition* (1929), established his reputation as a highly success-ful scientist. After 1927 Boyd Orr changed his research focus to human nutrition and began to investigate how to improve people's diets. His first work devoted to human nutrition, *Milk Consumption and the Growth of School Children* (1928), was based on dietary experiments carried out among schoolchildren in the mining districts. It was followed up by a whole series of papers dealing with the subject of human nutrition, the topic which led to Boyd Orr's growing concern with policy matters. This new focus prompted him to conclude that the United Kingdom needed a coordinated, scientifically based national food policy. His innovative projects on how to improve the nation's diet were, however, at odds with official views on the matter. Unable to win government support for his proposals, he became an active lobbyist and propagandist for enriching people's nutrition.

During the 1930s, Boyd Orr engaged in large-scale surveys of nutri-tional problems in many nations. He became 'a research scientist who made the whole world his laboratory' (Calder 1966: 23). This wider focus facilitated links with international institutions and brought many foreign scholars and students to the institute. The expansion of the research on human and animal nutrition also brought the institute into contact with a number of government-sponsored or other semi-governmental organisa-tions (Boyd Orr 1966: 109). Although very realistic and still needing to raise money, he continued to be very critical of official policies, pushing for reforms to ensure improvements to diets and campaigning for changes in food policy. For example, he agitated against the establishment of food monopoly boards in the interests of producers. In 1934, during the Chadwick Lecture, Boyd Orr criticised the agricultural marketing boards and urged the establishment of a comprehensive food and agricultural policy based on human needs, which would absorb all home-produced surpluses. This 'annoyed the Ministry', and Boyd Orr was of the opinion that, since the institute was maintained by a government grant, the director 'ought not to be allowed to engage in propaganda against the government' (Boyd Orr 1966: 113).

The real confrontation with the government, however, came later over the publication in 1936 of *Food, Health and Income*, which was based on the extensive dietary surveys that had been carried out by John Boyd Orr and his team. The study, which analysed the nutritive value of the diet for each income group, found evidence that a large proportion of the British population – nearly 50 per cent of the nation at that time (1933–4) – was unable to afford an adequate diet and that 10 per cent of the population was malnourished. When these results revealing the high level of malnutrition in the United Kingdom were about to be published, the authorities ordered civil servants who cooperated with Boyd Orr to withdraw their names from the publication (Boyd Orr 1966: 114). The report, being the first scientific evidence for the nutritional state of the British people, was 'political dynamite', especially in the run-up to a general election (Calder 1966: 15). Fearing that publication might be prevented, Boyd Orr decided to make the results public as soon as possible. Accordingly, he presented the figures at the British Science Association's annual meeting in 1935, and later issued a general statement about the food position in the country (Boyd Orr 1966: 114–15). He also engaged in a series of lectures, press interviews and presentations.

Although his disclosures were criticised and many newspapers carried sensational reports, Boyd Orr had managed to ensure publicity for the research results, and, consequently, in the 1935 election campaign every candidate had to be ready to answer questions on nutrition (Calder 1966: 17). Nonetheless, the ministry continued to put up strong resistance to informing the public of the undernourishment affecting many citizens; even just before the book was to be published, 'a Minister in the government came to me and suggested that the report should be not made public' (Boyd Orr 1966: 117). Boyd Orr proposed that, instead of trying to prevent the publication of the results of his research, 'the government should take the line that, owing to the great advance in the science of nutrition, they had promoted this inquiry' (117). Later that year, 'typically, in the British tradition, the government, which he had so embarrassed' gave Boyd Orr a knighthood (Calder 1966: 15).

The publication of *Food, Health and Income* the next year widened the debate about nutritional problems, led to a public outcry and laid the foundations for a positive nutritional policy. With the creation of the

Committee against Malnutrition and with new social programmes, such as milk at schools, starting to be publicly discussed, John Boyd Orr had achieved his main goal: a close connection between health and agriculture was established. Furthermore, the *Food, Health and Income* survey and the public discussion that followed were also responsible for the sensible measures introduced by the British during the Second World War. Boyd Orr, moreover, was directly involved, as a member of Winston Churchill's Scientific Committee on Food Policy, in the formulation of the war rationing policy (Calder 1966: 15). The British government's war food policy also benefited from a book that Boyd Orr co-authored with David Lubbock, *Feeding the People in Wartime* (1940), which outlined a policy for the government that included rationing, price controls and the regulation of agricultural production. 'This application of Boyd Orr's ideas resulted in a far higher level of health among the population than anyone had expected' (Jahn [1949] 2006: 3). Yet Boyd Orr himself played 'a curious role' during the war, because, although he had been the author of so much that was then put into effect, 'the establishment was still distrustful of him and his ideas about feeding the people of the world' (Calder 1966: 18). While the British authorities were prepared to listen to him 'as an adviser, and as a member of commissions, on the practical needs of Britain in war-time, they still regarded him as a visionary' (18). Soon Boyd Orr had even more proof that being a visionary pioneer, especially in wartime, could be a cause of many problems.

Despite the fact that he was carrying heavy wartime responsibilities, he also began to plan for the post-war years, especially the problem of how to repair the damages to world food production and nutrition programmes (Abrams 1988: 152). With the *Food, Health and Income* survey also making diet an international issue, the League of Nations appointed a special commission, the Technical Commission on Nutrition, to enquire into world food needs and their relationship to agriculture, health and economics. Boyd Orr, as a member of that commission, helped to prepare statements of dietary standards and projects to link the issues of health and agriculture on a world scale. In 1942, because of his leading role in the international plans to address the war devastation and to improve levels of nutrition around the world, he was invited by the Milbank Memorial Fund to visit the United States to help to draft a world food policy based on human needs (Wasson 1987: 133). The trip was also envisaged as 'free-lance diplomacy' to get 'the Roosevelt administration to revive the League of Nations plan for food and agriculture' (Calder 1966: 18). Subsequently, in 1943, Franklin Roosevelt invited delegates from the Allied nations to Hot

Springs, Virginia, to begin implementing plans for the third of his four Atlantic Charter pledges, 'Freedom From Want'. The UK government did not appoint Boyd Orr to its national delegation, however, 'in part because he advocated international measures that might infringe upon Great Britain's ability to compete in the free market' (Wasson 1987: 133). Moreover, Boyd Orr's ideas on food policy were not in agreement with 'the traditional British view for cheap imported food and better profits in industrial exports' (Boyd Orr 1966: 160). In short, the British government did not want him to go because 'his views were, said one telegram, "unorthodox"' (Calder 1966: 18). Nevertheless, despite the fact that he did not participate in the Hot Springs conference, his views strongly influenced its discussions and the projects that were adopted. The resolutions of the conference, which called for the establishment of a new world organisation, were 'wholly in accordance with the line taken by Boyd Orr' (Jahn[1949] 2006: 3).

In 1945 John Boyd Orr retired from the Rowett Research Institute and accepted two new positions: a three-year term as rector of Glasgow University and a seat in the Commons representing the Scottish universities.[3] In his many public appearances and newspaper articles he expressed his support for the creation of the United Nations and its objectives, and especially for its goal of banishing hunger and malnutrition in the world, as he saw this aim as 'the necessary step to remove the potential cause of social and international unrest ... Some may think that this suggestion is impracticable idealism. It is the only realistic approach to the problem facing mankind' (Boyd Orr 1945: 163). Yet, despite his public voice in support of the idea of internationalising food policy, the British government, while selecting the members of a delegation to a conference in Quebec, once again overlooked Boyd Orr. The UK delegation to this meeting consisted 'of active or retired civil servants who could be trusted to say what they were told' (161). Boyd Orr, who interpreted the British political elite's opposition to his idea for the global coordination of food policy as resistance to any economic changes that might threaten their financial interests, concluded that 'the fight for a sane policy for peace and economic prosperity was lost' (Boyd Orr 1966: 161). All the same, when in November 1945, at the last moment, he was asked to join the British delegation as an adviser, he accepted the offer, because 'it was my duty to go' (162).

At the conference Boyd Orr, although unprepared, gave one of his best speeches, in which he criticised politicians for having little interest in alleviating hunger and poverty and urged delegates to give a new agency not only advisory but broad executive powers (Keene 1998: 137). The gathering showed its appreciation by appointing Boyd Orr as the first director general of the FAO.[4] He led this organisation, despite its initial lack of authority and funds, in such a way that it became a major arm of the United Nations for improving the world production and equitable distribution of food. During his years in office Boyd Orr, who regarded himself as 'the torchbearer for the organisation and his job as the firing of public imagination' (Calder 1966: 20), made very valuable contributions to averting famine in many developing countries, while at the same time planning for their long-term food needs (Abrams 1988: 151). He began by addressing the most pressing issue: the post-war food crisis. Under the FAO's umbrella he succeeded in creating the International Emergency Food Council, an organisation that was in existence for three years and that saved millions from death by starvation (Stenersen, Libaek and Sveen 2001: 147).

Boyd Orr regarded the establishment of this organisation as one of his most important achievements. His next idea was the establishment of a World Food Board, which would be invested with strong executive powers so as to be able to stabilise food prices on world markets, stockpile food stores and make grants of surplus food to the neediest countries. He travelled extensively throughout the world trying to get support for his idea. Harold Wilson, the British Labour Party leader, in his book *The War on World Poverty* (1953), explained that the main reason why the proposal failed was that neither the United Kingdom nor the United States would vote for it. The idea of the World Food Board was 'the first courageous attempt at supra-nationalism in history', and Boyd Orr was 'two jumps ahead of history' (Calder 1966: 21) – or, in other words, the World Food Board was 'too big a step to be taken all at once' (Jahn [1949] 2006: 4). The rejection of his proposal confirmed Boyd Orr's conviction that the FAO could not work for world unity and that only a world government could take the necessary action. Thus it was that in 1948, 'very depressed' that he had failed to get the nations of East and West to cooperate in the fight against poverty, he resigned his position as director-general of the FAO (Boyd Orr 1966: 217).

The next year, 1949, John Boyd Orr received the Nobel Peace Prize. Jahn ([1949] 2006: 2), in his presentation speech, emphasised the originality of Boyd Orr's research, his unique ability to combine science and policy, and his devotion to the coordination of agricultural and nutritional policies, 'not only in order to free mankind from want, but also to create a basis for peaceful cooperation between classes, nations, and races'. In his Nobel lecture, Boyd Orr ([1949] 2006: 5) singled out the disparity between the standards of living in different countries as one of the main factors behind international tensions. He donated the entire amount of the prize to organisations devoted to world peace and a united world government. As a strong advocate of world unity and peace, Boyd Orr believed in cooperation between all countries irrespective of their political and economic systems. As he did not belong to any political party, he thought that he 'might be able to smooth over any differences' that might arise between delegations from different ideological camps (Boyd Orr 1966: 287). Worried about 'the lack of vision of the politicians concerned with international affairs today' (211), he became a member, often holding office, of many of the non-governmental organisations working for a world government that would be able to prevent war and bring about the cooperation of governments for the promotion of human welfare (Stenersen, Libaek and Sveen 2001: 147).

Boyd Orr was granted the highest scientific status for producing authoritative works as a result of his agricultural studies. Nevertheless, as he moved from the study of agricultural problems and formulated the foundations for a positive nutritional policy, and as his ideas gradually became more comprehensive, some of his colleagues were soon 'denouncing him for "bringing politics to science"' (Calder 1966: 16). In reality, however, Boyd Orr was bringing science to politics. He demonstrated that, in contrast to many press presentations of him as 'a simple-minded idealist trying to promote an impractical project', he was a scientist worth listening to because of the depth of his scientific argument and because of his courage in submitting suggestions dealing with world economic affairs (Boyd Orr 1966: 174). In short, John Boyd Orr was 'the embodiment of the social-purpose of science' (Calder 1966: 23). This, together with the firmness of his devotion to his principal objectives, his antipathy to social injustice, and his resistance to the expediency of politics and the 'realism' of conventional economists, allows us to see him as a visionary pioneer.

Linus Carl Pauling: opposed to making science a 'handmaiden of war'

Linus Carl Pauling (1901–94), one the most important American scientists of the twentieth century, laid the foundations for the discovery of the structure of DNA and was responsible for many cutting-edge discoveries in chemistry, physics, crystallography and molecular biology.[5] A survey in the British journal *New Scientist* in the mid-1970s ranked him among the twenty most outstanding scientists of all time (Richards 1991: 34). He is the only person ever to have won two undivided Nobel Prizes: in 1954 he was awarded the Nobel Prize in Chemistry for his research into the nature of the chemical bond and in 1963 he received the Nobel Peace Prize for his very successful efforts to mobilise the international scientific community against nuclear testing.

Linus Pauling, the pioneer of chemical bond theory, was a scientist who turned his energies to warning the public about the dangers of nuclear war. Pauling published more than 1,000 articles and many books, testifying to his originality and the wide range of his interests.[6] Pauling's high status within the scientific community is reflected in the fact that he was the most decorated scientist of recent times, holding honorary doctoral degrees from about fifty universities, including Yale, Harvard, Cambridge and Oxford, receiving dozens of other awards and being a member of some sixty scientific societies.[7] He spent thirty-seven years as a professor at the California Institute of Technology (Caltech), which he left in search of greater freedom to continue his work for peace. His life as an academic nomad lasted until 1973, when he started his new institute to study nutrition and medicine. During the period of McCarthyism in the United States, Pauling's public protests against nuclear testing and other allegedly 'subversive' activities made him a controversial figure in American scientific and public life. He was subject to a temporary withdrawal of his passport and called to appear before an investigative congressional subcommittee, and he was often criticised in the media for his alleged leftist sympathies. Despite this, his protests against further nuclear testing contributed to the signing of the 1963 Nuclear Test Ban Treaty, which outlawed all but underground nuclear testing.

Linus Carl Pauling was born in Portland, Oregon. His father, a pharmacist, died when Linus was nine. Although the family lost the shop, Pauling maintained the interest in chemistry that he had first acquired by helping in his father's pharmacy. It was this early curiosity about how two different substances could turn into a third entirely different one that fuelled Pauling's career for the next eighty years. In 1917 he entered Oregon Agricultural State College. He worked in various jobs through his undergraduate study to support himself and his mother. After receiving a bachelor's degree in chemistry and physics in 1922, he attended graduate school at the California Institute of Technology in Pasadena. In his first year there he published his first scientific paper, on the molecular structure of crystals, followed by four more papers in his second year at the institute. In 1925 he was awarded his PhD with the highest honours as well as receiving the Guggenheim Foundation fellowship, which allowed him to study atomic physics in Munich and in Copenhagen.

In 1927 Pauling returned to Caltech and took a job there as an assistant professor of chemistry, in 1932 becoming a full professor. Over the next few years he revolutionised chemistry, first with the use of X-rays to examine the molecular structure of crystals and later with his application of quantum physics to the study of chemistry. The importance of his research in physical chemistry was recognised as early as 1931, when the American Chemical Society awarded him its prestigious Langmuir Prize. With the publication in 1939 of *The Nature of the Chemical Bond*, which earned him the Nobel Prize in Chemistry in 1954 and which is the most influential chemistry book of the last century, Pauling established his reputation as the world's best chemist (Abrams 1988; Keene 1998).

In the mid-1930s Linus Pauling turned his attention to biochemistry, with a particular focus on proteins and their main constituents. In 1936 he was appointed chairman of the Division of Chemistry and Chemical Engineering and director of the Gates and Crellin Laboratories of Chemistry at Caltech, positions that he held for more then twenty years (Wasson 1988: 799). During the Second World War he aided the US government's defence efforts. Although he was a consultant to the explosives division of the National Defense Research Commission and had many contacts with governmental institutions, he did not have access to any classified information about the atomic bomb because he had rejected Oppenheimer's offer to go to Los Alamos as head of the chemistry section of the atomic bomb project (Pauling, quoted in Kreisler 1983: 1). In 1942 Pauling and his colleagues succeeding in producing the first synthetic antibodies, a substitute for human serum in medical treatment. For his contribution to national defence he was awarded the Presidential Medal of Merit in 1948 (Keene 1998: 173).

'The nuclear attacks on Hiroshima and Nagasaki became a turning point in Pauling's life' (Stenersen, Libaek and Sveen 2001: 176). They led him to take an ethical stand and get involved in anti-nuclear activism. Pauling, who believed that it was his duty as a scientist to inform people of the consequences of radioactive fallout, began giving talks – 'popular talks ... which were purely education, descriptive in nature, with little political content. Rather soon, they began to involve the expression of my own ideas ... that the time has come when we must give up war' (Pauling, quoted in Kreisler 1983: 1). In 1946 Linus Pauling was asked by Albert Einstein to join the Board of Trustees of the Emergency Committee of Atomic Scientists, popularly known as the Einstein Committee. The most important task of this committee was to inform and educate people about the change that had taken place in the world since the invention of the atomic bomb. From the late 1940s on Pauling emerged as a leading war activist, continuously campaigning against the testing of nuclear weapons and the production of the hydrogen bomb. He and his wife, Ava Helen Pauling, were both active in the movement, lecturing, holding conferences, petitioning the government and making known to the public the issues surrounding nuclear weapons (Goertzel 1995).

During the McCarthy era Pauling was criticised for working for disarming the United States, accused of 'un-American antiwar' activism and of being pro-Soviet or a communist. 'A statement was made that my anticommunist statements hadn't been strong enough' (Pauling, quoted in Kreisler 1983: 3). Although the harassment and intense interest in his public activities by the authorities initially silenced him, the testing of hydrogen bombs in the mid-1950s led to a new period in his political activism. Pauling gave over 500 public lectures and wrote more than 100 papers and a book arguing strongly against the development of nuclear weapons (Hager 1995: 549). In 1955, together with another fifty-one Nobel Prize-winners, Pauling signed the Mainau Declaration, which called for a renunciation of force as the final resort of policy (Wasson 1987: 800).

In the early 1950s the authorities withheld his passport, on the grounds that it was in the best interests of the United States. He was prevented from travelling abroad even when he wished to attend scientific congresses; for example, he was prevented from participating in the Royal Society's symposium in London on the biochemistry of DNA, and consequently he miss the chance to view the crucial X-ray photographs that inspired Watson and Crick's vision of the double helix (Keene 1998: 174). As a result of the McCarthy period's harassment, Linus Pauling became isolated and ostracised. Believing that scientists had a special moral responsibility to make generally known the consequences of nuclear weapons and mobilise public opinion against their construction and usage, he continued expressing his opinions, however. He was threatened by the Internal Security Subcommittee of the Senate with a year in jail for contempt of the Senate and harassed by the Internal Security Subcommittee (Pauling, quoted in Kreisler 1983: 3), but he refused to answer any question about his political beliefs and affiliations as he perceived the McCarthy hearings as a threat to democracy (Hager 1995: 361). When asked by the California State Investigation Committee on Education whether he was a member of the Communist Party, Pauling said: 'It seems to be that the beliefs that I have about the proper working of democracy, the way that we can save this nation by preserving democracy against attacks that are being made against it, require that I refuse to answer any question as to my political beliefs and affiliations. And so I say that I shall not answer' (quoted in Hager 1995: 361).

Using his skills as a prolific letter writer and his network resources, Linus Pauling initiated several international appeals (Hager 1995: 549).

His best-known appeal is the 1958 petition, which was signed by 9,235 scientists from many countries, including some 2,000 American scientists, protesting against further nuclear testing and asking nations to reach an agreement to stop all testing of nuclear weapons.[8] The petition asked for 'cessation of the testing of nuclear weapons on the atmosphere where they were liberating radioactive fallout over the whole world that would cause defective children to be born and that would damage living human beings, causing cancer and other diseases' (Pauling in Kreisler 1983: 3). It also made an issue of the responsibility of scientists for the knowledge they create being central to the debate over the development of the hydrogen bomb, and, later, to the justification of its manufacture. It was in 1958 as well that Pauling published *No More War!*, a book that shows how science had become 'the handmaiden of war' – that is, how it helped people to think about war, to define new instruments of warfare and to define new strategies. It also presents a rationale for abandoning not just the further testing – and use – of nuclear weapons but even war itself, and proposes that science should became a 'handmaiden of peace' (Kreisler 1983: 8). The same year Pauling participated in a widely broadcast television debate on disarmament with Edward Teller, a physicist who supported the project and helped to build the hydrogen bomb (White 1988).

Pauling kept up the pro-ban momentum through such actions as writing letters to world leaders (for example, he wrote to Khrushchev, the Soviet leader), appearances on television, writing articles, giving public talks, initiating lawsuits against the US Department of Defense and the US Atomic Energy Commission, and the organisation of an international conference of sixty scientists from fifteen countries in Oslo to discuss the spread of nuclear weapons. His direct involvement in the anti-nuclear activism and his argument that no human being should be sacrificed to a scientific project finally brought some results. In 1963 the Nuclear Test Ban Treaty, which outlawed all but underground nuclear testing, was signed by the United States, the Soviet Union and the United Kingdom. Noticing that the language President Kennedy used in his speech announcing the signing of the partial test ban was very similar to the language that he himself had used in defining the debate, Pauling asked if this 'was ... an instance of power listening to science' (quoted in Kreisler 1983: 4). The event also illustrates the change in Pauling's status: the transition from isolation to being listened to, a transition that began with Kennedy putting political pressure on the senate to approve the test ban treaty. This political sequence, from the persecution of intellectuals during the era of McCarthyism to 'the attention and favours perceived as being lavished on selected intellectuals during the Kennedy administration' (Collini 2006: 232), formed the context of Pauling's political activism.

The year that the Nuclear Test Ban Treaty was signed the Norwegian Nobel Committee announced that the Peace Prize reserved in the year 1962 was to be awarded to Linus Pauling. Jahn ([1963] 2006: 8), in his presentation speech, emphasised that the treaty would not have been concluded if 'there had been no responsible scientist who, tirelessly, unflinchingly, year in year out, had impressed on the authorities and on the general public the real menace of nuclear tests'. While the committee appreciated the fact that Pauling, through his courageous efforts, had contributed 'to restoring to science its ideals' (8), in the United States his Nobel Peace Prize was not always seen in a positive light. For example, *Life Magazine* published an editorial with the heading 'A weird insult from Norway – the Norwegian Nobel Committee awards the Peace Prizes', suggesting that Pauling's highly ethical attitude and campaign were of no value for the nation (Kreisler 1983: 3). In his Nobel Peace Prize lecture, Pauling ([1963] 2006: 1) said that war and science are connected and that scientists have an ethical responsibility to work to prevent the use of nuclear weapons and to abolish war. He spoke as a man of science who had great faith in the role of science, and was optimistic that these great tasks could be achieved and that the discoveries of scientists would benefit mankind. Pauling summarised his intellectual position by saying that, while it was his ethical principles that caused him to reach the conclusion that war had to be abolished, it was his scientific calculation of the amount of human suffering that was behind his protests against nuclear testing and nuclear war.

In 1964 Pauling left the California Institute of Technology to become a professor at the Center for the Study of Democratic Institutions, where he stayed until 1969. In 1967 he also became a chemistry professor, first at the University of California, San Diego, and two years later at Stanford University (Goertzel 1995). In 1973, when his interest switched to researching the impact of vitamins, he established the Linus Pauling Institute of Science and Medicine in Palo Alto, California, a non-profit organisation dedicated to biomedical research and nutritional education (Keene 1998: 175). His public campaign propagating the benefits of vitamin C and his book *Vitamin C and the Common Cold* established his new image as a self-promoting pioneer of this vitamin. Again, Pauling's new mission made him a controversial figure. Although his powerful connections drew the attention of many scientists to his claims about the importance of vitamin C, the results of their testing were negative. Despite the resultant rejection of his new idea by the medical establishment, Pauling continued to seek recognition and evaluation of his claims, and he 'persistently brought his considerable energy and well-developed political skills, along with his powerful scientific and public prestige, to bear on these ends' (Richards 1991: 37). To the end of his life, when he was ninety-three years old, Pauling remained devoted to the issue of world peace as well as the work of educating people about health concerns. A believer in science and in its discoveries, he also continued his research: at the age of ninety-one, he claimed that he had published twice as many papers between the ages of seventy and ninety as he had in the preceding twenty years (Csikszentmihalyi 1996: 211).

Linus Pauling exemplified 'the optimism and success of science in postwar America' (Hager 1995: 289). He was responsible for many cutting-edge discoveries in chemistry, physical chemistry and molecular biology. He understood the spirit of scientific discovery and the conditions necessary for its generation. Pauling was passionately curious about the universe, and consequently his work crossed the boundaries of disciplines. As a young scientist, he had first revolutionised chemistry by using the methods of physics, and later enhanced our understanding of biology by using chemistry. His curiosity, his competitive attitude and his interdisciplinary approach led him to move from chemistry to physical chemistry and then to biological chemistry, and later in his life to medicine. Pauling's successes in science can be attributed to his interdisciplinary, innovative approach, his curiosity, his application in testing a wide range of ideas and his participation in many loosely structured networks, which facilitated the exchange of information without, however, limiting his freedom to experiment or change his interests. The geographical dispersion of institutions, the lack of cohesiveness of American intellectual life and the trend towards specialisation meant that the research community was bound together only through the exchange of ideas in journals and during scientific gatherings. Although the postwar period, characterised by a broad acceptance of the importance of science, saw an increasing recourse to large-scale programmed research, which therefore increased the centrality of the research community, Pauling's status, originality and wide-ranging interests, coupled with the fragmentation and diversification of the scientific field, decreased the likelihood of his participation in strong and closed networks. Despite mainly working on his own, without being a member of an inclusive research community, and despite crossing many disciplinary boundaries, Pauling became a part of the scientific establishment thanks to his pioneering achievements, and was honoured by academia and professional societies.

In the public sphere, by contrast, his work 'appeared distinctly non-conformist, where he battled the establishment, openly and defiantly'

(Hager 1995: 358) and found himself at the centre of many controversies. In his efforts to promote the ban on nuclear testing and his peace activism, Pauling, while always only representing himself, relied on the peace organisations and other associations and networks that supported the opposition to the spread of nuclear weapons. Despite the fact that more and more scientific research began to be sponsored and financed by the federal government, and despite the fact that many scientists considered it 'dangerous' to take stands on public issues (Coser 1965: 308), Pauling waged a constant campaign against war and its potentially nuclear nature. His leadership 'points to the way that we can move beyond that particularism, that nationalism, toward a universalism' (Kreisler 1983: 8).

Linus Pauling was a courageous public intellectual whose campaign to stop nuclear tests and whose brave defence of democratic rights during the McCarthy period exposed him to considerable risk. This, together with his participation in many loosely structured networks, which facilitated exchange without limiting his freedom to choose either his topics or his methods, allows us to describe Pauling not only as the pioneer of chemical bond theory and the pioneer of vitamin C, but also as a highly important public intellectual who 'put pace in the peace race' (Hager 1995: 459).

Norman Borlaug: the father of the 'green revolution'

Norman E. Borlaug (1914–), received the Nobel Peace Prize in 1970 for his contributions to the world food supply. He is an American scientist, plant pathologist and geneticist whose success in creating new varieties of wheat has earned him an international reputation as the father of the so-called 'green revolution', the dramatic increase worldwide in food production in developing countries since the middle of the twentieth century. Borlaug's outstanding contribution to the advancement of agricultural science – that is, breeding short, stiff-strawed, fertiliser-responsive wheat varieties – was significantly 'complemented by his leadership in gaining rapid adaptation and adoption of the new wheats and accompanying technology, particularly in Mexico, India and Pakistan' (Havener 1987). He has also been concerned with the human right of freedom from hunger. Being a 'refreshingly unconventional research scientist' (Lionaes [1970] 2006: 2), Borlaug was instrumental in exploiting the results of research and technology in agriculture to enhance food production. Through his public stand, which has emphasised that access to adequate food is the moral right of all mankind and that the most important factor in alleviating the food crisis is the commitment of governments to agricultural investment, he has become influential in shaping public policy in many developing countries. He is no mere scientist interested in wheat. For him, 'wheat is merely a catalyst, a part of the picture', while his main interest lies in 'the total economic development in all countries' (Borlaug, quoted in Lionaes [1970] 2006: 6).

Norman Borlaug has published several books and more than seventy articles,[9] in which he not only discusses the scientific aspects of food production but also addresses the social, economic and political obstacles to and consequences of the green revolution. He is not only 'a much-sought-after public speaker' but also a frequent contributor to articles in influential publications such as the *New York Times* and the *Wall Street Journal* (Hesser 2006: x). In addition to his scientific and humanitarian work, Borlaug has been 'an inspiring leader for many young scientists' (Lionaes [1970] 2006: 3). In order to train young scientists from all over the world in all scientific disciplines associated with food production, Borlaug took an active role in the construction of a worldwide network of international, national and local research and training centres. He is also a founder of the World Food Prize (a 'Nobel-like' prize for food and agriculture), which since 1986 has been providing monetary recognition for agricultural scientists who have made inspiring contributions to improving the quality and availability of food in the world. For his contributions to the development of agriculture through cutting-edge science and his work in hunger alleviation, Borlaug has received more than fifty honorary degrees from institutions in eighteen countries and has been awarded the United States' Medal of Freedom, the country's highest civilian award, and many other civic and scientific awards.[10]

Norman Borlaug was born and raised on a small farm in Iowa run by his parents, second-generation Norwegian immigrants. Borlaug acknowledges that his childhood on a farm influenced his lifework. 'I was born out of the soil of Howard County. It was that black soil of the Great Depression that led me to a career in agriculture' (Borlaug 2005: 1). After graduating from a high school at a nearby small town, Creaso, in 1932 he studied forestry and plant pathology at the University of Minnesota, while supporting himself by working in various jobs. In 1937 Borlaug received a BS in forestry and started to work as a forester, but later he decided to resume his postgraduate studies in plant pathology at the University of Minnesota (Stenersen, Libaek and Sveen 2001: 192). He obtained an MS in 1940 and a PhD in plant pathology two years later. For the next two years he worked as a microbiologist at E. L. du Pont de Nemours in Wilmington, Delaware, where he was in charge of research on industrial and agricultural bactericides (Wasson 1987: 119).

In 1944 Borlaug went to Mexico as a member of a four-person team of agricultural researchers commissioned by the Rockefeller Foundation, to train Mexican agricultural scientists and teach farmers new farming methods. As a head of the newly established Cooperative Wheat Research and Production Program in the country, Borlaug was assigned to organise the wheat-breeding project. As a geneticist and plant pathologist, he was interested in research in genetics, plant breeding, plant pathology, entomology, agronomy, soil science and cereal technology. Aiming to increase wheat production in Mexico, which at the time was experiencing severe crop failures and had to import more than 50 per cent of its wheat, he began to breed a high-yield, disease-resistant type of wheat (Wasson 1987: 119). Soon, in conjuction with Mexican scientists, he started achieving success in trials to improve the quality and quantity of Mexican wheat output. Borlaug's feeling of urgency at this stage (1948), dictated by his understanding of the needs of the Mexican people, meant that research from the outset was production-oriented. As he and his team 'never waited for perfection' (Borlaug, quoted in Wasson 1987: 119), they accelerated crop production. 'By 1948 Mexican wheat yields had increased dramatically', but in the 1950s 'much wheat was lost' as the plants, mainly because of the excessive use of fertilisers, grew too tall (119). So, in 1954, Borlaug crossed Mexican wheat with a dwarf wheat strain from Japan. The resulting semi-dwarf plant was a great success, as it was a tougher variety of wheat: very high-yielding, disease-resistant and more suitable for Mexican conditions (Stenersen, Libaek and Sveen 2001: 192–3). In just two years, by 1956, as a result of the progress achieved under Borlaug's management, Mexico was self-sufficient in wheat for the first time. In seven years' time almost all Mexico's wheat crop came from the semi-dwarf varieties developed by Borlaug; the harvest in 1963 was six times larger than in 1944, the year that Borlaug had arrived there (Hanson, Borlaug and Anderson 1982).

At the beginning of the 1960s Norman Borlaug became director of the International Maize and Wheat Improvement Center (known by its Spanish acronym CIMMYT) at Texcoco, close to Mexico City, and he stayed in this position until his retirement in 1979. He spent these sixteen years breeding high-yield dwarf wheat that resisted a range of plant pests and diseases and yielded two to three times more grain than traditional varieties. The Mexican experiments provided Borlaug with important lessons about social (such as the old customs and habits of farmers) and political (chiefly bureaucratic chaos and inertia) obstacles to new methods. He also learned from his mistakes and 'corrected them before the production programs in India and Pakistan began' (Borlaug, quoted in Stenersen, Libaek and Sveen 2001: 193). These new projects started in the early 1960s, when the Rockefeller Foundation and the

Mexican government sent Borlaug's team to India and Pakistan, where famine was imminent. Their task was to teach local farmers how to cultivate these high-yielding wheat varieties with the aim of doubling yields in both countries in the first year of implementation (Wasson 1987: 120).

Initially, however, Borlaug's efforts to persuade the political leaders of Pakistan to recognise the advantages of introducing the new Mexican breeds of wheat into their country were slowed down by political barriers, the local bureaucracies and the region's cultural opposition to new agricultural techniques. Despite this institutional resistance – being 'confronted with bureaucratic chaos, resistance from local breeders and centuries of farmers' habits and customs' (Borlaug 2004a: 2) – he stayed in Pakistan and India, persistently working to convince all the parties involved of the benefits of his project. His frequent confrontations with officials, in which he was aiming to convince them of the merits of introducing a new economic policy to encourage farmers to use new production technologies, were not always easy. For example, after Borlaug's presentation of his argument to India's deputy prime minister Ashok Mehta, for several minutes 'there was chaos with both of us talking in loud voices at the same time. A flood of loud angry words was emitted by both of us until we both ran out of breath and began to talk in rational tones once again' (Borlaug, quoted in Hesser 2006: 88).

By 1965 the threat of starvation convinced the governments to allow Borlaug's scheme to go ahead. 'After a successful struggle to overcome bureaucracy, prejudice, and even rumours to the effect that Dr Borlaug's variety of wheat would produce sterility and impotence among the population', Borlaug managed to secure the import of large quantities of the new Mexican breed of seeds for Pakistan and India (Lionaes [1970] 2006: 4). In spite of many difficulties, and in spite of the war between India and Pakistan, Borlaug went on to organise the growing of sufficient wheat to seed all the fields in both nations the following year. By 1968 Pakistan was already self-sufficient in wheat production, while India, although not self-sufficient that year, achieved its best results ever (Hanson, Borlaug and Anderson 1982). 'This event was celebrated in India with the issue of a new postage stamp bearing the inscription "The Indian Wheat Revolution 1968"' (Lionaes [1970] 2006: 5).

Following the successful results achieved in Mexico, India and Pakistan, the new varieties of wheat were introduced into many developing countries. By the end of the 1960s the impact of Norman Borlaug's work with wheat varieties had become known as the 'green revolution' (Stenersen, Libaek and Sveen 2001: 193). In 1970 the Norwegian Nobel Committee, in 'the hope that providing bread will also give the world peace' (Lionaes [1970] 2006: 1), defined Borlaug's achievement as essential in any struggle for the basic human right of freedom from starvation and declared that his work 'had helped to turn pessimism into optimism in the dramatic race between population explosion and food production' (Stenersen 2006: 4). The chairman of the committee, Aase Lionaes ([1970] 2006: 1), in her presentation speech said that Borlaug was receiving the award because, 'more than any other single person of this age, he has helped to provide bread for a hungry world'. She stressed his courageous fight to reverse the food shortage and the fact that he was 'not only a man of ideals but essentially a man of action', as the green revolution was not only about 'weeds and rust fungus but just as much about the deadly procrastination of the bureaucrats and the red tape that thwart quick action' (2).

Borlaug saw his Nobel Peace Prize as recognition of the social and economic achievements of the green revolution. In his Nobel lecture, he emphasised that adequate food was the moral right of all mankind and called on all countries to stop military spending and invest the money saved in research and education designed to sustain and humanize life (Borlaug [1970] 2006). He also expressed his belief in progress and claimed that all successful action programmes had to be preceded and accompanied by research. While acknowledging that there were still many unsolved social and economic problems, he optimistically assumed that, since human beings are rational, it would be possible in the next couple of decades to eliminate hunger. To achieve actual progress, however, he declared that we need scientific and organisational leadership (11–13).

Helping to develop the training necessary for a new generation of scientists and scientific leaders has, consequently, become one of his main goals. Realising, on the basis of his Mexican experience, that one of the greatest obstacles to the improvement of agriculture in the developing countries is the scarcity of trained people, Norman Borlaug has been promoting and supporting international research and training institutes and calling for an integrated international approach to the issue. He encourages the development of independent, non-political international training and research centres, as they are in a unique position to assist national programmes and to develop international collaboration (Borlaug [1970] 2006: 14). In order to increase the opportunities for young scientists from developing countries further still, Borlaug has initiated several projects, such as the World Food Prize Global Youth Institute, the Norman E. Borlaug International Agricultural Science and Technology Fellows Program (which consists of scientist exchange programmes with developing countries) and the Norman Borlaug University, an internet-based learning company for agriculture and food industry personnel. Borlaug (2005: 1), despite his impressive success in agricultural research and production, believes that his 'most important legacy will be the young students who I inspire to follow careers in science and agriculture'.

In the 1970s Borlaug's humanitarian efforts continued in China, where his technology, his policy suggestions and his training of young scientists helped to increase wheat production by millions of tonnes per year (Hesser 2006: 147–52). At the same time, however, environmentalists' criticism of Borlaug's green revolution for its reliance on large-scale monoculture, input-intensive farming techniques, cross-breeding, chemical fertilisers and pesticides ensured that 'the man who fed the world' became the 'forgotten benefactor of humanity' (Easterbrook 1997: 74). Thus it was that, despite his achievements and many rewards, Borlaug remained unknown to the general public in the United States. Moreover, many international organisations, such as the Ford Foundation, the Rockefeller Foundation and the World Bank, which once sponsored his work, gave him 'the cold shoulder' (Easterbrook 1997: 74). With the intensification of environmentalists' attacks on his agricultural programmes and practices, Borlaug tried to address some of these environmental concerns. For example, he declared in his Nobel lecture that he shared with the environmentalists their concern about the unintended consequences of the agricultural improvements and about the relationship between food supply and population growth. He also admitted that he realised that he had been too optimistic about the green revolution, as it had not solved 'the problem of poverty and chronic under-nutrition afflicting hundreds of millions of people around the world' (quoted in Hesser 2006: 171). Nonetheless, he continuously restates his belief that the green revolution was a change in the right direction, as it 'has won a temporary success in man's fight against hunger and deprivation: it has given man a breathing space' (Borlaug [1970] 2006: 17). It is 'far better for mankind to be struggling with new problems caused by abundance rather than with the old problem of famine' (17). Moreover, he warns us not confuse the use of organic and chemical fertilisers: 'Use all the organic fertilizer that is available, but don't try to tell the world we can produce all the food that is needed without chemical nitrogen or other chemical fertilizers' (quoted in Schuff 2005: 2).

Since 1986 Norman Borlaug, as president of the Sasakawa Africa Association, a non-profit, humanitarian foundation, has been working to raise agricultural productivity in Africa (Pawson 1996). He is still actively engaged in introducing small farmers in Africa to the best possible farming practices. This task requires, as Borlaug (2004a: 2) knows from his previous experiences, confrontation with both bureaucratic constraints and resistance from local farmers. Working with local breeders means fighting old habits and customs, demonstrating to farmers the values of science and technology, convincing them to adopt new ways of farming and turning their new ways of farming, as soon as possible, into routine and habitual behaviour (Borlaug 2004a: 2). In addition, since 2000 Borlaug has been working on ways to improve agricultural technology in Africa in a partnership with the Carter Center, set up by former US president Jimmy Carter in Atlanta. Their combined programme, Sasakawa-Global 2000, aims to alleviate the food crisis in Africa through teaching agricultural methods and through working with African governments to implement effective agricultural polices (Pawson 1996). In his writings, speeches and interviews, Borlaug underlines the message that African governments need to address such issues as the funding of research in the public sector, educating the public about agricultural science and technology, and the unintended consequences of cheap food policies in their countries (Borlaug 2000). Borlaug also takes the case of Africa to the American public and their political leaders. He repeatedly tells the US authorities and people that political stability in the developing world is directly linked to the food supply. Warning that Africa could face a human catastrophe on a scale the world has never seen, he calls for a Marshall Plan for Africa. For many years Borlaug has publicly endorsed, testified at Senate hearings and lobbied Congress in support of an African Growth and Opportunity Act, a measure aimed at encouraging investment in Africa (Hagstrom 1997).

Apart from his public stand and his work for these African programmes, Borlaug's current visibility on the public scene is connected with his renewed confrontation with environmentalism. This time his views on the issue of the application of biotechnology are a source of controversy with the environmentalists. Complaining that, despite the fact that the past fifty years have been the most productive period in global agricultural history, agricultural science is increasingly criticised and undermined by the opponents of biotechnology, Borlaug worries that the debate over biotechnology in the industrialised countries 'continues to impede its acceptance in most poor, food-insecure countries', while new science and biotechnology have the power to address these countries' problems (Borlaug and Carter 2005). Recently, Borlaug has publicly expressed his anger with attacks on agricultural science by people who, 'for political rather than scientific reasons, are campaigning to limit advances, especially in new fields such as genetic modification (GM) through biotechnology' (Borlaug and Carter 2005). According to him, such attacks, when there are so many hungry and suffering people, particularly in Africa, are especially destructive. Borlaug's view is that we must be more rational about our approach to risks and need to think in broader terms, recognising, for example, 'that the world cannot feed all its 6.3 billion people from organic farms or power all its cities and industries by wind and solar energy' (Borlaug 2004b: 6). While the benefits of technology should always be weighed against its risk in the absence of sufficient experience to make a confident assessment of risk we should not compensate for our lack of knowledge by simply over-estimating the risk (2004b).

Now in his nineties, Norman Borlaug continues to work, dividing his time between the Texas A&M University and CIMMYT in Mexico. He still serves as ex officio consultant on wheat research and production problems to many governments in Latin America, Africa and Asia. Borlaug also continues to write and travel in the hope of inspiring further breakthrough achievements to increase the quality and availability of food throughout the world. In order to educate the public and the authorities alike about what needs to be done to combat hunger, he is a frequent contributor to newspapers and a regular speaker at international conferences and various other public forums. He believes that agricultural scientists 'have a moral obligation to warn the political, educational, and religious leaders of the world about the magnitude and seriousness of the arable land, food and population problems that lie ahead' (Hesser 2006: 205).

Borlaug's significant contribution to today's world is his insistence that our priority should always be the alleviation of hunger and that decisions as to what technology should be used for this purpose need to be based on informed debates about the limits and potential of science and technology. Borlaug is a 'distinguished scientist-philosopher' who has been 'demonstrating practical ways to give the people of the entire world a higher quality of life' (Carter 2006: 1). His 'unique combination of technical innovation, idealism, energy, and impatience with bureaucratic inefficiency took entire countries from starvation to self-sufficiency in the space of a few years' (Hesser 2006: 193). Norman Borlaug holds the record 'for longevity as a "persistent pioneer" in the development of a new cooperative approach among the countries of the world in the alleviation of hunger' (Wellhausen 1997: 7).

Scientists addressing the problems that affect humanity

All three of these pioneering scientists, John Boyd Orr, Linus Pauling and Norman Borlaug, won the Nobel Peace Prize not for their scientific inventions but for the way they employed their discoveries to improve human life and promote cooperation between nations. Although one of the most important traits of scientific visionaries is utter absorption in their projects, this single-mindedness did not prevent these three pioneers from becoming deeply involved with one or other of the two great concerns: the nuclear arms race and hunger.

Pioneers, in their belief that society should be founded on reason, aim to apply science in the best interests of humanity. They see science as a path to a happier life for people – in other words, using science for the purposes of advancing society's well-being. They are opposed to making science into a tool for the goal of undermining the welfare of all because they believe that, when science is transformed into a means for the state, it can become, for example, a 'handmaiden of war' (Kreisler 1983: 8). We saw Linus Pauling's efforts to prevent scientific discoveries from being used for military purposes. His opposition to making science a servant of the state helped American politicians and public to construct their rationale for abandoning the testing of nuclear weapons and to define new strategies. Moreover, Pauling's opposition to making science a 'handmaiden of war' raised the question of what the most intelligent way is of dealing with the uses to which scientific discoveries can be put. This issue presented a big challenge to Boyd Orr and Borlaug too, who also used science to advance the purposes of general societal well-being. All three pioneers believed that scientists are responsible for the use made of scientific discoveries. Each of them felt that scientists have a moral obligation to see that the uses that society makes of scientific discoveries are beneficent. While Pauling was involved in trying to ban the manufacture of hydrogen bombs and nuclear testing, Borlaug was active in ensuring the usage/implementation of his agricultural inventions, and Boyd Orr worked to make certain that his advances in the science of nutrition were adopted as the basis of food policy.

Although the societies in which our three pioneers lived, in contrast to the conditions in which the dissidents worked, provided them with the ability to discharge their moral responsibility, there was still some cost attached to exercising their judgement. These pioneers, despite living in modern, mobile and competitive societies that were prepared to embrace change, and despite responding to the perceived dangers of hunger or war, were still running risks in pursuing their beliefs. All three of them, while addressing the problems that affect humankind in general, faced the possibility of being criticised (Boyd Orr, Borlaug, Pauling), being overlooked (Boyd Orr, Borlaug) and even being harassed (Pauling). The case of Pauling's mistreatment shows what it entailed for scientists to assume moral and political responsibilities during the

McCarthy period. The cases of Boyd Orr and Borlaug illustrate the process whereby links were first established and then strengthened between the spheres of knowledge and enquiry and institutions of the economy and the state, and how scientists can use these institutions as instruments to advance their purposes even though their origins and ends were entirely extrinsic to the institutions themselves. All three cases demonstrate that the existence of international status, affiliations and widely spread networks diminishes dependence on institutions.

In searching for the proper role of a scientist in a democracy, Boyd Orr, Borlaug and Pauling felt that, as scientists, they had a special contribution to make to society by virtue of their technical expertise. Boyd Orr, who thought that as a scientist he had an obligation to be involved in the political process, tried to became an adviser to the government on the role of biological research in promoting human welfare. However, as a visionary he complicated 'the tidy files of government departments' (Calder 1966: 15), and he was not always ready to accept the compromises that the role of adviser necessarily demanded. Boyd Orr's efforts to apply the truth of science to removing the root cause of the twin injustices of hunger and poverty led him to advocate in his House of Commons speech that 'the great advance of science which had been applied in war' should also be applied in times of peace, so as to give 'every citizen social and economic security' (Boyd Orr 1966: 147). Borlaug was a trusted technical adviser to several governments (in Mexico, India and Pakistan) while working at his research institute, yet he assumed an outsider's critical stance when he felt that either moral scruples or technical considerations required a position different from that 'officially' advocated. Pauling felt that, as a responsible scientist, it was his duty to inform the public and protest against nuclear testing and the development of hydrogen bombs and the justification for their manufacture.

Pioneers have great faith in the role of science, which, to some extent, exemplifies the optimism and success of science since the nineteenth century. Their optimism, their belief that science could change the world for the better, kept them involved. 'The hope is that wisdom may prevail and the great powers of science be applied in co-operation by all nations to create a wonderful new era free from the intolerable evils of war, poverty and disease' (Boyd Orr 1966: 289). This anticipation of success was also sustained by the research nature of the pioneers' work. Working in the laboratory offered them 'a freer and more humane experience in which all share and to which all contribute' – one that was full of the excitement of the discovery, decentralised and uncoerced in the setting of its goals and agenda (Schweber 2000: 17). Comparing this type of working environment to a model of Dewey's communicative community, Silvan S. Schweber observes that such a context satisfies 'one of the most exalted of human aspirations – to be a member of a society which is free but not anarchical' (17).

The pioneers' creative production and scientific discoveries were results, at least to some degree, of their crossing the boundaries of various disciplines. Our three cases show that this switching from one discipline to another happened not only because the 'chances of success (i.e. getting recognition, gaining a full chair at a relatively young age, making an outstanding contribution) in one discipline are poor' (Ben-David and Collins 1966: 460). Rather than the motivation of a self-interested competition for status, the case study of the pioneers demonstrates that crossing boundaries enhances scientific creativity, both through what has been called 'role hybridisation' – that is, 'fitting the methods and techniques of the old to the materials of the new ones, with the deliberate purpose of creating a new role' (Ben-David and Collins 1966: 460) – and through such factors as the urgency of causes, curiosity, ethical responsibility and the attractiveness of new networks.

The second stage in the process of discovery or innovation is routinisation. In other words, the role hybridisation, which is 'facilitated by the American university tradition of decentralization and competition' (Bourdieu 2004: 68), is followed by the routinisation of new habits and practices. While opening up a new line of thought and research is helped by more informal, flexible structures that give individuals more autonomy in seeking solutions to decision problems, the implantation of new products and policies is enhanced by formalisation. All three pioneers realised that formalisation is beneficial in the final stages of an innovation, and all three fought for the establishment of new rules, practices and habits that could reduce the potential ambiguity surrounding new roles, new demands and new products. For instance, Borlaug stressed the need to routinise farmers' new agricultural practices in order to take full advantage of the agricultural innovation.

Pioneers' belief that the use of science is in the best interests of humanity is similar to heroes' aspirations to employ reason to enhance societal well-being and cooperation between nations. They differ as well, though, and this difference between heroes and pioneers can best be illustrated by the similarities between Borlaug's and Boyd Orr's ideas on the relationship between peace and food production and Jane Addams' thoughts in her book *Peace and Bread in Time of War*. While all three were concerned with the links between hunger and international tensions, the pioneers brought a depth of scientific argument and policy vision to the line of reasoning, while Addams drew a general moral vision. In contrast to pioneers' aims of addressing the problems that affect all humankind, champions try to use science as a solution to a specific problem or a group's concerns. As already mentioned, dissidents, because of the closed nature of their political context, lack pioneers' wide network of contacts and their independence from the institutions of the state. To conclude, pioneers are courageous public intellectuals whose actions are invoked at the frontiers of knowledge and experiment and who try to use the advances of modern science for the benefit of all.

Notes

1 John Boyd Orr's books are *Milk Consumption and the Growth of School Children* (1928), *Minerals in Pastures and Their Relation to Animal Nutrition* (1929), *The National Food Supply and Its Influence on National Health* (1934), *Food, Health and Income* (1936), *Food and the People* (1943), *Fighting for What?* (1942), *Food: The Foundation of World Unity* (1948), *Feeding the People in Wartime* (1940; with David Lubbock), *The Wonderful World of Food: The Substance of Life* (1958) and *As I Recall* (1966).

2 Boyd Orr received many academic rewards and titles. Apart from being a member of the Royal Society, he was also an honorary member of the American Public Health Association and the New York Academy of Sciences. His other honours included the Harben Medal of the Royal Institute of Public Health, the Lasker Award of the American Public Health Association and membership of the French Légion d'honneur. Boyd Orr was also awarded two medals for his contribution to the First World War (Wasson 1987: 134).

3 Boyd Orr was elected as Member of Parliament for the Combined Scottish Universities in a by-election in April 1945 as an independent, and kept his seat at the general election held shortly afterwards. He resigned in 1946 (Wasson 1987: 134).

4 Initially Boyd Orr accepted the position of director general of the FAO only for two years, arguing that it 'was long enough to get the organisation established with executive powers if governments could be pursuaded to agree, and not too long if that should prove impossible' (Boyd Orr 1966: 163). He wanted the FAO to be an answer to the atomic bomb.

5 Although the race for the discovery of the structure of DNA was won by James Watson and Francis Crick of Cambridge University, who in 1953 discovered the double-helix shape of DNA (for which they were jointly awarded the Nobel Prize in Physiology and Medicine in 1962), it was Pauling's work that had laid the foundations for the discovery. Watson himself acknowledges that when he says that, if Pauling had not been there, and if it had not been for their big rivalry, it probably would have been much more difficult for him and Crick to have made the discovery (Goertzel 1995).

6 Among Linus Carl Pauling's books are *The Nature of the Chemical Bond* (1939), *The Structure of Molecules and Crystals* (1942), *No More War!* (1958), *Vitamin C and the Common Cold* (1970) and *How to Live Longer and Feel Better* (1986).

7 In addition to his two Nobel Prizes, Pauling received the Award in Pure Chemistry of the American Chemical Society (1931), the Davy Medal of the Royal Society of London (1947), France's Pasteur Medal, the International Lenin Prize (1971), the National Medal of Science of the National Science Foundation (1975), the Award in Chemical Sciences of the National Academy of Sciences (1979) and the Priestley Medal of the American Chemical Society (1984) (Wasson 1987: 801).

8 The Bomb Test Appeal said in its first two paragraphs: 'We, the scientists whose names are signed below, urge that an international agreement to stop the testing of nuclear bombs be made now. Each nuclear bomb test spreads an added burden of radioactive elements over every part of the world. Each added amount of radiation causes damage to the health of human beings all over the world and causes damage to the pool of human germ plasm such as to lead to an increase in the number of seriously defective children that will be born in future generations' (Pauling [1962] 2006: 3).

9 Among Norman Borlaug's publications, the most important are *Wheat Breeding and Its Impact on World Food Supply* (1968), *Norman Borlaug on World Hunger* (edited by Anwar Dil; 1997), *Land Use, Food, Energy and Recreation* (1987), *Meeting the Challenges of Population, Environment, and Resources: The Costs of Inaction* (co-authored with several other distingushed scientists; 1996), *Finite Resources and the Human Future* (also co-authored; 1976). For the whole list of Borlaug's writings and speeches, see Hesser (2006: 233–7), and for his speeches online visit www.usda.gov/oce/forum.

10 Among these many honours and rewards, Borlaug values especially the naming of a street after him in Ciudad Obregon, the wheat capital of Mexico. In 2002 he was awarded the Public Welfare Medal from the US National Academy of Sciences and in 2003 he was a recipient of Sigma Xi's John P. McGovern Science and Society Award. In 2006 Borlaug was awarded the Padma Vibhushan, India's second highest civilian honour, by the president of India (Keene 1998: 136). His boyhood home in Howard County, Iowa, is being preserved and run by the Norman Borlaug Heritage Foundation.

Conclusion

The *via contemplativa* and the *via activa*

The Nobel Peace Prize honours the highest achievements in creativity and courage: it shows 'modern fame at its most dignified' (Feldman 2001: x). It bestows recognition and authority and confers upon the laureates some kind of nobility: 'The Nobels are really knighthoods of a new and unusual kind, perhaps the only true aristocracy in our democratic levelling age' (Feldman 2001: 1). This book's aim in embodying the four types of creative and courageous public intellectual in the twelve 'Nobels' has not been to offer us idols to worship but to illustrate the different ways in which intellectuals can contribute to societal wellbeing and democracy. Its goal has been to sketch a perspective from which can be derived a more general typology of intellectuals' public involvement, which, I hope, can advance our understanding of intellectuals' public practice.

To develop a theoretical framework for an understanding of intellectuals' contributions towards the betterment of society and the enrichment of democracy, we started with the question of what gives intellectuals the authority to speak out to a general audience on broad issues. The comparison of the four types – dissidents, heroes, champions and pioneers – allows us to say that the public intellectual's special authority is constructed through his or her performance of the role with a sense of creativity and the effectiveness of his or her own voice in effecting social change within a set of historically specific cultural and social relations. Public authority, rooted in the intellectual's creative imagination and civic courage, develops in the course of what she or he does and depends upon a variety of conditions and resources, among which the nature of her or his networks and the costs of nonconformity are the most crucial. It starts with the recognition of creative achievements. The creative figure is in a position to capitalise on his or her reputation by speaking to a non-specialist audience on broader public issues. The reputation for scientific or artistic achievements can be traded or exploited in order to advance a specific cause or issue. In their pursuit of public authority intellectuals compete with one another, and this competition is helped by creative achievements and creativity in constructing their networks, along which others can be recruited and ideas can be exchanged.

Our outstanding exemplars also show a unique capacity to reduce tensions between specialism and generalism, between engagement and detachment and between intellectual action and civic responsibility – or, in other words, the tensions between the *via contemplativa* and the *via activa*. Their lives and careers confirm Weber's ([1918] 1978: 212) observation that, in order to achieve the optimum balance of intellectual engagement and detachment, there is a need to discover how to combine the ability to 'contemplate things as they are with inner calm and composure before allowing them to affect one's action' with 'a passionate commitment to a realistic cause'. All twelve public intellectuals in our sample, at different times in their lives and in different ways, but all with relative success, managed to combine 'hot passion and cool judgment [...] within the same personality' (Weber [1918] 1978: 213). Their examples illustrate that a solution to this ancient dilemma – the relationship of the *via contemplativa* to the *via activa* (where the latter, as active engagement in doing something, is always rooted in the world of people) – is associated with the possession of good judgement in the public domain. Since there are no methods that have turned out to have a clear advantage in this respect, and although there is some knowledge that can illuminate a given situation and therefore can be useful (Berlin 1996), what makes intellectuals' contribution to the democratic project successful is their democratic imagination, which is itself stimulated by their knowledge of a given specific area and their democratic values. While creative thinking and imagination are indispensable ingredients of good political judgement, intellectuals' knowledge and comprehension of the specific issues and their civic concern with justice and other matters of human significance, especially when supported by some understanding of the workings of the world of politics, can lead to inspiring insights and the actions that flow from them.

Traditionally, until the beginning of the modern age, the *via activa* had a negative connotation, while the appreciation of contemplation as the philosopher's way of life ensured the primacy of contemplation (Arendt 1958: 12–15). It is in Plato's writings that 'the eternal and the life of the philosopher are seen as inherently contradictory and in conflict with the striving for immortality, the way of life of citizens' (Arendt 1958: 20). With the modern age came a reversal of the traditional hierarchy between action and contemplation; the problem now is not how to embrace the *via contemplativa* and stand apart and alone, as Benda ([1927] 1980) suggested, but how to ensure that both contemplative and active attitudes contribute to our lives. Nonetheless, in contrast to Benda's claim, intellectuals do not inhabit a realm of pure values. Our exemplars were firmly rooted within their respective societies and their values, norms and laws, and they were concerned and affected by their communities' problems and dilemmas. The nature of their contexts enhanced or obstructed their capacity for finding a solution to the tension between engagement and detachment, yet all twelve intellectuals in our sample achieved some success in combining the *via contemplativa* and the *via activa*, even though in all cases the tension between these two states was never totally eliminated.

The lives of our public intellectuals show that the tension between intellectual action and civic responsibility is a result of several factors. In broad terms, such a conflict arises from the fact that intellectual and political actions are different kinds of action and because they cannot be practised simultaneously. The tension is also a result of the fact that intellectuals 'have had more sense of responsibility for the maintenance of traditions of intellectual achievement than they have for the well-being of their political and civil collectivities' (Shils 1990: 306). The majority of our twelve intellectuals, although they sometimes entered the political fray, tried to stay above all political parties and work towards finding common ground, without, however, compromising their democratic convictions. Despite their persistent nonconformity, they believed that public intellectuals had a duty not only to criticise but to affirm as well.

The tension between engagement and detachment was solved differently in different socio-political contexts. For example, under conditions of political closure, we witnessed the politicisation of the intellectual, as illustrated by the case of Ossietzky's attempt to alert Germany to the dangers of militarisation. On the other hand, in relatively informal and open systems, the perception of opportunities for change enhanced champions' optimistic engagements. Generally, it can be said that the nature and scope of engagement is influenced by the level of risk – that is, the anticipated danger of engaging in a specific public activity. If we are resistant to the intellectual's function, as some scholars are (for instance, Jennings 2000a), we should, like Habermas (2001), look forward to a new, cosmopolitan model of the intellectual.

Our discussion of what gives intellectuals the authority to exercise their judgement shows a wide range of intellectuals' input into societal well-being, their relations with different publics and different dimensions along which intellectuals relate to, and help shape, the political process. Our twelve public intellectuals who won the Nobel Peace Prize, while establishing the link between academia and non-specialist publics, courageously upheld and acted upon core civic values. They provide us with evidence of the importance of civil courage, because the risk was an inherent part of all their activities, including the creative process of constructing the new, solving the difficulties of social and political life and building a reputation for making important contributions to societal well-being. Thus, while remembering Aron's (1957) observation that in Western democracies criticism can no longer be regarded as proof of courage, and admitting that democracy offers many incentives for engagement, it can still be argued that courage is needed. If we want to have an educated public and educated politicians, we need to continue to find among our ranks the successors – the contemporary reincarnations – of our exemplars. In that way we can make our own contribution to reinforcing the view expressed forty years ago by the sociologist Lewis Coser (1965: 312), that there 'are good reasons to believe that a breed that has produced ... Linus Pauling ... is nowhere near extinction'.

References

Aarvik, E. [1982] 2006. Nobel Peace Prize presentation speech, at http://nobelprize.org/peace/laureates/1982/press.htm (last accessed 1 March 2006).

[1986] 2006. Nobel Peace Prize presentation speech, at http://nobelprize.org/peace/laureates/1986/presentation-speech (last accessed 16 April 2006).

Aaseng, N. 1987. *The Peace Seekers: The Nobel Peace Prize*. Minneapolis: Lerner Publications.

Abrams, I. 1988. *The Nobel Peace Prize and the Laureates: An Illustrated Biographical History, 1901–1987*. Boston: G. K. Hall.

1994. 'The many meanings of the Nobel Prize', in: K. Holl and A. C. Kjelling (eds.), *The Nobel Peace Prize and the Laureates*. Frankfurt: Peter Lang, 13–35.

Abrams, P. 1982. *Historical Sociology*. Bath: Open.

Addams, J. 1902. *Democracy and Social Ethics*. New York: Macmillan.

1922. *Peace and Bread in Time of War*. New York: Macmillan.

[1910] 1925. *Twenty Years at Hull House*. New York: Macmillan.

[1893] 2002a. 'The subjective necessity for social settlements', in: J. Bethke Elshtain (ed.), *The Jane Addams Reader*. New York: Basic, 14–29.

[1893] 2002b. 'The objective value of a social settlement', in: J. Bethke Elshtain (ed.), *The Jane Addams Reader*. New York: Basic, 29–46.

Adorno, T. [1946] 1984. *Minima Moralia: Reflections from Damaged Life* (trans. E. F. N. Jephcott). London: Verso.

Albert, R. S., and M. Runco 1999. 'A history of research on creativity', in: R. J. Sternberg (ed.), *Handbook of Creativity*. Cambridge: Cambridge University Press, 16–34.

Alonso, H. H. 1994. 'Jane Addams and Emily Greene Balch: two women of WILPF', in: K. Holl and A. C. Kjelling (eds.), *The Nobel Peace Prize and the Laureates*. Frankfurt: Peter Lang, 201–26.

Amabile, T. M. 1999. *Creativity in Context*. Cambridge, MA: Harvard University Press.

Angell, N. 1910. *The Great Illusion: A Study of the Relation of Military Power in Nations to Their Economic and Social Advantage*. London: Heinemann.

1914. *The Foundations of International Polity*. London: Heinemann.

1926. *The Public Mind: Its Disorders; Its Exploitation*. London: Noel Douglas.

1933. 'The international anarchy', in: L. Woolf (ed.), *The Intelligent Man's Way to Prevent War*. London: Gollancz, 19–66.

1951. *After All: The Autobiography of Norman Angell*. London: Hamish Hamilton.

[1934] 2006. Nobel lecture at http://nobelprize.org/peace/laureates/1933/angell-lecture.html (last accessed 8 May 2006).

Antoine, C. 1983. 'Introduction', in: A. Pérez Esquivel, *Christ in a Poncho: Witnesses to the Non-Violent Struggles in Latin America*. New York: Orbis, 1–12.

Arendt, H. 1958. *The Human Condition*. Chicago: University of Chicago Press.

1961. *Between Past and Future*. London: Faber and Faber.

1963. *On Revolution*. London: Faber and Faber.

1978. *The Life of the Mind*. New York: Harcourt Brace.

Arieti, S. 1976. *Creativity: The Magic Synthesis*. New York: Basic Books.

Aristotle [350 BC] 1962. *Nicomachean Ethics* (trans. M. Ostwald). New York: Macmillan.

Aron, R. 1957. *The Opium of the Intellectuals*. London: Routledge.

Asmis, E. 1992. 'Plato on poetic creation', in: R. Kraut (ed.), *The Cambridge Companion to Plato*. Cambridge: Cambridge University Press, 338–64.

Bacon, A. 1999. 'Peace profile: Adolfo Pérez Esquivel', *Peace Review* **11** (3): 471–7.

Bailey, G. 1990. *The Making of Andrei Sakharov*. London: Penguin.

Bailyn, B. 2003. *To Begin the World Anew*. New York: Alfred A. Knopf.

Bain, J.A. 1897. *Fridtjof Nansen: His Life and Explorations*. London: S.W. Partridge.

1898. *Life and Explorations of Fridtjof Nansen*. London: Walter Scott.

Bakhtin, M. 1968. *Rabelais and His World*. Cambridge, MA: MIT Press.

1981. *The Dialogic Imagination: Four Essays* (ed. M. Holquist, trans. M. Holquist and C. Emerson). Austin: University of Texas Press.

Balton, R.K. 2004. 'The dark side of democratic courage', *Social Research* **71** (1): 73–105.

Barbour, L.G. (ed.) 1976. *Finite Resources and the Human Future*. Minneapolis: Augsburg Publishing.

Baudrillard, J. 1990. *Seduction*. New York: St Martin's Press.

Bauman, Z. 1987. *Legislators and Interpreters*. Cambridge: Polity Press.

1992a. 'Love in adversity: on the state and the intellectuals, and the state of the intellectuals', *Thesis Eleven* **31**: 81–104.

1992b. *Intimations of Postmodernity*. London: Routledge.

1995. *Life in Fragments*. Oxford: Blackwell.

2002. 'A sociological theory of postmodernity', in: C. Calhoun, C.J. Gerteis, J. Moody, S. Pfaff and L. Virk (eds.), *Contemporary Sociological Theory*. Oxford: Blackwell, 419–29.

Ben-David, J., and R. Collins 1966. 'Social factors in the origin of new science: the case of psychology', *American Sociological Review* **31**: 451–65.

Benda, J. [1927] 1980. *The Treason of the Intellectuals* (trans. R. Aldington). New York: Norton.

Berger, S. 2000. 'Globalization and politics', *Annual Review of Political Science* **3** (1): 43–62.

Berlin, I. 1979. *Russian Thinkers*. London: Pelican.

1996. 'On political judgment', *New York Review of Books*, **3** (October): 26–30.

1999. *The Roots of Romanticism* (ed. H.H. Hardy). Princeton, NJ: Princeton University Press.

Berman, M. 2002. *Silence in the Fiction of Elie Wiesel.* Cape Town: ComPress.

Bernhard, C. G. 1987. 'The Nobel Prizes and Nobel institutions', in: T. Wassan (ed.), *Nobel Prize Winners: An H. W. Wilson Bibliographical Dictionary.* New York: H. W. Wilson Co., xxix–xxxiii.

Bernik, I. 1999. 'From imagined to actually existing democracy: intellectuals in Slovenia', in: A. Bozoki (ed.), *Intellectuals and Politics in Central Europe.* Budapest: CEU Press, 101–18.

(ed.) 2002a. *The Jane Addams Reader.* New York: Basic.

2002b. *Jane Addams and the American Dream of Democracy.* New York: Basic.

Bethke Elshtain, J., and S. Tobias (eds.), 1990. *Women, Militarism, and War: Essays in History, Politics, and Social Theory.* Savage, MD: Rowman and Littlefield.

Bickford, S. 1996. *The Dissonance of Democracy: Listening, Conflict and Citizenship.* Ithaca, NY: Cornell University Press.

Biddulph, H. 1975. 'Protest strategies of the Soviet intellectual opposition', in: R. L. Tokes (ed.), *Dissent in the USSR: Politics, Ideology, People.* Baltimore: Johns Hopkins University Press, 96–115.

Bisceglia, L. 1982. *Norman Angell and Liberal Internationalism in Britain, 1931–1935.* New York: Garland Publishing.

Bloom, A. 1988. *The Closing of the American Mind.* New York: Simon and Schuster.

Boden, M. A. 1994. 'Introduction', in: M. A. Boden (ed.), *Dimensions of Creativity.* Cambridge, MA: MIT Press, 1–12.

Bohm, D. 1998. *On Creativity* (ed. L. Nichol). London: Routledge.

Bohm, D., and D. F. Peat 1987. *Science and Creativity.* London: Routledge.

Bok, S. 1991. *Alva Myrdal: A Daughter's Memoir.* Reading, MA: Addison Wesley.

Bonner, E. 1986. *Alone Together* (trans. A. Cook). London: Collins Harvill.

Borlaug, N. 1968. *Wheat Breeding and Its Impact on World Food Supply.* Canberra: Australian Academy of Science.

1987. *Land Use, Food, Energy and Recreation.* New York: Rowman and Littlefield.

2002. *Biotechnology and the Green Revolution: Interview with Norman Borlaug*, American Institute of Biological Sciences, Washington, DC, at www. ActionBioscience.org/biotech/borlaug.html (last accessed 21 May 2006).

2004a. 'Battle to avoid compromising potential for biotech progress', *Western Farm Press* **24** (20): 2–6.

2004b. 'Foreword', in: H. Miller and G. Conko (eds.), *The Frankenfood Myth: How Protest and Politics Threaten the Biotech Revolution.* New York: Praeger, 1–23.

2005. *World Food Prize Foundation News*, World Food Prize Foundation, Des Moines, Indiana, at www.worldfoodprize.org.

[1970] 2006. Nobel lecture, at http://nobelprize.org/peace/laureates/1970/borlug-lecture.html (last accessed 8 May 2006).

Borlaug, N. E., and J. Carter 2005. 'Food for thought', *Wall Street Journal* 14 October: 10.

Boswell, J. [1791] 1998. *Life of Samuel Johnson* (eds. R. Chapman and J. D. Fleeman). Oxford: Oxford University Press.

Bourdieu, P. 1977. *Outline of Theory of Practice*. Cambridge: Cambridge University Press.

1988. *Homo Academicus* (trans. P. Collier). Stanford, CA: Stanford University Press.

1989. 'The corporatism of the universal: the role of intellectuals in the modern world', *Telos* **81** (Fall): 99–110.

1992. 'For a socio-analysis of intellectuals: an interview with L. J. D. Wacquant', *Berkeley Journal of Sociology* **1**: 1–29.

1993. *Sociology in Question* (trans. R. Nice). London: Sage.

2004. *Science of Science and Reflexivity* (trans. R. Nice). Cambridge: Polity Press.

Bourdieu, P., and L. J. D. Wacquant 1992. *An Invitation to Reflexive Sociology*. Oxford: Polity Press.

Boyd Orr, J. 1936. *Food, Health and Income*. London: Macmillan.

1943. *Food and the People*. London: Pilot Press.

1945. 'Food, health and education for the world', *The Friend* 5 October: 661–3.

1948. *Food: The Foundation of World Unity*. London: National Peace Council.

1966. *As I Recall*. London: MacGibbon and Kee.

[1949] 2006 Nobel lecture, at nobel.org/peace/laureates/1949/orr-lecture.html (last accessed 21 April 2006).

Boyd Orr, J., and D. Lubbock 1940. *Feeding the People in Wartime*. London: Macmillan.

Bozoki, A. 1999. 'Introduction', in: A. Bozoki (ed.), *Intellectuals and Politics in Central Europe*. Budapest: CEU Press, 1–18.

Breit, W., and B. T. Hirsch 2004. *Lives of Laureates: Eighteen Nobel Economists*. Cambridge, MA: MIT Press.

Brown Bissell, V. 2004. *The Education of Jane Addams*. Philadelphia: University of Pennsylvania Press.

Brym, R. J. 1980. *Intellectuals and Politics*. London: Allen and Unwin.

1988. 'Structural location and ideological divergence', in: B. Wellman and S. D. Bewoitz (eds.), *Social Structures: A Network Approach*. Cambridge: Cambridge University Press, 359–80.

Burns, T. R., and G. Stalker 1961. *The Management of Innovation*. London: Tavistock.

Bussey, G., and M. Tims 1965. *Women's International League for Peace and Freedom, 1915–1965*. London: Allen and Unwin.

Calder, R. 1966. 'Introduction', in J. Boyd Orr, *As I Recall*. London: MacGibbon and Kee, 10–26.

Camic, C., and N. Gross 2004. 'The new sociology of ideas', in: J. Blau (ed.), *The Blackwell Companion to Sociology*. Oxford: Blackwell, 236–51.

Campbell, J. 1949. *The Hero with a Thousand Faces*. New York: Pantheon.

Canguilhem, G. 1989. *The Normal and the Pathological*. New York: Zone.

Carey, J. 1992. *Intellectuals and the Masses: Pride and Prejudice among the Literary Intelligentsia 1880–1939*. London: Faber.

Cargas, H. J. 1976. *In Conversation with Elie Wiesel*. New York: Paulist Press.

Carlyle, T. [1840] 1924. *On Heroes, Hero-Worship and the Heroic in History* (ed. G. Wherry). Cambridge: Cambridge University Press.

Carter, J. 2006. 'World hunger', AgBioWorld, Tuskegee Institute, Alabama, at agbioworld.org/biotech (last accessed 12 April 2006).

Castoriadis, C. 1987. *The Imaginary Institution of Society*. Cambridge: Polity Press.

Chomsky, N. 1989. *Necessary Illusion*. London: Pluto Press.

Cole, J. R., and S. Cole 1973. *Social Stratification of Knowledge*. Chicago: University of Chicago Press.

Collini, S. 2006. *Absent Minds: Intellectuals in Britain*. Cambridge: Cambridge University Press.

Collins, H. M. 1974. 'The TEA set: tacit knowledge and scientific networks', *Science Studies* 4: 165–86.

Collins, R. 1998. *The Sociology of Philosophies: A Global Theory of Intellectual Change*. Cambridge, MA: Harvard University Press.

    2004. *Interaction Ritual Chains*. Princeton, NJ: Princeton University Press.

Comte-Sponville, A. 2003. *A Short Treatise on the Great Virtues*. London: Vintage.

Coser, L. 1965. *Men of Ideas*. New York: Free Press.

Coughlin, W. P. 1986. 'Alva Myrdal, Nobel winner', *Boston Globe* 5 February: 45.

Crane, D. 1972. *Invisible Collages*. Chicago: University of Chicago Press.

Crawford, E. 1984. *The Beginnings of the Nobel Institution: The Science Prizes, 1901–1915*. Cambridge: Cambridge University Press.

    1992. *Nationalism and Internationalism in Science, 1880–1939*. Cambridge: Cambridge University Press.

    1998. 'Nobel: always the winners, never the losers', *Science* 282: 1256–7.

Csikszentmihalyi, M. 1988. 'Society, culture, and person', in: R. J. Sternberg (ed.), *The Nature of Creativity: Contemporary Psychological Perspectives*. Cambridge: Cambridge University Press, 325–39.

    1996. *Creativity: Flow and the Psychology of Discovery and Invention*. New York: HarperCollins.

    1999. 'Implications of a system perspective for the study of creativity', in: R. J. Sternberg (ed.), *Handbook of Creativity*. Cambridge: Cambridge University Press, 313–38.

Dahl, R. A. 1973. 'Introduction', in: R. A. Dahl (ed.), *Regimes and Oppositions*. New Haven, CT: Yale University Press, 1–16.

Dalton, B. 2004. 'Creativity, habit and the social products of creative action: revising Joas, incorporating Bourdieu', *Sociological Theory* 22 (4): 603–22.

Davis, A. F. 1973. *American Heroine: The Life and Legend of Jane Addams*. Oxford: Oxford University Press.

Davis, J. 1994. 'Social creativity', in: C. M. Hann (ed.), *When History Accelerates*. London: Athlone Press, 95–110.

de Jouvenel, B. 1960. 'The treatment of capitalism by continental intellectuals', in: G. B. de Huszar (ed.), *The Intellectuals: A Controversial Portrait*. Glencoe, IL: Free Press, 387–98.

de Solla Price, D. J. 1963. *Little Science, Big Science*. New York: Columbia University Press.

Deak, I. 1968. *Weimar Germany's Left-Wing Intellectuals*. Berkeley: University of California Press.

Debray, R. 1981. *Teachers, Writers, Celebrities: The Intellectuals of Modern France* (introd. B. Mulhern, trans. D. Macey). London: Verso.

Deegan, M. J. 1988. *Jane Addams and the Men of the Chicago School*. New Brunswick, NJ: Transaction.

des Peres, T. 1978. 'The authority of silence in Elie Wiesel's art', in: A. H. Rosenfeld and I. Greenberg (eds.), *Confronting the Holocaust*. Bloomington: Indiana University Press, 49–57.

Dewey, J. 1917. 'The need for a recovery of philosophy', in: J. Dewey et al., *Creative Intelligence: Essays in the Pragmatic Attitude*. New York: Henry Holt, 3–69.

  1934. *A Common Faith*. New Haven, CT: Yale University Press.

Dil, A. (ed.) 1997. *Norman Borlaug on World Hunger*. San Diego: Bookservice International.

Donaldson, T., and P. H. Werhane (eds.) 1995. *Ethical Issues in Business*. New York: Prentice Hall International.

Dornan, P. 1975. 'Andrei Sakharov: the conscience of a liberal scientist', in: R. L. Tokes (ed.), *Dissent in the USSR: Politics, Ideology, People*. Baltimore: Johns Hopkins University Press, 354–417.

Douglas, W. O. 1960. 'Introduction', in: E. C. Johnson (ed.), *J. Addams: A Centennial Reader*. New York: Macmillan, xvii–xix.

Durkheim, E. [1895] 1966. *The Rules of Sociological Method*. New York: Free Press.

  [1912] 1971. *Elementary Forms of Religious Life*. New York: Free Press.

  [1915] 1973. *On Morality and Society* (ed. and introd. R. N. Bellah). Chicago: University of Chicago Press.

Easterbrook, G. 1997. 'Forgotten benefactor of humanity', *Atlantic Monthly* **279** (1): 74–82.

Ekerwald, H. 2000. 'Alva Myrdal: making the private public', *Acta Sociologica* **43** (3): 342–52.

  2001. 'The modernist manifesto of Alva and Gunnar Myrdal', *International Journal of Politics, Culture and Society* **14** (3): 539–61.

  2005. *The Private Life of a Public Intellectual: Alva Myrdal in the Service of the United Nations 1949–1955*. Paper presented at the Thirty-Seventh World Congress of the International Institute of Sociology, Stockholm, 5–9 July.

Engell, J. 1981. *The Creative Imagination: Enlightenment to Romanticism*. Cambridge, MA: Harvard University Press.

Ericsson, D. 2002. *Caught in the Iron Cage of Creativity*. Paper presented at the European Academy of Management's Second Conference on Innovative Research in Management, Stockholm, 9–11 May. Available at www.sses.com/.public/events/eurocram/complete_tracks/managemnt_play/ericsson.pdf (last accessed 23 July 2006).

Etzioni-Halevy, E. 1985. *The Knowledge Elite and the Failure of Prophecy*. London: Allen and Unwin.

Euripides [410 BC] 1978. *Iphigeneia at Aulis* (trans. W. S. Merwin and G. E. Dimock, Jr.). Oxford: Oxford University Press.

Eyerman, R. 1994. *Between Culture and Politics: Intellectuals in Modern Society.* Cambridge: Polity Press.

Farrell, M. P. 2001. *Collaborative Circles: Friendship Dynamics and Creative Work.* Chicago: University of Chicago Press.

Fassin, E. 1998. 'Play it again, Sartre? New Dreyfusards in search of a new Dreyfus', *French Politics and Society* **16** (1): 23–37.

Feifer, G. 1975. 'No protest: the case of the passive minority', in: R. L. Tokes, (ed.), *Dissent in the USSR: Politics, Ideology, People.* Baltimore: Johns Hopkins University Press, 418–38.

Feldman, B. 2001. *The Nobel: A History of Genius, Controversy and Prestige.* New York: Arcade Publishing.

Ferree, M. M., W. A. Gamson, J. Gerhards and D. Rucht 2002. 'Four models of the public sphere in modern democracies', *Theory and Society* **31** (3): 289–323.

Fettweis, C. 2003. 'Revisiting Mackinder and Angell: the obsolescence of Great Power geopolitics', *Comparative Strategy* **22** (2): 109–29.

Fiedor, K. 1986. *Carl Von Ossietzky: Zycie i Walka.* Warsaw: Pańtwowe Wydawnictwo Warszawa.

Finkelstein, N. G. 2000. *The Holocaust Industry: Reflections on the Exploitation of Jewish Suffering.* London: Verso.

Foucault. M. 1975. *Discipline and Punish: The Birth of the Prison.* New York: Vintage.

   1977. *Language, Counter-Memory, Practice: Selected Essays and Interviews* (ed. D. F. Bouchard and S. Simon). Ithaca, NY: Cornell University Press.

Frangeur, R. 2002. *The Feminism of Alva Myrdal and the Patriarchy.* Paper presented at the conference 'Alva Myrdal's questions to our time', Uppsala, Sweden, 6–8 March.

Frei, B. (ed.) 1971a. *The Stolen Republic: Selected Writings of Carl von Ossietzky.* London: Lawrence and Wishart.

   1971b. 'Carl von Ossietzky and his time', in: B. Frei (ed.), *The Stolen Republic: Selected Writings of Carl von Ossietzky.* London: Lawrence and Wishart, 11–30.

Friendly, A., Jr. 1979. 'Introduction', in: A. Sakharov, *Alarm and Hope* (eds. E. E. Yankelevich and A. Friendly, Jr.). London: Collins Harvill, xi–xix.

Fromm, E. 1998. *On Being Human.* New York: Continuum.

Fuchs, S. 2001. *Against Essentialism.* Cambridge, MA: Harvard University Press.

Fuller, S. 2003. 'The critique of intellectuals in a time of pragmatist captivity', *History of Human Science* **16** (4): 19–38.

   2005. *The Intellectual.* London: Icon.

Furedi, F. 2004. *Where Have All the Intellectuals Gone?* London: Continuum.

Gardner, H. 1988. 'Synthetic scientific growth', in: R. J Sternberg (ed.), *The Nature of Creativity: Contemporary Psychological Perspectives.* Cambridge: Cambridge University Press, 298–324.

   1993. *Creating Minds: An Anatomy of Creativity.* New York: Basic.

Gerth, H. H., and C. W. Mills (eds.) 1946. *From Max Weber: Essays in Sociology.* Oxford: Oxford University Press.

Glassner, B. 2004. 'Narrative techniques of fear-mongering', *Social Research* 7 (4): 819–27.

Glover, J. 1999. *Humanity: A Moral History of the Twentieth Century.* London: Jonathan Cape.

Goertzel, T. G. 1995. *Linus Pauling: A Life in Science and Politics.* New York: Basic.

Goldfarb, J. C. 1998. *Civility and Subversion: The Intellectual in Democratic Society.* Cambridge: Cambridge University Press.

Goldgar, A. 1995. *Impolite Learning: Conduct and Community in the Republic of Letters, 1680–1750.* New Haven, CT: Yale University Press.

Gouldner, A. W. 1979. *The Future of Intellectuals and the Rise of the New Class.* New York: Seabury.

Gramsci, A. 1971. *Selections from the Prison Notebooks* (ed. O. Hoare and G. Smith). London: Lawrence and Wishart.

Grossmann, K. R. 1963. *Ossietzky: Ein deutsches Patriot.* Munich: Kindles.

Gruber, H. E. 1980. 'Cognitive psychology, scientific creativity and the case study method', in: M. D. Graek, R. S. Cohen and G. Cimion (eds.), *On Scientific Creativity.* Amsterdam: D. Reidel, 259–322.

  1981. 'Breakaway minds', *Psychology Today* **15**: 68–73.

  1983. 'History and creative work: from the most ordinary to the most exalted', *Journal of History and the Behavioral Sciences* **19**: 4–15.

Gussejnow, G. 1994. 'Andrei Sakharov and Mikhail Gorbachev', in: K. Holl and A. C. Kjelling (eds.), *The Nobel Peace Prize and the Laureates.* Frankfurt: Peter Lang, 277–93.

Habermas, J. 1989. *The New Conservatism.* Cambridge: Polity Press.

  1997. *A Berlin Republic: Writing on Germany* (trans. S. Rendall). Lincoln: University of Nebraska Press.

  2001. *The Postnational Constellation: Political Essays.* Cambridge: Polity Press.

  2002. 'Civil society and the political public sphere', in: C. Calhoun, J. Gerteis, J. Moody, S. Pfaff and I. Virk (eds.), *Contemporary Sociological Theory.* Oxford: Blackwell, 358–77.

Hacking, I. 1990. *The Taming of Chance.* Cambridge: Cambridge University Press.

Hager, T. 1995. *Force of Nature: The Life of Linus Pauling.* New York: Simon and Schuster.

Hagstrom, J. 1997. 'Nobel laureate urges aid for Africa', *National Journal* **29** (38): 18–37.

Hagstrom, W. 1965. *The Scientific Community.* New York: Basic.

Hall, H. 1960. 'Introduction: social work', in: E. C. Johnson (ed.), *J. Addams: A Centennial Reader.* New York: Macmillan, 2–6.

Hamilton, R. F. 2003. 'American sociology rewrites history', *Sociological Theory* **21** (3): 281–97.

Hanson, H., N. E. Borlaug and R. G. Anderson 1982. *Wheat in the Third World.* Boulder, CO: Westview Press.

Hastrup, K. 2001. 'Othello's dance: cultural creativity and human agency', in: J. Liep (ed.), *Locating Cultural Creativity*. London: Pluto Press, 31–45.

Havel, V. 1991. *Disturbing the Peace: A Conversation with Karel Hvizdala*. New York: Vintage.

Havener, R. D. 1987. 'Scientists: their rewards and humanity', *Science* 237:1281.

Hayek, F. A. 1960. 'The intellectual and socialism', in: G. B. de Huszar (ed.), *The Intellectuals: A Controversial Portrait*. Glencoe, IL: Free Press, 371–86.

Heller, S. 2004. 'The ministry of fear', *Social Research* 7 (4): 849–963.

Henley, J. 2005. 'Nobel's changing landscape', *The Guardian* 4 October: 1–2.

Herman, S. R. 1993. 'From international feminism to feminist internationalism: the emergence of Alva Myrdal, 1936–1955', *Peace and Change* 18 (4): 325–46.

Hesser, L. 2006. *The Man Who Fed the World: An Authorized Bibliography*. Dallas: Durban House.

Hirschman, A. O. 1970. *Exit, Voice, and Loyalty*. Cambridge, MA: Harvard University Press.

Hobbes, T. [1651] 1991. *Leviathan* (ed. Richard Tuck). New York: Cambridge University Press.

Hobbs, A. 2000. *Plato and the Hero: Courage, Manliness and the Impersonal Good*. Cambridge: Cambridge University Press.

Hobsbawm, E. 2002. *Interesting Times*. London: Abacus.

Holl, K., and A. C. Kjelling (eds.) 1994. *The Nobel Peace Prize and the Laureates*. Frankfurt: Peter Lang.

Hollander, D. 1975. 'Political communication and dissent in the Soviet Union', in: R. L. Tokes (ed.), *Dissent in the USSR: Politics, Ideology, People*. Baltimore: Johns Hopkins University Press, 233–75.

Holmwood, J. 2000. 'Three pillars of the welfare state theory: T. H. Marshall, Karl Polanyi and Alva Myrdal', *European Journal of Social Theory* 3 (1): 23–50.

Hoyer, L. 1957. *Nansen: A Family Portrait* (trans. M. Michael). London: Longman.

Huizinga, J. 1955. *Homo Ludens: A Study of the Play-Element in Culture*. Boston: Beacon Press.

Hunt, G. (ed.) 1995. *Whistleblowing in the Health Service: Accountability, Law and Professional Practice*. London: Edward Arnold.

Huntford, R. 1998. *Nansen: The Explorer as Hero*. London: Duckworth.

Ignatieff, M. 1997. 'The decline and fall of the public intellectual', *Queen's Quarterly* 104: 395–403.

Jacoby, R. 1987. *The Last Intellectuals: American Culture in the Age of Academe*. New York: Basic.

1999. *The End of Utopia: Politics and Culture in an Age of Apathy*. New York: Basic.

Jahn, G. [1946] 2006. Nobel Peace Prize presentation speech, at http://nobelprize.org/peace/laureates/1946/presentation-speech (last accessed 5 March 2006).

[1949] 2006. Nobel Peace Prize presentation speech, at http://nobelprize.org/peace/laureates/1949/press.html (last accessed 7 June 2006).

[1963] 2006. Nobel Peace Prize presentation speech, at http://nobelprize.org/ peace/laureates/1962/presentation-speech (last accessed 16 March 2006).

James, W. 1890. *The Principles of Psychology*, vol. II. New York: Henry Holt.

Jasper, J. M. 1997. *The Art of Moral Protest: Culture, Biography, and Creativity in Social Movements*. Chicago: University of Chicago Press.

Jay, M. 1973. *The Dialectical Imagination*. New York: Little, Brown.

Jellinek, F. [1937] 1965. *The Paris Commune of 1871*. New York: Gross and Dunlap.

Jennings, J. 2000a. 'Intellectuals and political culture', *The European Legacy* 5 (6): 781–95.

2000b. '1889–1998: from Zola's '*J'accuse*' to the death of the intellectual', *The European Legacy* 5 (6): 829–44.

Jennings, J., and A. Kemp-Welch 1997. 'The century of the intellectual', in: J. Jennings and A. Kemp-Welch (eds.), *Intellectuals in Politics: From the Dreyfus Affair to Salman Rushdie*. London: Routledge, 1–24.

Joas, H. 1996. *The Creativity of Action*. Cambridge: Polity Press.

Johnson, E. C. (ed.) 1960. *Jane Addams: A Centennial Reader*. New York: Macmillan.

Johnson, P. 1988. *Intellectuals*. London: Weidenfeld and Nicolson.

Judt, T. 1992. *The Past Imperfect: French Intellectuals 1944–1956*. Berkeley: University of California Press.

Karabel, J. 1996. 'Towards a theory of intellectuals and politics', *Theory and Society* 25 (2): 205–33.

Karazijal, R., and A. Momkauskait 2004. 'The Nobel Prize in Physics: regularities and tendencies', *Scientometrics* 61 (2):191–205.

Kateb, G. 2004. 'Courage as a virtue', *Social Research* 71 (1): 39–72.

Kauffman, G. B. 2001. 'The Nobel centennial 1901–2001', *Chemical Educator* 6 (6): 370–84.

Kauppi, N. 1996. *French Intellectual Nobility: Institutional and Symbolic Transformations in the Post-Sartrian Era*. Albany, NY: SUNY Press.

Keene, A. T. 1998. *Peacemakers: Winners of the Nobel Peace Prize*. Oxford: Oxford University Press.

Kelly, A. 2002. 'Keeping the sparks alive', *New York Review of Books* 9 May: 13–15.

Kempny, M. 1999. 'Between tradition and politics', in: A. Bozoki (ed.), *Intellectuals and Politics in Central Europe*. Budapest: CEU Press, 151–67.

Kendall, H. W., K. Arrow, N. E. Borlaug, P. R. Ehrlich, J. Lederburg, J. I. Vargas, R. T. Watson and E. O. Wilson 1996. *Meeting the Challenges of Population, Environment, and Resources: The Costs of Location*. Washington, DC: World Bank.

Kennedy, J. F. [1956] 1965. *Profiles in Courage*. London: Hamish Hamilton.

Kenny, M. 2004. 'Reckless minds or democracy's helpers? Intellectuals and politics in the twentieth century', *Contemporary Political Theory* 3 :89–103.

Kilpinen, E. 1998. 'Creativity is coming', *Acta Sociologica* 41 (2): 173–79.

King, M. L. 1963. *Letter from Birmingham Jail*. San Francisco: Harper.

Kline, E. 1990. 'Foreword', in: A. Sakharov, *Memoirs* (trans. R Lourie). London: Hutchinson, xiii–xix.

Knight, L. W. 1997. 'Jane Addams and the settlement house movement', in: P. A. Cimbala and R. M. Miller (eds.), *Against the Tide: Women Reformers in American Society*. Westport, CT: Praeger, 85–112.

2005. *Citizen Jane Addams and the Struggle for Democracy*. Chicago: University of Chicago Press.

Koestler, A. 1964. *The Act of Creation*. London: Macmillan.

Koht, P. [1931] 2005. Nobel Prize presentation speech, at http://nobelprize.org/peace/laureates/1931/press/html (last accessed 6 June 2006).

Kohut, H. 1985. *Self Psychology and the Humanities*. New York: Norton.

Kolakowski, L. 1971. 'The priest and the jester', in: L. Kolakowski (ed.), *Marxism and Beyond: On Historical Understanding and Individual Responsibility*. London: Pall Mall Press, 56–65.

Konrad, G., and I. Szelenyi 1979. *The Intellectuals on the Road to Class Power* (trans. A. Arato and R. E. Allen). New York: Harcourt.

Korosenyi, A. 1999. 'Intellectuals and democracy: political thinking of intellectuals', in: A. Bozoki (ed.), *Intellectuals and Politics in Central Europe*. Budapest: CEU Press, 227–44.

Kreisler, H. 1983. 'Linus Pauling: the peace movement in historical perspective', *Conversations with History*, Institute of International Studies, University of California, Berkeley, at globetrotter.berkeley.ed.u/conversations/Pauling/pauling1.html (last accessed 11 July 2006).

Kris, E. 1952. *Psychoanalytic Exploration in Art*. New York: International Universities Press.

Kuhn, T. S. 1962. *The Structure of Scientific Revolutions*. Chicago: University of Chicago Press.

Kurzman, C., and E. Leahey 2004. 'Intellectuals and democratisation, 1905–1912 and 1989–1996', *American Journal of Sociology* **109** (4): 937–86.

Kurzman, C., and L. Owens 2002. 'The sociology of intellectuals', *Annual Review of Sociology* **28**: 63–90.

Lange, C. L. [1934] 2006. Nobel Peace Prize presentation speech, at http://nobelprize.org/peace/laureates/1933/presentation–speech (last accessed 16 February 2006).

Laqueur, W. 1974. *Weimar: A Cultural History 1918–1933*. London: Weiderfeld and Nicolson.

Lasch, C. (ed.) 1965. *The Social Thought of Jane Addams*. New York: Irvington Publishers.

1966. *The New Radicalism in America, 1999–1963: The Intellectual as a Social Type*. London: Chatto and Windus.

Lassman, P. 2000. 'Enlightenment, cultural crisis and politics', *The European Legacy* **5** (6): 815–28.

Lasswell, H. D., and D. Lerner (eds.) 1965. *World Revolutionary Elites*. Cambridge, MA: MIT Press.

Latour, B., and S. Woolgar 1986. *Laboratory Life: The Construction of Scientific Facts*. Princeton, NJ: Princeton University Press.

Leavitt, H. J., and J. Lipman-Blumen 1995. 'Hot groups', *Harvard Business Review* **73** (4): 110–17.

Lemert, C. C. 1991. 'The politics of theory and the limits of academia', in: C. C. Lemert (ed.), *Intellectuals and Politics: Social Theory in a Changing World*. London: Sage, 177–88.

Lemmel, B. 2001a. 'The Nobel Foundation: a century of growth and change', in: A. Wallin Levinovitz and N. Ringertz (eds.), *The Nobel Prize: The First 100 Years*. Stockholm: Nobel Foundation, 13–25.

2001b. 'The nomination and selection of the Nobel laureates', in: A. Wallin Levinovitz and N. Ringertz (eds.), *The Nobel Prize: The First 100 Years*. Stockholm: Nobel Foundation, 25–31.

Levine, D. H. 1971. *Jane Addams and the Liberal Tradition*. Madison: State Historical Society of Wisconsin.

1986. 'Is religion being politicized and other pressing questions Latin America poses', *Political Studies* **19** (4): 825–31.

Levinowitz, W. A., and N. Ringertz (eds.), 2001. *The Nobel Prize, The First 100 Years*. Stockholm: Nobel Foundation.

Levy, L. W., and A. Young 1965. 'Foreword', in C. Lasch (ed.), *The Social Thought of Jane Addams*. New York: Irvington Publishers, vii–ix.

Liep, J. (ed.) 2001. *Locating Cultural Creativity*. London: Pluto Press.

Lilla, M. 2001. *The Reckless Mind: Intellectuals in Politics*. New York: New York Review.

Lin, N. 2001. *Social Capital: A Theory of Social Structure and Action*. Cambridge: Cambridge University Press.

Lionaes, A. [1970] 2006. Nobel Peace Prize presentation speech, at http:// nobelprize.org/peace/laureates/1970/press.html (last accessed 4 March 2006).

[1975] 2006: Nobel Peace Prize presentation speech, at http://nobelprize.org./ peace/laureates/1975/press.html (last accessed 16 April 2006).

Lipset, S. M. 1963. *Political Man: The Social Bases of Politics*. Garden City, NY: Doubleday.

Lockwood, D. 1992. *Solidarity and Schisma*. Oxford: Clarendon Press.

Lofgren, O. 2001. 'Celebrating creativity: on the slanting of a concept', in: J. Liep (ed.), *Locating Cultural Creativity*. London: Pluto Press, 71–81.

Lourie, R. 2002. *Sakharov: A Biography*. Hanover, NH: Brandeis University Press.

Luke, T., P. Piccone, F. Siegel and M. Tave 1987. 'Roundtable on Intellectuals and the Academy', *Telos* **71** (Spring): 5–37.

Lundestad, G. 1994. 'Reflections on the Nobel Peace Prize', at http:// nobelprize.org/nobel/ (last accessed 6 April 2006).

2001a. 'Introduction', in: Ø. Stenersen, I. Libaek and A. Sveen (eds.), *The Nobel Peace Prize*. Oslo: Cappelen, 8–9.

2001b. 'The Nobel Peace Prize', in: A. Wallin Levinovitz and N. Ringertz (eds.), *The Nobel Prize: The First 100 Years*. Stockholm: Nobel Foundation, 173–88.

Lyon, E. S. 2001. 'Education for modernity: the impact of American social science on Alva and Gunnar Myrdal', *International Journal of Politics, Culture and Society* **14** (3): 513–37.

Lyotard, J.-F. 1984. *The Postmodern Condition*. Minneapolis: University of Minnesota Press.

Machiavelli, N. [1513] 1988. *The Prince* (eds. Q. Skinner and R. Price). Cambridge: Cambridge University Press.

Mannheim, K. 1949. *Ideology and Utopia* (trans. L. Wirth and E. Shils). San Diego: Harcourt Brace Jovanovich.

Marcuse, H. 1966. *One-Dimensional Man*. Boston: Beacon Press.

Marrin, A. 1979. *Sir Norman Angell*. Boston: Twayne Publishers.

Martin, B. 1999. 'Whistleblowing and nonviolence', *Peace and Change* 24 (1): 16–28.

Martin, P. 2002. 'Spontaneity and organization', in: M. Cooke and D. Horn (eds.), *Cambridge Companion to Jazz*. Cambridge: Cambridge University Press, 130–44.

Mayer, R. E. 1999. 'Fifty years of creative research', in: R. J. Sternberg (ed.), *Handbook of Creativity*. Cambridge: Cambridge University Press, 445–60.

McGown, J. 1999. 'Toward a pragmatic theory of action', *Sociological Theory* 16 (3): 292–312.

McLaren, R. 1993. 'The dark side of creativity', *Creativity Research Journal* 6: 137–44.

Mead, G. H. 1932. *The Philosophy of the Present*. Arthur E. Murphy (ed.), LaSalle, IL: Open Court Publishing.

Merton, R. K. 1959. 'Social conformity, deviation and opportunity structures: a comment on the contributions of Dubin and Cloward', *American Sociological Review* 24 (2): 177–89.

[1949] 1968. *Social Theory and Social Structure*. New York: Free Press.

[1938] 1970. *Science, Technology and Society in Seventeenth-Century England*. New York: Harper.

1973. *The Sociology of Science: Theoretical and Empirical Investigations* (ed. N. Storer). Chicago: University of Chicago Press.

Michels, R. 1932. 'Intellectuals', in: E. Seligman and A. Johnson (eds.), *Encyclopaedia of the Social Sciences*, vol. VIII. New York: Macmillan, 118–26.

Miller, W. I. 2000. *The Mystery of Courage*. Cambridge, MA: Harvard University Press.

Mills, C. W. 1963. *Power, Politics and People*. New York: Ballantine.

Misztal, B. A. 2000. *Informality: Social Theory and Contemporary Practice*. London: Routledge.

Montesquieu, C.-L. [1748] 1989. *The Spirit of the Laws* (eds. A. M. Cohler, B. C. Miller and H. S. Stone). Cambridge: Cambridge University Press.

Mooney, R. L. 1963. 'A conceptual model for integrating four approaches to the identification of creative talent', in: C. W. Taylor and F. Barron (eds.), *Scientific Creativity: Its Recognition and Development*. New York: Wiley, 331–40.

Myrdal, A. 1941. *Nation and Family*. New York: Harper and Brothers.

1976. *The Game of Disarmament: How the United States and Russia Run the Arms Race*. New York: Pantheon.

[1982] 2006. Nobel lecture, at http://nobelprize.org/peace/laureates/1982/myrdal-lecture.html (last accessed 9 June 2006).

Myrdal, A. and V. Klein 1956. *Women's Two Roles*. London: Routledge and Kegan Paul.

Nansen, F. [1922] 2005. Nobel speech, at http://nobelprize.org./peace/laureates/1922/nansen-lecture.html (last accessed 12 May 2006).

Near, J.P., and M.P. Miceli 1985. 'Organizational dissidence: the case of whistleblowing', *Journal of Business Ethics* 4: 1–16.

Nettl, J.P. 1969. 'Ideas, intellectuals, and structures of dissent', in: P. Rieff (ed.), *On Intellectuals: Theoretical Studies, Case Studies*. Garden City, NY: Doubleday, 53–124.

Nietzsche, F. [1911] 1990. *Beyond Good and Evil*. Harmondsworth: Penguin.

Norwegian Nobel Committee [1986] 2006. Press release, at http://nobelprize.org/peace.laureates/1986/press.html (last accessed 11 April 2006).

Oliner, S.P., and P.M. Oliner 1988. *The Altruistic Personality: Rescuers of Jews in Nazi Europe*. New York: Free Press.

Oppenheimer, A. 2004. 'West German pacifism and the ambivalence of human solidarity', *Peace and Change* 29 (3 & 4): 353–79.

Ortega y Gasset, J. [1929] 1961. *The Revolt of the Masses*. New York: Allen and Unwin.

Osborne, P. (ed.) 1996. *A Critical Sense: Interviews with Intellectuals*. London: Routledge.

Osborne, T. 2003. 'Against "creativity": a philistine rant', *Economy and Society* 21 (4): 507–23.

Palmieri, P.A. 1996. 'The simplest of New England: becoming Emily Greene Balch, 1867–1961', in: S.L. Porter (ed.), *Women of the Commonwealth: Work, Family and Social Change in Nineteenth-Century Massachusetts*. Amherst: University of Massachusetts Press, 283–306.

Parsons, T. 1969. 'The intellectual: a social role category', in: P. Rieff (ed.), *On Intellectuals: Theoretical Studies, Case Studies*. Garden City, NY: Doubleday, 3–24.

Passy, F. 2001. 'Political altruism and solidarity movements: an introduction', in: M. Giugni and F. Passy (eds.), *Political Altruism and Solidarity Movements*. Lanham, MD: Rowman and Littlefield, vii–ix.

2003. 'Social networks matter', in: M. Diani, and M. McAdam (eds.), *Social Movements and Networks*. Oxford: Oxford University Press, 21–48.

Patterson Meyer, E. 1959. *Champions of Peace*. Boston: Little Brown.

1978. *In Search of Peace*. Nashville: Abingdon.

Pauling, L.C. 1958. *No More War*. San Francisco: Dodd Mead.

1970. *Vitamin C and the Common Cold*. San Francisco: W.H. Freeman.

1986. *How to Live Longer and Feel Better*. Corvallis: Oregon State University Press.

[1963] 2006. Nobel lecture, at nobel.org/peace/laureates/1962/pauling-lecture.html (last accessed 16 March 2006).

Pawson, L. 1996. ' "Green" revolution for Africa?', *African Business* 211: 25.

Pears, D. 2004. 'The anatomy of courage', *Social Research* 71 (1):1–12.

Pels, D. 1995. 'Knowledge politics and anti-politics', *Theory and Society* 24 (1): 79–104.

1999. 'Privileged nomads: on the strangeness of intellectuals and the intellectuality of strangers', *Theory, Culture and Society* **16** (1): 63–86.

Pérez Esquivel, A. 1983. *Christ in a Poncho: Witnesses to the Non-Violent Struggles in Latin America*. New York: Orbis.

[1980] 2006. Nobel Peace Prize acceptance speech, at http://nobelprize.org/peace/laureates/1980/acceptance-speech (last accessed 17 January 2006).

Perrin, A. 2006. *Citizen Speak: The Democratic Imagination in American Life*. Chicago: University of Chicago Press.

Phillips, J. O. C. 1974. 'Education of Jane Addams', *History of Education Quarterly* **14** (1): 49–67.

Plato [380 BC] 1896. *The Laches of Plato* (introd. and notes M. T. Tatham). London: Macmillan.

Polanyi, M. 1951. *The Logic of Liberty*. London: Routledge.

Pope, R. 2005. *Creativity: Theory, History, Practice*. London: Routledge.

Popper, K. R. 1959. *The Logic of Scientific Discovery*. London: Hutchinson.

Porter, R. 2001. *The Enlightenment: Britain and the Creation of the Modern World*. Harmondsworth: Penguin.

Posner, R. A. 2001. *Public Intellectuals: A Study of Decline*. Cambridge, MA: Harvard University Press.

Pyszczynski, T. 2004. 'What are we so afraid of? A terror management theory perspective on the politics of fear', *Social Research* 7 (4): 827–49.

Rachman, S. J. 1978. *Fear and Courage*. New York: W. H. Freeman.

2004. 'Fear and courage: a psychological perspective', *Social Research* **71** (1): 149–76.

Randall, M. M. 1964. *Improper Bostonian: Emily Greene Balch*. New York: Twayne.

(ed.) 1972. *Beyond Nationalism: The Social Thought of Emily Greene Balch*. New York: Twayne.

Reichmann, W., G. Beidernikl and C. Fleck 2005. *Nobel Prize Nominations in Physics*. Paper presented at the thirty-seventh World Congress of the International Institute of Sociology, Stockholm, 5–9 July.

Reynolds, E. E. 1949. *Nansen*. Harmondsworth: Penguin.

Richards, E. 1991. *Vitamin C and Cancer: Medicine or Politics?* London: Macmillan.

Richmond, S. 2005. 'Credit agency: politics and paradox in Sartre's life and work', *Times Literary Supplement* 4 November: 3–4.

Rieff, P. 1969. 'The case of Dr Oppenheimer', in: P. Rieff (ed.), *On Intellectuals: Theoretical Studies, Case Studies*. Garden City, NY: Doubleday, 314–40.

Riesman, D. 1950. *The Lonely Crowd*. New Haven, CT: Yale University Press.

Ringer, F. K. 1969. *The Decline of the German Mandarins: the German Academic Community, 1890–1933*. Cambridge, MA: Harvard University Press.

Ritzer, G. 2001. *Explorations in Social Theory: From Metatheorizing to Rationalization*. London: Sage.

Robbins, B. 2006. 'Martial art', *London Review of Books* 20 April: 18–19.

Robin, C. 2000. 'Fear: a genealogy of morals', *Social Research* **67** (4): 1085–102.

Rogers, C. R. 1973. 'Towards a theory of creativity', in: P. E. Vernon (ed.), *Creativity*. Harmondsworth: Penguin Education, 137–52.

Rorty Oksenberg, A. 1988. *Mind in Action*. Boston: Beacon Press.

Rosaldo, R., S. Lavie and K. Narayan 1993.' Introduction', in: S. Lavie, K. Narayan and R. Rosaldo (eds.), *Creativity/Anthropology*. Ithaca, NY: Cornell University Press, 1–8.

Rossbach, S. 1999. *Gnostic Wars: The Cold War in the Context of the History of Western Spirituality*. Edinburgh: Edinburgh University Press.

Ruff, G., and S. Korchin 1964. 'Psychological responses of the Mercury astronauts to stress', in: G. Grosser, H. Wechsler and M. Grenblatt (eds.), *The Threat of Impending Disaster*. Cambridge, MA: MIT Press, 23–45.

Safire, W. 1993. *The First Dissident: The Book of Job in Today's Politics*. New York: Random House.

Said, E. 1994. *The Representation of the Intellectual: The 1993 Reith Lectures*. London: Vintage.

1996. 'Orientalism and after', in: P. Osborne (ed.), *A Critical Sense: Interviews with Intellectuals*. London: Routledge, 65–89.

Sakharov, A. 1979. *Alarm and Hope* (eds. E. Yankelevich and A. Friendly). London: Collins and Harvill.

1990. *Memoirs* (trans. R. Lourie). London: Hutchinson.

Sanness, J. [1980] 2006. Nobel Peace Prize presentation speech, at http://nobelprize.org/peace/laureates/1980/presentation-speech (last accessed 16 June 2006).

Sartre, J.-P. 1972. *The Psychology of Imagination* (trans. H. Barnes). London: Methuen.

1974. *Between Existentialism and Marxism* (trans. J. May). London: New Left Review.

Sawyer, R. K. 2001. *Creating Conversations*. Cresskill, NJ: Hampton Press.

Schaffer, S. 1994. 'Making up discovery', in: M. A. Boden (ed.), *Dimensions of Creativity*. Cambridge, MA: MIT Press, 13–51.

Schuff, S. 2005. 'Borlaug drives home message', *Feedstuffs* **77** (9): 1–2.

Schumpeter, J. 1947. *Capitalism, Socialism, and Democracy*. London: Allen and Unwin.

1991. *Essays on Entrepreneurs, Innovations, Business Cycles and Evolution of Capitalism* (ed. R. V. Clemence). New Brunswick, NJ: Transaction.

Schutz, A. 1964. *Collected Papers: Studies in Social Theory*, vol. II. The Hague: Martinus Nijhoff.

Schwan, G. 2004. 'Civil courage and human dignity: how to regain respect for the fundamental values of Western democracy', *Social Research* **71** (1): 107–16.

Schwartz, N. L. 2004. 'Dreaded and dared: courage as a virtue', *Polity* **36** (3): 341–66.

Schweber, S. S. 2000. *In the Shadow of the Bomb*. Princeton, NJ: Princeton University Press.

Scorza, J. A. 2001. 'The ambivalence of political courage', *Review of Politics* **63** (4): 637–62.

Sejersted, F. 2004. 'The Nobel Peace Prize: from peace negotiations to human rights', at http://nobelprize.org/nobel/.

Shils, E. 1955. 'The intellectuals: Great Britain', *Encounter* **4**: 5–16.

1968. 'Charisma', in: *International Encyclopaedia of the Social Sciences*, vol. II. New York: Macmillan, 386–90.

1972. *The Intellectuals and the Powers and Other Essays*. Chicago: University of Chicago Press.

1981. *Tradition*. Chicago: University of Chicago Press.

1990. 'Intellectuals and responsibility', in: I. Maclean, A. Montefiore, A. Winch and P. Winch (eds.), *The Political Responsibility of Intellectuals*. Cambridge: Cambridge University Press, 257–307.

Shils, E. and M. Janowitz 1948. 'Cohesion and disintegration in the Wehrmacht in World War II', *Public Opinion Quarterly* **12**: 280–315.

Shklar, J. N. 1989. 'Liberalism of fear', in: N. L. Rosenblum (ed.), *Liberalism of the Moral Life*. Cambridge, MA: Harvard University Press, 21–38.

Simmel, G. 1950. *The Sociology of Georg Simmel* (trans. and ed. K. M. Wolff). New York: Free Press.

Singer, P., and R. Singer (eds.) 2005. *The Moral of the Story: An Anthology of Ethics through Literature*. Oxford: Blackwell.

Skilling, H. G. 1973. 'Opposition in communist East Europe', in: R. A. Dahl (ed.), *Regimes and Oppositions*. New Haven, CT: Yale University Press, 89–120.

Sohlman, R. 1983. *The Legacy of Alfred Nobel* (trans. E. H. Schubert). London: Bodley Head (with appendix: Alfred Nobel's will, 136–9).

Sontag, S. 2003. *Regarding the Pain of Others*. London: Hamish Hamilton.

Spanish, D. 2002. 'Making the Celestial City', *Times Literary Supplement* 24 May: 5–6.

Sparks, H. 1997. 'Dissident citizenship: democratic theory, political courage, and activist women', *Hypatia* **12** (4): 74–111.

Stang, F. [1922] 2005. Nobel Peace Prize presentation speech, at http://nobelprize.org./peace/laureates/1922/press.html (last accessed 1 March 2006).

[1936] 2006. Nobel Peace Prize presentation speech, at http://nobelprize.org/peace/laureates/1936/press.html (last accessed 12 April 2006).

Stapleton, J. 2000. 'Cultural conservatism and the public intellectuals in Britain', *The European Legacy* **5** (6): 815–28.

Stenersen, Ø. 2006. 'The humanitarian Nobel Prizes', at http://nobelprize.org/nobel_prizes/peace/articles/stenersen/index.html (last accessed 16 June 2006).

Stenersen, Ø., I. Libaek and A. Sveen 2001. *The Nobel Peace Prize*. Oslo: Cappelen.

Sternberg, R. J. 1988. 'Introduction', in: R. J. Sternberg (ed.), *The Nature of Creativity: Contemporary Psychological Perspectives*. Cambridge: Cambridge University Press, 1–10.

Sternberg, R. J., and T. I. Lubart 1999. 'The concept of creativity: prospects and paradigms', in: R. J. Sternberg (ed.), *Handbook of Creativity*. Cambridge: Cambridge University Press, 3–15.

Stouffer, S. A., E. A. Suchman, L. C. DeVinney, S. A. Star and R. M. Williams 1949. *The American Soldier: Adjustment during Army Life*. Princeton, NJ: Princeton University Press.

Sustein, C. R. 2003. *Why Societies Need Dissent*. Cambridge, MA: Harvard University Press.

Swedberg, R. 1999. 'Civil courage (Zivilcourage): the case of Knut Wicksell', *Theory and Society* **28** (4): 501–28.

Szacki, J. 1990. 'Intellectuals between politics and culture', in: I. Maclean, A. Montefiore and P. Winch (eds.), *The Political Responsibility of Intellectuals*. Cambridge: Cambridge University Press, 229–46.

Sztompka, P. 1986. *Robert K. Merton: An Intellectual Profile*. London: Macmillan.

Tardif, T. Z., and R. J. Sternberg 1988. 'What do we know about creativity?', in: R. J. Sternberg (ed.), *The Nature of Creativity: Contemporary Psychological Perspectives*. Cambridge: Cambridge University Press, 429–40.

Taylor, C. M. 1989. *Sources of the Self: The Making of Modern Identity*. Cambridge: Cambridge University Press.

Taylor, C. W. 1988. 'Various approaches to and definitions of creativity', in: R. J. Sternberg (ed.), *The Nature of Creativity: Contemporary Psychological Perspectives*. Cambridge: Cambridge University Press, 99–121.

Taylor, M. 1982. *Community, Anarchy and Liberty*. Cambridge: Cambridge University Press.

Tec, N. 1986. *When Light Pierced the Darkness*. Oxford: Oxford University Press.

Theorin, B. M. 2001. *Alva Myrdal and the Peace Movement*. Paper presented at the conference 'Alva Myrdal's questions to our time', Uppsala, Sweden, 6–8 March.

Thomas, W. I. 1923. *The Unadjusted Girl*. Boston: Little Brown and Co.

Thoreau, H. D. [1849] 2005. *Resistance to Civil Government*. New York: Easton Press.

Tillich, P. 1961. *The Courage to Be*. London: James Nisbet.

Tilly, C. 1997. *Roads from Past to Future*. New York: Rowman and Littlefield.
  2000. 'How do relations store histories?', *Annual Review of Sociology* **26**: 721–3.

Tims, M. 1961. *Jane Addams of Hull House, 1860–1935*. London: Allen and Unwin.

Tocqueville, A. de [1835] 1968. *Democracy in America*, vol. II. London: Fontana.

Tonnesson, O. 2005. 'Controversies and criticism', at http://nobelprize.org/nobel/ (last accessed 13 March 2006).

Trilling, L. 1972. *Sincerity and Authenticity*. Oxford: Oxford University Press.

Turner, B. S. 1994. *Orientalism, Postmodernism and Globalization*. London: Routledge.

Turner, S. P., and R. A. Factor 1994. *Max Weber: The Lawyer as Social Thinker*. London: Routledge.

Vogt, C. E. 2005. 'Fridtjof Nansen and the Norwegian peace tradition', at www.hum.au.dk/forskerskoler/historiephd/papercarlemil2005.pdf (last accessed 15 January 2006).

von Mises, L. 1960. 'The resentment and the anti-capitalistic bias of American intellectuals', in: G. B. de Huszar (ed.), *The Intellectuals: A Controversial Portrait*. Glencoe, IL: Free Press, 365–70.

Wagner, P. 1996. 'Crisis of modernity: political sociology in historical context', in: S. P. Turner (ed.), *Social Theory and Sociology*. Oxford: Blackwell, 97–116.

Wallace, J. D. 1978. *Virtues and Vices*. Ithaca, NY: Cornell University Press.

Walton, D. N. 1986. *Courage: A Philosophical Investigation*. Berkeley: University of California Press.

Walzer, M. 2001. *The Company of Critics*. New York: Basic.

Ward, L. 2001. 'Nobility and necessity: the problem of courage in Aristotle's Nicomachean Ethics', *American Political Science Review* **95** (1): 71–86.

Wasson, T. (ed.) 1987. *Nobel Peace Prize Winners: An H. W. Wilson Bibliographical Dictionary*. New York: H. W. Wilson Co.

Weber, M. [1919] 1946a. 'Science as a vocation', in: H. H. Gerth and C. W. Mills (trans. and eds.), *From Max Weber: Essays in Sociology*. Oxford: Oxford University Press, 129–56.

[1915] 1946b. 'The social psychology of the world religions', in: H. H. Gerth and C. W. Mills (trans. and eds.), *From Max Weber: Essays in Sociology*. Oxford: Oxford University Press, 267–301.

[1914] 1964. *The Theory of Social and Economic Organization* (trans. and ed. T. Parsons). New York: Free Press.

[1914] 1968. *Economy and Society*, vol. II (trans. G. Roth and C. Wittich). Berkeley: University of California Press.

[1918] 1978. 'Politics as a vocation', in: W. G. Runciman (ed.), *Weber: Selections in Translation* (trans. E. Matthews). Cambridge: Cambridge University Press, 212–26.

Weisberg, R. W. 1993. *Creativity: Beyond the Myth of Genius*. New York: Freeman.

Wellhausen, E. J. 1997. 'Foreword', in: A. Dil (ed.), *Norman Borlaug on World Hunger*. San Diego: Bookservice International, 2–8.

West, C. 1993. 'On the responsibility of intellectuals', *Boston Review* **18** (1), available at http://bostonreview.net/BR18.1.responsibility.html.

1996. 'American radicalisms', in: P. Osborne (ed.), *A Critical Sense: Interviews with Intellectuals*. London: Routledge, 128–42.

1999. *The Cornell West Reader*. New York: Civitas.

White, F. M. 1988. *Linus Pauling: Scientist and Crusader*. New York: Walker.

White, H. 1992. *Identity and Control: A Structural Theory of Social Action*. Princeton, NJ: Princeton University Press.

Whyte, W. H. 1956. *The Organization Man*. New York: Touchstone.

Wiesel, E. 1966. *The Gates of the Forest* (trans F. Frenaye). New York: Holt, Rinehart and Winston.

1978. 'Why I write', in: A. H. Rosenfeld and I. Greenberg (eds.), *Confronting the Holocaust: The Impact of Elie Wiesel*. Bloomington: Indiana University Press, 200–6.

1995. *From the Kingdom of Memory*. New York: Schocken.

1996. *All Rivers Run to the Sea: Memoirs*, vol. I, *1928–1969* (trans. M. Wiesel). New York: HarperCollins.

1999. *And the Sea is Never Full: Memoirs*, vol. II, 1969– (trans. M. Wiesel). New York: Schocken.

[1986] 2006. Nobel lecture, at http://nobelprize.org/peace/laureates/1986/wiesel-lecture.html (last accessed 8 February 2006).

[1999] 2006. 'The perils of indifference', at http://historyplace.com/speeches/wiesel.htm (last accessed 16 April 2006).

Williams, R. 1961. *The Long Revolution*. London: Chatto and Windus.

1977. *Marxism and Literature*. Oxford: Oxford University Press.

1983. *Keywords*. London: Fontana.

Willis, P. E. 1977. *Learning to Labour: How Working Class Kids Get Working Class Jobs*. Farnborough: Saxon House.

1990. *Common Culture: Symbolic Work at Play in the Everyday Cultures of the Young*. London: Open University Press.

Wilson, M. 1953. *The War on World Poverty*. London: Macmillan.

Wolfe, A. 2003. *An Intellectual in Public*. Ann Arbor: Michigan University Press.

Znaniecki, F. 1940. *The Social Role of the Man of Knowledge*. New York: Columbia University Press.

Zuckerman, H. 1977. *Scientific Elite: Nobel Laureates in the United States*. New York: Free Press.

Index

Aarvik, E. 143, 147, 204
Aaseng, N. 116, 121
Aberdeen, University of 215
Abrams, I.
  champions and 182, 184, 185, 188, 192, 195, 197, 199, 201
  dissidents and 156, 161, 175
  heroes and 130, 137, 138, 143, 144
  Nobel Prize and 110, 111, 113–14, 115, 121
  pioneers and 212, 215, 217, 220
  on recurrent patterns 101
absence of intellectuals 14–15
academic-expert 29
Academy of Sciences (Russia) 165, 169
'Account rendered' (Ossietzky) 159
achievement 32
Act of Creation (Koestler) 46
action theory 42, 53–4, 54–5
Addams, Jane 122, 127–33, 235
  courage and 133
  creativity and 132–3
  Emily Greene Balch and 193, 194, 207
  hostility to 130
  Hull House and 127, 128–9, 132, 133
  migrants and 128
  networks and 133
  social reform and 128–9
  universities and 129
  wholeness of life/work 147
  women's rights and 130
  world peace and 130–1
adhocism 58
Adler, Alfred 145
Adorno, T. 90
Afghanistan 169
Africa 120, 144, 195
  Norman E. Borlaug in 230–1
African Growth and Opportunity Act 231
African National Congress 117, 120
African-Americans 95
Albert, R. S. 40, 41, 42

allegiances to group 86
Alonso, H. H. 130, 131
  Emily Greene Balch and 193, 194, 196, 198, 207
Altruistic Personality: Rescuers of Jews in Nazi Europe (Oliner and Oliner) 75
Amabile, T. M. 49
ambiguity 15, 63
American Academy of Arts and Letters 141
American Chemical Society 220
American culture 71, 80, 95
American Economic Association 191
American Journal of Sociology 130
American Sociological Society 129
American Union Against Militarism 194
Amnesty International 118, 119, 175
Amundsen, Roald 135
ancient Greeks 1, 39, 65–7, 68–70, 73, 125
Anderson, Hans Christian 154
andreia (military manliness) 68
Andropov, Yury 168
Angell, Norman 122, 182–91, 206
  cooperation and 184
  Great Illusion and 182, 184–5
  League of Nations and 187, 188
  Norman Angellism 184
anomie 79
anthropological studies 46–7
'anti-capitalist bias' 97
anti-democratic gestures 98
anti-Semitism 160
Antoine, C. 173, 175, 176
anxiety 59–60
apartheid 117
Approaches to the Great Settlement (Balch) 194
Aquinas, Thomas 74
Arctic expedition (Nansen) 134, 135
Arendt, H. 59–60, 64, 239
  authority sources and 33, 35, 39
  courage and 65, 68, 70, 177